TEA LOVER'S

TREASURY

James Norwood Pratt's

TEA LOVER'S

TREASURY

~

With an introduction by
M.F.K. FISHER

COLE GROUP

Publisher Brete C. Harrison
VP Publishing Robert G. Manley
VP and Director of Operations Linda Hauck
VP Marketing and Business Development John A. Morris
VP and Editorial Director James Connolly
Senior Editor Annette Gooch
Editorial Assistant Lynn Bell
Production Assistant Dotti Hydue

Cover design Candace J. Magee, Executive Edition, Atlanta, GA
Cover photography Michael Lamotte
Map John C. W. Carroll

Text © 1982 James Norwood Pratt
Illustrations © 1982 Sara Raffetto
Introduction © 1982 M.F.K. Fisher
A version of the introduction was originally published in *The New Yorker*.

Printed and bound in Hong Kong

Published by
Cole Group, Inc.
1330 N. Dutton Ave., Suite 103
Santa Rosa, CA 95401
(800) 959-2717   (707) 526-2682   Fax (707) 526-2687

F E D C B A
0 9 8 7 6 5

Library of Congress Catalog Card Number 94-46900
ISBN #1-56426-565-X

Distributed to the book trade by Publishers Group West.

FOR CHARLOT & OUR FIRST BORN
luxe, calme, et volupté

ACKNOWLEDGMENTS

I should like to thank, for kindness, interest, and help, Mr. Eustace G. C. Crawley of Jacksons of Piccadilly, Mr. Simpson Hemphill of Paloma Plantation, Mississippi, Miss Ruth Morrison of Ruth Morrison Associates, Mr. Richard Sanders of Grace Rare Tea, Mr. Michael Spillane of the G. S. Haly Company, and Mr. Ralph Starr of John Wagner & Sons. I am indebted to Mr. Tung Ying Fong of San Francisco for his calligraphy on page 239. Mr. William MacMelville, one of America's most eminent tea professionals, a past director of the Tea Association of the United States, and twice chairman of the United States Board of Tea Experts, very generously agreed to review the more technical sections in manuscript for errors of fact or emphasis: Such as remain I claim as my own. This book would never have attained its final form without the help of my brilliant and on the whole patient editor, Sharon Silva.

Grateful acknowledgment is made to the following for permission to reprint previously published material:

Dodd, Mead and Company, Inc.: For excerpts from *A History of the English-Speaking Peoples,* Volume III, *The Age of Revolution* by Sir Winston Churchill. Copyright © 1957 by The Right Honourable Sir Winston Leonard Spencer Churchill K.G. O.M. C.H. M.P. Reprinted by permission of Dodd, Mead and Company, Inc.

E. P. Dutton: For excerpts from *The Great Tea Venture* by J. M. Scott. Copyright © 1965. Reprinted by permission of E. P. Dutton.

Hutchinson Books Ltd.: For excerpts from *Tea & Coffee: A Modern View of 300 Years of Tradition* by Edward Bramah, Copyright © 1972. Reprinted by permission of Hutchinson Books Ltd.

Harcourt Brace Jovanovich, Inc.: For an excerpt from *The Idea of a Christian Society* by T. S. Eliot. Copyright © 1939 by T. S. Eliot; copyright renewed 1967 by Esme Valerie Eliot. Reprinted by permission of Harcourt Brace Jovanovich, Inc.

Harper & Row, Publishers, Inc.: For an excerpt from *A Military History of the Western World,* Volume III, by J.F.C. Fuller (Funk & Wagnalls Co.). Copyright © 1956 by J.F.C. Fuller. Reprinted by permission of Harper & Row, Publishers, Inc.

Farrar, Straus & Giroux, Inc.: For an excerpt from *The Confessions of Aleister Crowley: An Autohagiography* edited by John Symonds and Kenneth Grant. Copyright © 1969 by John Symonds and Kenneth Grant. Reprinted by permission of Hill and Wang, a division of Farrar, Straus & Giroux, Inc.

Houghton Mifflin Company: For an excerpt from *To Think of Tea!* by Agnes Repplier. Copyright © 1932 by Agnes Repplier. Copyright renewed 1960 by Fidelity Philadelphia Trust Company. Reprinted by permission of Houghton Mifflin Company.

Oxford University Press: For an excerpt from *The Culture and Marketing of Tea* by C. R. Harler (3rd ed. 1964). Reprinted by permission of Oxford University Press.

Prentice-Hall, Inc.: For an excerpt from *Dinner at Buckingham Palace* by Charles Oliver. Copyright © 1972. Reprinted by permission of Prentice-Hall, Inc.

St. Martin's Press: *The Book of Coffee & Tea* by Joel Schapira, David Schapira, and Karl Schapira. Copyright © 1975. Reprinted by permission of St. Martin's Press.

Tea & Coffee Trade Journal Co.: For excerpts from *All About Tea,* Volume I, by W. H. Ukers. Copyright © 1935. Reprinted by permission of Tea & Coffee Trade Journal Co.

John Wagner & Sons: For an excerpt from *Talking of Tea* by Gervas Huxley. Copyright © 1956. Reprinted by permission of John Wagner & Sons.

Contents

INTRODUCTION by M.F.K. Fisher   8

CHAPTER I   TEA TALES: The Greatest Stories Ever Told   15
A Truthful Relation of Tea History

CHAPTER II   TEA THINGS: Where Did That Come From?   103
An Introduction to Pottery, China, & Silver

CHAPTER III   TEA TYPES: What Do You Call This?   119
A Short Survey of the World of Tea

CHAPTER IV   TEA TIMES: What Is the Meaning of This?   171
A Commentary on Tea Ways & Means

CHAPTER V   TEA TRADE: Whose Business Is It Anyway?   183
A Miscellany of Curious Lore

CHAPTER VI   TEA PRODUCING: Why Does It Taste Like That?   211
A Somewhat Technical Excursus

Selected Bibliography   228

Index   231

Map of Major Tea-Growing Areas   164

 NE OF THE REWARDS of a long life of trying to use the language with respect as well as decency is that an occasional invitation is offered to write an introduction to a really good book produced by a younger and more agile mind. This explanation of my presence in Norwood Pratt's extraordinary essay on tea is more of an apology than a thank you, because I have not tasted even a sip from those cups "that cheer but not inebriate" for more than forty years. In other words, I have no right to be here at all.

Perhaps this introduction, though, will help to clarify my continuing love of the brew. If I need an excuse, I turn occasionally to George Saintsbury, who wrote the small classic called *Notes on a Cellarbook,* although he himself could not touch wine for the last decades of his life.

Tea makes me drunk, or as I usually think more coldly of it, "drunk as a skunk." I doubt that it has anything to do with my liver, as was Mr. Saintsbury's reason for total abstinence, but certainly the chemistry of my body has dictated my sad loss of enjoyment. I found this out, after what seemed to me at the time (I was then almost thirty!) a long life of true pleasure with teas, properly brewed.

To start, before my astonishing penance began, I first drank tea at lunch, when I was between five and eleven. Father came home at noon from his local daily newspaper, and we all sat down when he did; we ate and talked and smiled when he did too. And Bertha or whoever was in the kitchen brought a tall teapot of Dresden china and its matching cups and so on and put them in front of Mother, at the other end of the quiet but amiable table. We discussed love, money, and politics after dinner, but never in the middle of the day, largely because the *News* did not go to press until three, and it was Father's meal, easy-like.

There was always a pot of cool milk for my little sister Anne and me, because although Bertha served us just as shakily as she did Grandmother and our parents and anyone else there, we alone drank Cambric.

Does this book talk about Cambric Tea? It has undoubtedly been part of all sorts of cosmic finaglings, like the China Trade and other shapings-of-nations, from the nursery on to well-earned serenity and age. A good recipe calls for one part of strong tea in the bottom of a pretty cup or mug, and eight to ten parts of fine fresh milk, to be stirred by recipient with perhaps a little sugar or honey and of course politeness.

Cambric Tea, as I drank it at lunch time when I was little, was a privilege, and therefore lapped up like nectar. It made Anne and me feel almost accepted as people, this cool sop to our nascent self-images. The grown-ups drank it hot and dark, as we knew that someday we would too, and meanwhile our special brew was a fine way to practice.

Grandmother, born in County Tyrone, believed as a good Irishwoman that there were only three kinds of tea fit to drink, none of them store-bought. The first quality was kept, sensibly enough, in China. The second picking was sent directly to Ireland. The third and lowest grade went, of course, to the benighted British. And all the tea used in our house came once a year, in one or two beautiful soldered tin boxes, from Dublin. Then only would we know it to be second to what the Dowager Empress of China was drinking, while the other Old Lady in Buckingham Palace sipped our dregs, as served her right.

Grandmother also believed that tea, when properly made, should be served strong enough to trot a mouse on. I never tasted her noontime tipple, but feel sure that it was as bitter as it was black, beyond much help from milk or even sugar. I knew, though, that it made cheeks pink and tongues looser, as its potency warmed my parents' blood, and I enjoyed their innocent release.

Afternoon Tea was another matter, served to guests who came while Grandmother napped, and I suspect that along with her innate protest at anything English, fifty years on the Iowa prairies had dimmed the Anglican side of her daily needs, if she had ever had one. This was not true of Mother, though, and after Grandmother died when I was about twelve, tea was served every day at four o'clock, instead of at the lunch table. Father was never there, but there was always somebody to share it, in our warm dim living room at the Ranch, and I was increasingly on hand to produce it, so that our slavey-of-the-moment could catch a bit of rest before dinner was served promptly at six. Father must be off by seven, to cover the Chamber of Commerce or School Supervisors or Flood Control meetings for the next day's paper. Sometimes the cook and her boyfriend would want to catch a ride uptown to the movies. Dinner, in other words, was hurried and perfunctory if always polite, which may explain some of mother's sensuous enjoyment of Afternoon Tea, as well as my growing resentment of it.

The truth is that I was a pushover, a patsy, for any kind of slavish house-jobs, so long as I was assured at least weekly that nobody could churn butter on Saturdays as deftly and cleverly and neatly as I, or pick prettier posies, or make a nicer tea.

For several years I battened on this sly usage. By the time I was well into adolescence, though, I began to see where such flattery had landed me, and I began a long silent emotional simmer. Why was I always the one who had to come in early from playing one-a-cat with the kids on the next Ranch, or miss a meeting of the Latin Club, to perform the simple but demanding ritual of making tea for a few old ladies? I knew that I would keep on, because I loved Mother and enjoyed pleasing her, but it shamed me to realize my dangerous hunger for recognition. Of course I kept on with the pesky ceremony, and fawned for more praise by baking dainty little cakes, and slicing bread the right thinness for nasturtium-leaf sandwiches. As I look back on this silently snarling servitude, I think that I even grew the nasturtiums with Afternoon Tea in mind.... It was not admirable but it was fun, like scratching an old mosquito bite.

There were several teapots at home. I liked the one we always used for lunch when Grandmother was alive: tall, graceful, with little rosebuds here and there on it, and cups and saucers and cream pitcher and hot-water jug to match. There was a slop-bowl, of course, for the dregs of cups before fresh tea was poured. Then for two or three people, or Mother and me alone, there was the little Georgian silver set. And if duty called loudly enough to invite the members of the St. Matthias Ladies' Guild, there was the ugly big tea set that had been given to one of the Irish uncles when he was Lord Mayor or something. It was handsome and heavy, very Teutonic, not of sterling silver, and usually Mother kept it out of sight.

My favorite was the little Georgian set. It was lovely to touch, and it meant that only a couple of friends might be there by the glowing fireplace, to murmur over their scones and throw an occasional kind compliment toward me. I never joined them, of course, but grew deft at whisking things on and off Mother's low tea table set by her couch.

Cups and their saucers were pure pleasure from the start, and Mother taught me without words that beautiful objects are made to be used, so that even with palsied Bertha at the lunch table, and an occasional wince when a full cup would jig off its saucer before it got down the table to Father, we always used fine Dresden. Or Spode. Or Sèvres, from the corner cupboard. Or even Chinese porcelain, designed for the Anglo-Saxon tea trade.

In the glassed corner, both up in Whittier and then down at the Ranch after Grandmother died, there was an almost full set of Belleek, sent as a wedding present to Mother. My sister and I stared sometimes at the shells that they seemed made of. Who could ever keep the dust from going in and in, like sand, in the wee shells they stood on?

As I remember, the Belleek was used only once, when its Irish donors, rich titled linen weavers, stopped for tea in the Far West. The whole idea was a disaster, mostly because the shell-shaped cups, fairylike in their transparent delicacy, kept tipping over on their three little legs made of tinier rosy or pale-green shells. The pot, a larger one on three more substantial but still inadequate rosy shells, tipped over. The milk and the sugar spilled. The only thing that stayed upright was the slop-basin, empty because all the tea was here and there on people's knees and laps. And our cook-of-the-moment had tried to follow a recipe for Slim Johns as made in an Irish castle where Mother had once stayed, and they were burned black, inedible.

After the people left, Mother washed the fragile shells herself, and put them back in the glassed cupboard. We never knew whether there was any sand in all the tiny porcelain shells, but we often looked up respectfully at them, and long after our mother had died, Anne sold the set of Belleek to a stylish auctioneer for a startlingly fat sum.

In kitchen cupboards there were always a few clumsy thick cups with deep saucers, which we never used. I still have one of them, for special guests. It was made for Irishmen, Grandmother said, by the same Chinese who sent us their next-to-the-best tea. That was in the days when one was invited to have "a *dish* of tea." The brew was poured into the cup to cool and then it was poured into the deep saucer and drunk from there. I liked the uncouth romance of all this, and of course read sometimes in British novels about a dish o' tea, usually drunk by the lower-class characters.

Just lately I read an odd reminder of this, in a novel published in perhaps 1923 by Mrs. Belloc-Lowndes. A Kindly Old Country Doctor comes unexpectedly to the lawn where a lady is resting beside the little tea table that a parlormaid has trundled out to her chair. She is planning or recovering from the addition of cyanide to her enemy's nightly shandygaff. She likes the Kindly Old Country Doctor, and asks him to join her soothing ritual. He says, "I should be glad of some tea. But don't send for another cup. I'll have mine in this basin, for I'm in rather of a hurry."

Basin? Slop-bowl? Shallow saucer? Surely a genteel murderess on a country lawn in the twenties would not have been drinking from a "dish"! Norwood Pratt must be asked about this, as probably the only man in these parts who would know. . . .

Myself, I don't have a parlormaid, nor a lawn where a Kindly Old Country Doctor can join me for a basin of tea-without-arsenic. All this is unknown, where I live, except perhaps for rat poison. And I do not have a low dim sitting room, much less a sullenly happy young slave of a daughter. I live in a two-room *palazzino,* where people come to eat-drink-talk by a good fire in winter, and in cool breeziness in the hot months, but where serving tea and *then* dinner is too much of a hassle. Where do the tea things go, on my one long kitchen counter where I must cook after the first batch of people? How do I set the round dining table that is between the fireplace and the sink, a few minutes after I have said goodbye to the "tea set" and before I've turned on the oven for dinner? A glass of wine and some roasted nuts. . . .

Resentment of my self-invited indenture lessened as I grew up and out, and I made tea almost every afternoon for fellow students in France, because I was a married woman and therefore could invite people to my room when they could not, and also because I had a gas-ring and even running water. And none of us had enough money to go more than once a month or so to Duthu or Michelin, the best tearooms in Dijon, where we would have eaten delicious pastries and ices instead of slabs of the cheapest local gingerbread called *pavé de santé.*

When Mother came to Dijon in about 1930 and saw my prized tea equipment, she immediately bought me four pretty teacups and what she called "a decent pot." I still use it, an ugly Burgundian ceramic thing, but with a good spout. ("It pours well.")

After that, in my thirties and then until death, probably, my bitterness about the ceremony of Afternoon Tea, as seen by the pawn who makes and serves and then-un-serves it, has grown. When friends will "be along about tea time," often I say, "Or a glass of wine?" But when they mean tea, for cultural or any other of a dozen reasons, good tea is what I give them, and I do it conscientiously and well, and feel about fourteen.

Grandmother taught me, unwittingly, that tea must be hot and fresh, and of fine quality. Mother went on to show me that tea tastes best served from pleasant and elegant utensils. I could never brew tea strong enough to trot a mouse on. Neither would I affect only porcelain, for tea served from a silver or even a pewter pot, if made properly, can be as good as that made in the rarest of earthenware. Water is usually boiled in metal before it is poured over the dried leaves, and then is stirred with a silver spoon, here in the Western world, so why quibble?

My grandmother died before tea bags. I am thankful. My mother never admitted their existence. A friend has described them as boiled mice, and he is right too, but I have some teas in little white bags for people who have never known anything else, and who are adept enough to leave the wee tail hanging over the edge of the cup. I am told that these mice are often dried out and used again. . . .

I do not serve the black China tea that Grandmother liked for lunch. Occasionally I serve black Russian tea, but mostly Oriental greens, with beautiful names. I also serve herbal teas made of many leaves and blossoms (everything but alfalfa!), to people who are usually under thirty and prefer mugs to cups and saucers. I even have a silver teapot, although I prefer the good old mustard-and-green monster that Mother bought in Dijon, because it pours so truly.

But I never do more than sniff the stuff, as its first steam rises from its basin. If I did, as I learned some forty years ago, I would probably fall on my face, or go whirling off in a skunk-drunk dance. In other words, tea is my poison.

In about 1942, I spent a night with two friends who were flat broke. I felt poor myself, but did not realize that they actually had no money for toast for breakfast, much less butter or honey to put on it. I was worried for them, but we were young and strong, and we loved each other and still do.

So we sat for about three hours drinking tea. There was nothing like sugar or milk or an old cookie to blanket it. We talked and laughed and came to great conclusions, and I should have remembered how my grandmother and Father and Mother grew pink-cheeked and chatty after a couple of cups of the lunch-time brew from Dublin. Instead, I finally drove off to meet my mother at Great-Aunt Maggie's and then headed back to Whittier, and almost at once I knew that I should not be behind the wheel.

I was a good driver, and had been since I was eleven and Father taught me . . . pure Hell all the way, since like most loving parents who must cope with preadolescent vacuities he was harsh and mocking. Traffic laws were simple then, and there were no white lines down the middle of roads and no red and green lights. I knew all the rules, including my father's dictum that I should always drive as if everybody else on the road were either drunk or crazy. And that day, full of good company and tea, I knew I was.

Telephone poles were matchsticks, put there to be snapped off at a whim. Dogs trotting across the road were suddenly big trucks. Old ladies turned into moving vans. Everything was too bright, but very funny and made for my delight. And about half a mile from my long liquid breakfast I turned carefully down a side street and parked, and sat beaming happily through the tannic fog for about an hour, remembering how witty we all had been, how handsome and talented. . . .

By the time I got to Great-Aunt Maggie's, Mother was plainly a little put out by my lateness, but I was sober. We drove home in a good mood, and although I never told her why I was tardy, that afternoon we sat pleasurably together by her fire over a good cup of delicate green tea, and she did not see that I was not drinking it, then or ever again.

This deliberate and self-protective abstinence has often filled me with regret. Was I warned so dangerously because of my anger at my own docility for so many years? Did I find myself high-drunk on fury and frustration, or on other chemicals like caffeine? How can I know? And how can a maimed tea lover like me be writing an introduction to this story of one of the true refinements of our present culture?

Perhaps one answer is that the intoxication that lives in the way our language can be used is headier than any herbal or fermented brew. George Saintsbury knew it, and so do we, the fortunate many. Norwood Pratt's book about tea is written so deftly, in its heady combination of learning and pure love, that its pages will cheer us long after what's in the cup is cold and stale.

Tea grows on bushes, but good books about it do not. This one, though, will cheer us for a long time, and reassure of the potency of words well used.

—M.F.K. FISHER

Glen Ellen, California
Spring, 1982

CHAPTER ONE

TEA TALES

The Greatest Stories Ever Told

A TRUTHFUL RELATION OF TEA HISTORY

Surely every one is aware of the divine pleasures which attend a wintry fireside: candles at four o'clock, warm hearthrugs, tea, a fair tea-maker, shutters closed, curtains flowing in ample draperies to the floor, whilst the wind and rain are raging audibly without.
—*Thomas De Quincey*
CONFESSIONS OF AN ENGLISH OPIUM–EATER

ISTORIANS NOW agree the good Dr. Samuel Johnson was wrong in saying tea first came to England in 1666, but when exactly it did come they have not yet decided. I myself shall claim it was on 13 September 1658, and let it go at that. On that date tea was first advertised in a London journal by one Thomas Garway as "the excellent and by all physitians approved China drink, called by the Chineans Tcha, by other nations Tay, alias Tee." The somewhat wordy Mr. Garway offered this novelty for sale at his "Cophee-House, in Sweeting's Rents by the Royal Exchange." Two years later, in 1660, we find him publishing a pamphlet entitled "An Exact Description of the Growth, Quality and Vertues of the Leaf TEA" in which it is unblushingly urged for what it is—a stimulant. In his *Diary* this same year, Samuel Pepys notes, "I did send for a cup of tea (a China drink) of which I had never drank before." It was probably to Garway's he did send. The year 1660 also saw the beginning of that long contest between tea drinkers and tax collectors that is responsible for some of the liveliest pages of English and American history.

From the Oriental point of view, the enterprising Mr. Garway and his customers are late arrivals in the ancient and generally honorable history of tea. Wherever the plant itself may have originated, it was definitely the Chinese who discovered tea as a drink. They credit a legendary emperor named Shen Nung with its discovery around 2700 B.C. According to the story he only drank water that had been boiled, and one day leaves from the firewood, or perhaps a nearby bush, fell into his kettle, and the Chinese date tea drinking from this happy accident. The Chinese have never seemed troubled by the fact that more or less recognizable references to tea only appear in their writings about the time of the Roman Empire. (Tea only acquired its distinctive ideogram, *ch'a,* in the Chinese written language around A.D. 725, appearing for the first time in an herbal.)

The taste for tea must have spread beyond China during Roman days also, for Chinese records say Turkish barbarians appeared on their Mongolian frontier and bartered for tea the very year that the last emperor of Rome, young Romulus Augustulus, began his ill-fated reign. By the time Charlemagne was crowned the first so-called Holy Roman Emperor in the year 800, Lu Yu, a close contemporary of the poet Li Po, had just become recognized as patron saint of all the tea in China.

LU YU & THE *CH'A CHING*

Oh no—I was afraid of that!
—Harvard's Professor Wiesel on learning
he'd received the Nobel Prize, 1981

The Victorian art critic John Ruskin once said, "to see a thing and tell it in plain words is the greatest thing a soul can do"—and that's exactly what Lu Yu did. Lu Yu, if his biographers are to be believed, was an orphan raised by Buddhist monks. As an adolescent, he rebelled (as who does not?) against the pieties and practices of his received religion. One imagines that the long periods of sitting meditation got to him. Whatever the case, he fled from holiness and the prospects of enlightenment to enter show business, so to speak, as a comic and clown. He was a success, it is said, but still dissatisfied: He yearned for an education.

At about this point, an influential fan became his patron and enabled Lu Yu to make a scholar of himself, only to find him fired with a further ambition: He wanted to make a lasting contribution of his own to learning (as, again, who wouldn't?). Somehow Lu Yu wangled a contract for a book on tea. The tea interests wanted their haphazard methods of cultivation and production codified, compared, and analyzed in a clearly understandable report. Like the author of *Confessions of an English Opium-Eater,* Lu Yu saw it as the chance of a lifetime. He went into five years of hermithood and came out with the *Ch'a Ching*—the world's first "book of tea." In its own field, the *Ch'a Ching* was right away ranked alongside the *I Ching,* the "cyclopedia," "scripture," or "classic" of changes, for *ching* means much more than "book."

The *Ch'a Ching*'s masterful descriptions of tea cultivation and production, proper and otherwise, comprise only one part of Lu Yu's masterpiece. He goes into detail about the very best china to serve it in, gives exquisitely precise advice on brewing it, and winds up carried away with such a refined appreciation of tea that he recommends a respectful ceremonial as the best way to drink it. Lu Yu's ideal afternoon tea required twenty-four different objects and implements for measuring, preparing, serving, and enjoying a cup. As a native of southern China, his tea ceremony incorporated much of the Taoist symbolism current there. "Tao" is a Chinese term roughly equivalent to the Sanskrit-Buddhist "dharma" or the Greco-Christian "logos," all of which may be

translated "the way things are." Nor is it incidental that the insanely refined and mannered Lu Yu was a southern Chinese. These sons of the Tao are to their northern, Confucian brethren as Italians are to Germans or Rebel gentlemen to Yankees.

Suddenly Lu Yu was a celebrity. He'd had the last word on tea and every one agreed nobody could have said it better. Take his description of the best quality leaf: It should "curl like the dewlaps of a bull, crease like the leather boots of a Tartar horseman, unfold like mist rising over a ravine, and soften as gently as fine earth swept by rain." No wonder publication of the *Ch'a Ching* made Lu Yu tea's patron saint in China in his own lifetime. Nobody could think of anything to add! High and low revered the man; the emperor made him his friend. That he was not greatly affected by all this is to his credit—and probably also thanks to a comedian's view of life leftover from his earlier calling. Lu Yu ended up withdrawing—comfortably, I'm sure—from this world and going off to meditate the way the Buddhists always told him he should.

It is perhaps interesting to note that the (to be) Zen Buddhists introduced tea and Lu Yu's tea ceremony to Japan somewhat later and have preserved both to this day there, just as the Mongols and Tibetans have ever since made tea according to one of his most godawful recipes—with butter and ground barley. About a generation after Lu Yu, two Arab travelers wrote the first account of tea for non-Chinese, but nothing came of it. The Chinese weren't interested in creating foreign markets. They knew little about the rest of the world, which they perceived as populated by barbaric races who ought, if the least intelligent, to recognize their Yellow Emperor as the Son of Heaven and lord of everything under it. Meanwhile, they enjoyed undoubtedly the world's greatest civilization, entirely self-sufficient and supremely self-satisfied.

T'ANG, SUNG, & MONGOL

Tea is like the East he grows in,
A great yellow mandarin
With urbanity of manner
And unconsciousness of sin.
    —*G. K. Chesterton (1874–1936)*
    THE SONG OF RIGHT AND WRONG

About a century after the death of the patron saint of tea in China, the T'ang Dynasty (618–906), to which Lu Yu's emperor friend belonged, was deposed. Confusion reigned for the next fifty-odd years as no fewer than fifteen different emperors came and went. A functioning central government was finally restored with the advent of the Sung Dynasty in 960. Having no competence whatever as an Orientalist, I can only repeat here what the authorities claim: The T'ang Dynasty represents the "classic" and the Sung the "romantic" era of tea, society, and the arts. T'ang tea lovers used tea compressed into cakes, which were roasted over a fire "until soft as a baby's arm," as Lu Yu puts it. The cakes were then shredded and added to boiling salted water, sometimes with flavorings like dates, peppermint, or even onions. Under the Sung Dynasty, tea leaves were ground to a fine powder in a small stone mill and then whipped in hot water with a delicate whisk made of split bamboo. Salt and most other flavorings were discarded forever. The preferred chinaware for serving this new-style tea was also different. The cups Lu Yu liked best had an exquisite blue glaze, so that once the reddish-brown cake tea was served in them it would look jade green in the cup. The more delicately colored whipped tea inspired Sung ceramicists to come up with strangely beautiful teacups of blue black, black, dark brown, and deep purple.

The T'ang and Sung dynasties differed not only in their ideal teas, but also in their ideas of life. Where the largely Taoist T'ang found the Mystery of the Universe *represented* in the use of tea, the largely Buddhist Sung found it *realized* there. The T'ang mentality found everything "symbolic" of something else, so to speak, while the down-to-earth Sung made no distinctions between things of this world and things of any other. The Sung world was not just a reflection of the Cosmic Mystery but an actual part of it: Life in this world was no less significant than the goings-on beyond. From the Sung viewpoint, therefore, properly serving your guest a proper cup of tea was just as important as the Buddha's attaining enlightenment. If everything didn't mean something then nothing would mean anything, you might say.

To the Sungs, tea meant a great deal. The emperor Hui-Sung, who was much too great an artist to be a well-behaved monarch, spent fortunes developing rare tea varieties and wrote a treatise on twenty different kinds, selecting as rarest and finest a particular "white tea." The Sung emperors held undisputed sway over all China for almost two hundred and fifty years, until Genghis Khan & Sons began wresting their territory away from them in 1206. By 1275, the year Marco Polo reached China, the *Ch'a Ching* had been in circulation almost exactly five hundred years. Curious, is it not, that Messer Marco nowhere mentions tea? Historians assume that as guest of Kublai Khan and the Mongol barbarians who'd finally conquered the Chinese, he—like them—simply took no notice of the drink of the subject people. Historians also aver that these same Mongols damn nigh destroyed Chinese culture.

After ousting the Sungs and holding power some two hundred and fifty years, the Mongol, or Yuan, Dynasty was finally in its turn replaced on the throne by the native Chinese Ming emperors (1368–1644). Their imperial Ming majesties inherited few or none of the fruits of T'ang and Sung culture. Manners and customs had changed so radically that few vestiges of former times remained. To quote the Japanese Okakura Kakuzo, author of our own century's classic, *The Book of Tea*: "We find a Ming commentator at a loss to recall the shape of the tea whisk mentioned in one of the Sung classics. Tea is now taken by steeping the leaves in hot water in a bowl or cup. The reason why the Western world is innocent of the older methods of drinking tea is explained by the fact that Europe knew it only at the close of the Ming Dynasty."

TEA & THE JAPANESE

To a European the [tea] ceremony is lengthy and meaningless. When witnessed more than once, it becomes intolerably monotonous. Not being born with an Oriental fund of patience, he longs for something new, something lively, something with at least the semblance of logic and utility. But then it is not for him that the tea ceremonies were made. If they amuse those for whom they were made, they amuse them, and there is nothing more to be said. In any case, tea ceremonies are perfectly harmless. . . . Some may deem them pointless. None can stigmatise them as vulgar.
—Basil Hall Chamberlain (1849–1912)
JAPANESE THINGS

It would take as much diligence and time to unravel the history of tea in Japan as to write the rest of this book. Tea had long been the favorite beverage among the Buddhists of the mainland because it helped them stay awake and alert during their lengthy meditations.* It is therefore not surprising that a Japanese Buddhist, returning from studying in China, should become the first to bring tea seeds to Japan and plant them there. He accomplished this the very year of Lu Yu's death, 805, and Dengyo Daishi has been considered a saint in Japan ever since. Over the ensuing centuries tea was to pervade every aspect of Japanese culture, from *fellatio* and flower arranging to the art of suicide. It caught on fast. Almost as soon as the first tea was ready for plucking, the Japanese emperor Saga sampled some, liked it, and ordered that tea be cultivated in five different provinces near the capital. Imperial patronage lends a certain snob appeal in any time and place—tea throve in Japan. It seems more than likely that this agricultural experiment was an effort by the emperor of Japan to catch

---

*It was in this connection that the Japanese concocted a legend of their own to account for the origin of tea. They say the missionary monk Daruma, who brought Buddhism from his native India to China, took a vow in Nanking to sit facing a wall for nine years of unremitting and sleepless meditation, but after only five years he was overcome by drowsiness and dozed off for a moment. Filled with chagrin, he cut off his eyelids and flung them to the ground whereupon a tea bush miraculously grew up on the spot. The beverage he made from its leaves promptly refreshed the good Daruma and banished sleepiness for the remainder of his meditation. Believe it or not.

up with his Chinese counterpart, Lu Yu's T'ang patron and friend. Years later, for some reason, there suddenly occurred a break in relations between China and Japan that lasted some two hundred eighty years.

Contact between the two countries was resumed shortly before the year 1200, by which time a Japanese Buddhist version of Lu Yu's tea ceremony was already being taught as a practical spiritual exercise. It was also about 1200 that another Buddhist and foe of drowsiness during meditation, the abbot Myo-e, pioneered one of the finest tea gardens in the world in the neighborhood of Uji near Kyoto. Myo-e's small temple garden is still there, I am told, including offshoots of the original plantings. And tea, made from their leaves, continues to be served at the temple. Myo-e's seeds came from a tea-drinking friend and fellow Buddhist abbot who had already written the first book on tea in Japanese. All these beginnings were to bear unbelievable fruit.

As nearly as I can judge, the Japanese tea ceremonies have undergone at least three distinct stages in the seven hundred or so years of their existence. The first was a medico-religious stage. Myo-e's friend, the abbot Yeisei, tries to promote it as a sort of divinely mixed snake oil and holy water in his, the first Japanese tea book, *The Book of Tea Sanitation.* (This is the literal translation of the title, but knowledgeable friends assure me he meant "the salutary effects of tea drinking." As with all "Japanosities"— the transliteration of names above all—it is impossible there shall ever be agreement about these things.) It appears that Yeisei (or "Eisai" as others spell him) was summoned to the bedside of the youthful and reprobate shogun of the day to administer last rites. Finding that the shogun was merely—and I use the word respectfully— suffering from a terrible hangover, Yeisei endeavored to sober him up and save him from the wine cup by making him take tea and, in the manner of propagandists everywhere, he accompanied his prescription with a tract. The health claims he makes for tea are absurd, but the ceremonial he prescribed for the drinking of it was religious and a tinge of Buddhist ritual has adhered to the tea ceremony ever since. Perhaps this is not so surprising, considering it was this same Yeisei who introduced Zen to Japan.

It took little over a century from the time of Yeisei and Myo-e for tea drinking to reach a second stage, that of luxury. Well before 1330, the Japanese nobility had devised the "tea tournament" on the model of another of their rarified pleasures, "incense comparing." They continued to hang Buddhist scroll paintings in their tea rooms and to make offerings before them, to be sure, but that was the extent of religious observances. The guests, lolling about the spacious tea-drinking pavilion on leopard and tiger skins, were invited to admire their host's rich silks and brocades, gold and silver vessels, jewelry and inlaid armor and weapons. All these were "Chinese things" and treasured as such, for Japan still languished beneath the cultural shadow of her giant neighbor, whose fashions she aped in all things and whose fine arts her nobility admired to the exclusion of all things "domestic."

A tea tournament was rather like a wine tasting and not, one supposes, without the attendant foolishness. The point of this *jeu de société* was to guess which tea came from where, and the one who guessed rightly was awarded one of the treasures adorning the tea pavilion. The rules of the ceremony as it was then practiced, however, ordained that the winner should bestow his prize on one or more of the singing and dancing girls who were always present at these revels. Such affairs might be dubbed "10 bowl," "50 bowl," or even "100 bowl" tea tournaments, depending on how many teas were served. Japan's Lorenzo de' Medici, the shogun Yoshimasa, even abdicated the shogunate to devote himself to his art collecting and tea parties full time. (This in 1473.) His drinking buddy, so to speak, was an apparently lapsed Buddhist abbot named Shuko, who might be said to know both sides of a tea bowl. It's claimed he was once ousted from a temple for gambling in and judging tea tournaments. Shuko, pleasure-loving but a good Buddhist at heart, was the first to formulate the cult of tea as a sort of sacrament, a "way" as Asians put it, with something approaching the status of a separate religion. He attained *satori,* enlightenment, one day when it occurred to him that even the gesture of filling an ordinary tea bowl with hot water must express the Law of the Universe.

Having long since eclipsed the emperor, the shoguns of this so-called Muromachi period (1338–1568) were drawn, one and all, from the Ashikaga clan. Under their stewardship, things went from bad to worse, but in reading the melancholy annals of the Ashikaga—one long catalog of individual debauchery and tragedy and of ruinous wars between the great feudal houses—we must not forget that this was also the golden age of Japanese painting, when some of the best literature was produced, and the *noh* drama invented. A better scholar than I will someday explain how this happened. Assuredly, it was a great time to be rich and powerful. How working folks felt about the regime can be guessed from the fact that well into the nineteenth century citizens of

Kyoto would, in exchange for a few *yen* cheerfully paid, obtain permission to enter the family's shrine and beat the statues of the Ashikaga departed with a stick.

The principal strongman to emerge from the collapse of Ashikaga authority was a remarkably hideous peasant named, remarkably, Hideyoshi (1536–98). He was the sort of man who had his slain enemies' ears cut off, packed in barrels, and sent back to the capital at Kyoto for burial. It was largely his doing that the Japanese were united under one functioning government for the first time. One of the most influential of Hideyoshi's contemporaries and a principal adviser was the greatest of all Japanese tea masters, Sen-no Rikyu (1521–91). During his lifetime Japan was not only in the throes of the struggle for national unification, but also was having to deal with Westerners, merchants and missionaries from Portugal and Holland, for the first time.* Sen-no Rikyu took refuge from all this confusion in Zen meditation training, studying the way of tea, or *chado,* under a disciple of the great Shuko. If Shuko was the Saint Paul of *chado,* Rikyu was its Luther, for he became a different sort of tea prophet, spreading a doctrine of *wabi,* or "simple and natural," which spilled out of his teacup into every aspect of Japanese life.

Hideyoshi loved tea and he practiced *chado* after his own fashion. He sponsored probably the greatest tea party of all time, the invitation being in the form of an official edict, which is still preserved. All the tea lovers of the empire were summoned to assemble near Kyoto and bring along all their treasured tea utensils and wares. Rikyu planned everything to the last detail and the meeting lasted ten days, during which Hideyoshi fulfilled his promise to drink tea with each participant, whether nobleman, trader, or peasant—proof that *chado* had already begun to filter down into the lower strata of society.

Rikyu would also accompany Hideyoshi to the battlefield with a tiny portable tea house as a place of relaxation before the fighting, where the heart could be composed.

---

* The first missionary arrived from Portugal in 1549. By 1567, Christian converts included at least one great lord who gave land to the Jesuits, forced Christianity on his vassals by the most drastic means, and, to serve as the stronghold of the foreign religion, established the town of Nagasaki. Ironic, no?

But while Rikyu's pursuit of *wabi* became ever more simple and constantly more accessible to ordinary citizens, Hideyoshi, in the wake of his victories, triumphantly ordered all his tea vessels made of gold. The falling out between the two was perhaps foreordained, but to Western eyes it seems as mysterious and remote as a power struggle between an ancient Etruscan king and his augur.

One historian avers Rikyu's fall came about because he was "not indifferent to money" and abused his unrivaled skill as a connoisseur of tea wares to enrich himself and curry favor with the great. Others think it was Rikyu's irksome appearance of saintliness that eventually provoked Hideyoshi into ordering his death. (After all, any *wabi* tea master could have made do on Rikyu's annual stipend of three thousand bushels of rice.) Whatever the case and despite his seventy years, having composed a farewell poem and smashed his favorite tea bowl, Sen-no Rikyu enjoyed the privilege of dying by his own hand. Nothing became his life so much as the leaving of it, and the tea ceremony that he purified and codified has retained the form he gave it ever since, a "path to enlightenment" or "way of being" *unto itself.* Just fifty-four years after Rikyu's death, to illustrate, the greatest samurai Japan ever produced, Musashi, began his book on strategy as follows: "Strategy is the [way] of the warrior. . . . There are various ways. There is the way of salvation by the law of the Buddha, the way of Confucius governing the way of learning, the way of healing as a doctor, [poetry], tea, archery, and many arts and skills." Musashi's word for tea is *chado.*

Obviously with Rikyu and his doctrine of *wabi,* which he inherited in part from Shuko, the tea ceremony enters its aesthetic stage. But wait a minute, I hear you say: Tea drinking as a way of life? Tea as a path toward holiness? Whoa!

Sen-no Rikyu himself said "there are many ways to put into practice in our own lives the teachings of the great masters of the past. In Zen, truth is pursued through the discipline of meditation in order to realize enlightenment, while in Tea we use training in the actual procedures of making tea to achieve the same end."

But the most eloquent explanation I've read of tea's importance in life is to be found in *The Book of Tea* written in 1906 by Okakuro Kakuzo, who was born a decade after Commodore Perry's mission to Japan and was reared in the strict moral code of the samurai.

It is in the Japanese tea ceremony that we see the culmination of tea ideals. Our successful resistance to the Mongol invasion of 1281 had enabled us to carry on the Sung movement so disastrously cut off in China itself through the nomadic inroad. Tea with us became more than an idealisation of the form of drinking: It is a religion of the art of life. The beverage grew to be an excuse for the worship of purity and refinement, a sacred function. . . . The tea room was an oasis in the dreary waste of existence where weary travellers could meet to drink from the common spring of art appreciation. The ceremony was an improvised drama whose plot was woven about the tea, the flowers, and the paintings. Not a color to disturb the tone of the room, not a sound to mar the rhythm of things, not a gesture to obtrude on the harmony, not a word to break the unity of the surroundings, all movements to be performed simply and naturally—such were the aims of the tea ceremony. And strangely enough it was often successful. A subtle philosophy lay behind it all. Teaism was Taoism in disguise.

The ceremony invariably employs powdered tea whipped into a froth, Sung style. "The use of the steeped tea of the later China," Kakuzo adds, "is comparatively recent among us, being only known since the middle of the seventeenth century."

EAST MEETS WEST

"Take some more tea," the March Hare said to Alice very earnestly. "I haven't had any yet," Alice replied in an offended tone, "so I can't take more."
—*Charles Lutwidge Dodgson (Lewis Carroll, 1832–98)*
ALICE IN WONDERLAND

Apart from a stray Marco Polo or so, very few Occidentals and Orientals had ever met face to face until Vasco da Gama of Portugal sailed around Africa's Cape of Good Hope and reached India in 1498. True, the Romans had been the first Europeans to trade with the Chinese even though this trade was carried on indirectly via middlemen. One theory blames Rome's decline and fall on the constant flow of Roman gold over the caravan routes to China in exchange for silks. But it was some twenty years after da Gama's voyage that, for the first time, a European vessel stood to off the coast of China. The ship was Portuguese and was over fifteen thousand sea miles and almost two years'

sail from home. To return, her captain had to find his way through a maze of uncharted rocks, shoals, and islands, cross the Indian Ocean, beat his way back around the cape into the Atlantic, and then face a still-considerable voyage to Lisbon, all in a small, square-rigged ship that was hard to handle under the best of circumstances and absolutely helpless in a storm or against a headwind.

Since there was no question of sailing so far without places to put in for repairs and fresh supplies, the Portuguese' first order of business was to found in China a base like those they had established in Africa and India. In sign language, one supposes, permission was denied. The Chinese authorities greeted these *yang-kuei-tze* or "foreign devils" (what a name for the courteous Portuguese!) with the suspicion and disdain they reserved for all outsiders. But if East and West did not exactly meet, at least they'd made contact—and somehow the Portuguese maintained that contact.

The Portuguese carried on a sort of buccaneering trade up and down the coast of China for forty years, until the emperor finally relented and granted them a legal port of entry and base of operations—just one. This way he could at least receive the import and export duties he was losing otherwise, while keeping the "foreign devils" under the Ming thumb. The place selected was a rocky peninsula about three miles long that jutted off an island in the Pearl River delta, some miles down river from the major port of Canton. The Portuguese named it Macao and hold it to this day. They traded there, not for tea, but for the silks, brocades and velvets, the exotic wares and condiments to season food and drink that the European upper classes had hitherto received, when at all, through Venice. When Portugal received the exclusive right to trade in Macao in 1557, the Venetian connection was doomed. More and more of this rich produce was shipped to Lisbon whence, it was the Dutch for the most part who transported it to the ports of France, Holland, and the Baltic. After about fifty years of this commerce, Europe began to receive her first shipments of tea through these Dutch merchants. The year was 1610.

RUMORS OF TEA

Rumoresque senum severiorum
Omnes unius aestimemus assis.
—*Catullus (84–54* B.C.)

Europe had heard of tea years before that first chance to try some, but what a surprise the real article must have been! Not one of the half dozen or more descriptions fairly widely circulated by 1610, would have enabled Europeans to imagine what tea was like—or even to recognize it.

The earliest-known mention of tea in Europe was published in 1559, and, not surprisingly, at Venice. A certain Giambattista Ramusio had served as secretary to the ruling Council of Ten there and was charged with entertaining numerous foreign visitors and collecting such information of commercial value as he could from them. These intelligence reports were published in a volume titled *Voyages and Travels,* along with earlier narratives like that of Marco Polo, a Venetian no one in Venice had believed before. Tea appears in Ramusio's "Tale of Hajji Mohammed," a Persian traveler he'd entertained.

> He told me that all over Cathay [China] they made use of another plant, or rather of its leaves. This is called by those people *Chai Catai,* * and grows in the district of Cathay which is called *Cacian-fu* [Szechwan]. They take of that herb, whether dry or fresh, and boil it well in water. One or two cups of this decoction taken on an empty stomach removes fever, headache, stomach ache, pain in the sides or in the joints, and it should be taken as hot as you can bear it. He said, besides, that it was good for no end of other ailments which he could not remember but gout was one of them. And if it happens that one feels incommoded in the stomach [has indigestion] from having eaten too much, one has but to take a little of this decoction. . . . And it is so highly valued and esteemed that every one going on a journey takes it with him, and those people would gladly give a sack of rhubarb for one ounce of *Chai Catai.*

Chai catai means "tea of China (Cathay)." *Chai,* a corruption of *ch'a,* persists to this day through India, Afghanistan, Iran, and who knows where else as the word for "tea."

This last obscurity was illumined when I discovered the Chinese used rhubarb medicinally as an aid to digestion.

Rhubarb aside, Ramusio's Persian informant was most impressed with tea's value as a medicine. One feels he's heard an all-purpose Dramamine described, some Oriental antidote to their own version of Montezuma's revenge. A year after its publication, Ramusio's hearsay was shakily substantiated in the travel diary of a Portuguese Jesuit, freshly returned from Macao: "Whatsoever person or persons come to any man's house of quality, he hath a custome to offer him . . . a kind of drink they called *Ch'a,* which is somewhat bitter, red, and medicinall." Quickly translated and reprinted, such travel accounts were not meant as entertainment only, but serious reading for merchants looking for profitable ventures in the East. But who could have guessed from any of them what tea really is?

The Dutch not only brought the first tea to Europe but also the name by which it is known. As we have seen, tea is *ch'a* to the Chinese—but not to all of them. Denied access to Canton or Macao, the Dutch conducted their early China trade from Java in what is now Indonesia and was then a regular port of call for Chinese merchant junks. They must have obtained their first tea from junks out of Amoy, the Chinese port opposite Formosa (Taiwan), and therefore adopted the Amoy dialect term *t'e* (pronounced "tay") for the stuff. Portuguese retains the Cantonese-derived *cha* to this day. All other European countries, except Russia, bought their first tea from the Dutch and learned from them to call it "tay" as well.

TEA'S RECEPTION IN EUROPE

The progress of this famous plant has been something like the progress of truth; suspected at first, though very palatable to those who had the courage to taste it; resisted as it encroached; abused as its popularity seemed to spread; and establishing its triumph at last, in cheering the whole land from the palace to the cottage, only by the slow and restless efforts of time and its own virtues.

—*Isaac D'Israeli (1766–1848)*
in a 1790 EDINBURGH REVIEW

When the Dutch brought the first tea to Europe in 1610, England's Good Queen Bess had been dead seven years, Shakespeare had six years to live, and Rembrandt was four years old. After decades of Portuguese middlemanship, the Dutch East India Company had been formed in 1602, to establish bases in Indonesia and Japan and trade directly with the Orient. And by 1637 the Company's directors, the "Lords Seventeen," were writing their governor-general in Indonesia: "As tea begins to come into use by some of the people, we expect some jars of Chinese as well as Japanese tea with each ship." They got their jars on a regular basis thereafter, it appears, for within a few years tea had become a fashionable, if expensive, beverage among high society at The Hague. And if it sometimes cost the equivalent of a hundred dollars or more per pound, so what? The people Vermeer pictured for us in rooms rich with colored maps and intricate Oriental carpets were nothing if not affluent. At first they bought their tea from apothecaries, who added it and other such luxury items as sugar and ginger and spices to their line of medicines. By the year of Vermeer's death (1675, six years after Rembrandt's), tea was being sold in grocery stores to rich and poor alike and was in general use throughout Holland.

It is about this time we find a certain Dr. Bontekoe advising his Dutch readers to use eight or ten cups of tea daily, hastily adding he sees no reason to object to fifty, a hundred or two hundred cups, as he frequently consumed that much himself! History whispers that Dr. Bontekoe may have been in the pay of the Dutch East India Company, which promptly made him a handsome honorarium for the impetus he'd given their tea sales. Tea soon became a daily necessity in Dutch life.

In the light of more recent history, it seems strange that tea drinking encountered no official intolerance in Europe—no rabid prohibitionists, no self-perpetuating anti-drug agency. You can, however, trace the spread of tea from Holland by the proliferation of medical Viewers with Alarm. Even before regular imports began, the first of these had warned in a Latin treatise that tea "... hastens the death of those that drink it, especially if they have passed the age of forty years." This same medical authority, Dr. Simon Paulli, also assured his readers that "girls' breasts that are rubbed with the juice of hemlock do not grow thereafter, but remain properly small and do not change the size they are." Prior to Bontekoe's pronouncements, even a Dutch physician, prejudiced by a moldy batch it sounds like, could deride tea as "groats and dishwater, a tasteless and disgusting beverage!" Soon after tea reached Germany we find a German medico gravely blaming tea for the "dried-up" appearance of the Chinese and exclaiming, "Down with tea! Send it back!"

The mid-1600s saw tea set off the kind of raging debate the French are famous for, a famous Parisian doctor becoming the first to denounce it as "the impertinent novelty of the century." A colleague of his was soon complaining that "the Dutch bring tea from China to Paris and sell it at thirty francs a pound, though they have paid but eight or ten *sous* in that country, and it is old and spoiled into the bargain. People must regard it as a precious medicament. . . ." You can just see how he must have shook his head. Nonetheless, before the century is finished, poems to tea appear in French. In one of her letters, Madame de Sévigné finds it worthy of note that a friend of hers takes her tea with milk—imagine!—and the aged Racine, who died in 1699, begins every day drinking tea with his breakfast. There is a painting in the Louvre by a certain Olivier depicting perhaps the most famous French tea. It is entitled *Tea à l'anglaise in the Grand Salon of the Temple, with the Court of the Prince de Conti listening to the Young Mozart,* and it is dated nigh a century after the honest de Sévigné's gossip. It is precisely this depiction of how the French nobility gave an "English-style" tea party that assures us the French had given up on tea for themselves. Once the "novelty of the century" had worn off, almost all Frenchmen returned to the beverages traditionally associated with their national life—wines, mostly cheap and occasionally divine, and dark-roasted coffee. The Germans likewise, after the first flurry of excitement, came to ignore the new drink, preferring their old and true favorite, beer. A European tea merchant of 1700 would have recognized only two growing markets outside Holland—England and Russia.

RUSSIA DISCOVERS TEA

This will last out a night in Russia,
When nights are longest there.
—William Shakespeare (1564–1616)
the magistrate Angelo in MEASURE FOR MEASURE

About the time that first tea order from the Dutch "Lords Seventeen" reached their agent in the Orient, the Mogul emperor of north India, Pakistan, Afghanistan, and elsewhere was entertaining the first agent or ambassador from his fellow despot to the

north, Czar Michael Romanov, the founder of Russia's Romanov dynasty. Though introduced to tea himself, the ambassador declined an offer to take a gift of it back to the czar as something his master would have no use for, thereby blowing one more chance the Russians had had to make tea's acquaintance. They finally did so only after 1689, when Russia and China signed a treaty establishing a boundary between them and, at Chinese insistence, confining all trade between the two to a single frontier town.* In the middle of nowhere thenceforth, at Usk Kayakhta, a thousand miles across the Gobi Desert from Peking and over three thousand miles from Moscow, Russian government caravans would arrive laden with furs and load up with tea for the return journey.

Ordinary caravans numbered two hundred to three hundred camels and took almost a year for the trip from Moscow to Usk Kayakhta and back. Reckoning about six hundred pounds to the camel, more knowledgeable authorities than I estimate Russia was receiving over six hundred camel loads of tea annually soon after 1700. It was so costly—fifteen rubles per pound in 1735—that only aristocrats could afford to buy tea at first. But in that year the Czarina Elizabeth—whether with an eye to profit or a taste for tea is not recorded—established a regular private caravan trade and tea became increasingly plentiful.

By the time Catherine the Great died in 1796, Russia was consuming over six thousand camel loads of tea per annum—better than three and a half million pounds! This is especially impressive when you reflect that nobody had invented a faster camel. What they had invented, probably as early as Elizabeth's time, was the samovar. The likeliest explanation I can come up with for this invention is that the samovar is a modification of the Mongolian firepot, which operates on the same principle and was used by the trans-Ural nomads for cooking. Be that as it may, the samovar soon became

---

*European Jesuits played an interesting role in these negotiations. A number of them were allowed to live (though not to proselytize) at the Chinese court, where they instructed the Imperial Manchu Majesty in such Western novelties as the heretic Galileo's astronomy and the music of J. S. Bach. Two of these, the Portuguese Pereira and the Frenchman Gerbillon, served as interpreters between the Chinese and Russians. They drew up the treaty in Latin, making copies in the Tartar and Muscovite languages.

a feature of everyday life throughout Russia. For reasons of tradition and economy, Russians were accustomed to a single, if mammoth, daily meal and high and low resorted to the samovar the rest of the time, generally sipping their tea from glasses through a sugar cube held between the teeth.

Since the Chinese refused to let Russian ships trade in their ports, the caravan trade went on growing in volume right up to 1880, when the first link of the Trans-Siberian Railroad was opened. With the completion of the railway in 1900, the caravans passed into history, finally returning Usk Kayakhta to the obscurity it so richly deserves. The tea that had formerly required many months to reach Russian samovars made the trip by rail in seven weeks. By this time Russia was importing even more Chinese tea than England, the Western country whose history is most intimately associated with that shrub.

ORIGINS OF THE JOHN COMPANY

Corporations, like people, are often better understood by looking at their past. In the business world, where eyes are usually firmly fixed on the road ahead, this exercise is seldom performed.

—*Michael Katz (1942–   ) et al*
EVERYBODY'S BUSINESS: THE IRREVERENT
GUIDE TO CORPORATE AMERICA

Sixty years before Samuel Pepys first "did send for a cup of tea" in London, Queen Elizabeth had had to face up to one of the most important decisions of her reign. Her valiant little navy had broken the Spanish Armada, but in international commerce the Spanish remained supreme in the West, just as Portugal was rivaled only by the Dutch in the East. As a lady with a wardrobe of three thousand costumes, mostly made of Oriental fabrics, Elizabeth was in a position to guess at the enormous profits to be had from direct trade for such goods with the Far East. And once the Dutch and Portuguese conspired to fix the price of pepper and other spices, Elizabeth realized it was time England did her own importing. On the last day of 1600, therefore, "for the honor of the nation, the wealth of the people . . . the increase of navigation and the advancement of lawfulle traffic," she chartered the Honorable East India Company.

The "John Company," as this group came to be called, was granted a monopoly on all trade east of the Cape of Good Hope and west of Cape Horn. This organization of wealthy merchants was to play a central role in the creation of the British Empire. Over the years to come, its far-reaching powers would be extended even further. It was granted the right to acquire territory, coin money, maintain armies and forts, form foreign alliances, declare war, conclude peace, and try and punish law breakers. And as the basis of its power, the John Company was to become the biggest and mightiest monopoly in any commodity that the world has ever known. That commodity? Tea.

Only six weeks after receiving their charter, the East India merchants dispatched their first fleet of five ships and four hundred men under the command of one James Lancaster. Sixteen months later, he found himself anchored off Sumatra and disinclined to venture farther east into seas the Portuguese claimed as their own. He collected a certain amount of cargo in trade with a fat and aged local king and assigned men to stay and start a "factory"—not a place of manufacture in the parlance of the times, but a fortified trading establishment complete with offices, warehouses, and living quarters. On the way back, Lancaster captured more Oriental produce from a Portuguese ship and reached home to discover that one out of every three Londoners had perished of the plague and James I occupied the throne. And the Company discovered it had a 90 percent profit on capital and expenses to pocket!

A company "factor" (head of a "factory," what else?) in Japan became the first English tea drinker of record, writing a colleague in Macao in 1615, for "a pot of the best sort of chaw." (It seems inexplicable that a man stationed in Japan would not have noticed the innumerable native tea drinkers and simply asked them for some; this blindness to local ways was to prove typical of the British trader and lead to monumental blunders.) By the time of this letter the Company had eighteen "factories" in the Orient, including the one in Japan and several in India, but England had come no nearer her first "pot of chaw."

TEA REACHES ENGLAND AT LAST

Thank God for tea! What would the world do without tea? How did it exist? I am glad I was not born before tea.

—*Sidney Smith (1771–1845)*
the English Billy Graham of his day, in a letter

I shall repeat here my assertion that tea only came onto the English scene in September of 1658, the very month that Oliver Cromwell died and presumably went to hell. There is an interesting connection between these two events. Holland was at the height of her power when Cromwell took over in England and beheaded Charles I. If any English merchant of the day wanted to import wine from Bordeaux, say, or ship masts from the Baltic, he was likely to employ Dutch ships as the most economical. Cromwell's regime soon passed laws providing that European goods must be imported to England in English vessels or in those of the producing nation, but not via Dutch middlemen. The Amsterdam harbor was transformed into a forest of masts and idle ships and the Dutch chose war with England over the threat of financial ruin. They lost the war, but the English lost the chance to make tea's acquaintance at the same time as the rest of Europe. Thus it was ten years after "the impertinent novelty of the century" had come to France before tobacconist and coffee-house keeper Thomas Garway became the first to offer it to England. It may have been an English ship that brought it, but it must have come from Holland, for it was ten years more before the John Company imported its first tea from the East—some one hundred forty pounds of it.

The son of the martyred king had in the meantime been restored to the English throne as Charles II, after having grown up in exile at The Hague. He had brought home with him a taste for tea and soon acquired a Portuguese wife, Catherine of Braganza, who shared it. This explains the earliest Company reference to tea: two pounds were purchased from a coffee-house proprietor as a gift for His Majesty lest "he find himself wholly neglected by the Company." (Tea cost over one hundred shillings the pound at this time.) A couple years later the Royal Pair received over twenty pounds from the same source. In contrast to Elizabeth, who breakfasted each day on bread, meat, and a gallon of beer, Catherine was soon known as a tea-drinking queen—England's first. Before Catherine's day, sniffed a Victorian biographer in her praise, English ladies and

gentlemen "habitually heated or stupefied their brains morning, noon, and night." As it was, the Royal Pair started a trend.

Had tea been introduced earlier, the English coffee houses—the first of which was established in 1650—would have been known as "tea houses." By the time of the Restoration, they were all offering tea as a wonderful health drink, but, being made by the barrel, one that must also have tasted like medicine. It is doubtful if tea could have caught on had the court not made it fashionable (or Charles and Catherine not known the proper method of preparing it). Courtiers of theirs, the Lords Arlington and Ossory, gave the fashion a major impetus when they returned from a mission to The Hague with a quantity of tea they had bought there. Their wives proceeded to give enormous teas after the newest and most elegant Continental manner. Many an Englishman heard of tea for the first time in connection with these entertainments, the apothecaries of London hastened to add it to their stock in trade, and the ladies of the realm acquired a sudden interest in the vogue.

Thus, seven years after Mr. Pepys drank his first cup of tea, Mrs. Pepys enjoyed a similar experience. Quoth his *Diary* for 1667: "Home and found my wife making of tea; a drink Mr. Pelling, the potticary, tells her is good for her cold and defluxions." Defluxions notwithstanding, it must be a matter of regret that Mr. Pelling and his brethren degraded tea from a pure pleasure to the lowly status of a remedy. All the same, "tea had come," as Alice Repplier writes in her now almost unobtainable *To Think of Tea!*, "as a deliverer to a land that called for deliverance; a land of beef and ale, of heavy eating and abundant drunkenness; of grey skies and harsh winds; of strong-nerved, stout-purposed, slow-thinking men and women. Above all, a land of sheltered homes and warm firesides—firesides that were waiting—waiting, for the bubbling kettle and the fragrant breath of tea."

A couple years after Mrs. Pepys' experience, the John Company's first shipment of tea arrived from the East and, by a strange coincidence, tea imports from Holland were forbidden by English law. The Company was not exactly a Young Men's Christian Association; it deliberately kept the cost of tea high till well after 1700, by which year the average annual importation was about twenty thousand pounds, occasionally twice that. Although the cheap cotton cloth imported from its three main factories in India was the chief reason for the Company's rising profits—annual dividends were reaching

20 or even 50 percent—the tea business was looking up. Tea was in continually greater demand and the Company had finally managed to establish a "factory" in China, up river from Portuguese-held Macao right outside the very walls of Canton. Thus by 1702, the directors were able to order an entire ship's cargo of tea, well and closely packed in chests or boxes, to be two-thirds Singlo, one-sixth Imperial, and one-sixth Bohea.*

THE CENTURY OF THE COFFEE HOUSE

> . . . *for tea, though ridiculed by those who are naturally coarse in their nervous sensibilities, or are become so from wine-drinking, and are not susceptible of influence from so refined a stimulant, will always be the favored beverage of the intellectual.* . . .

—*Thomas De Quincey (1785–1859)*
CONFESSIONS OF AN ENGLISH OPIUM–EATER

The eighteenth century was thus underway. "Slack about morals, strict about the proprieties," as an old author has well said, "it produced far and away the most amusing and attractive society that England has ever known." It was a society addicted to, among other things, tea. They must have drunk that first ship's load down and sent it back for more at once, for by 1725, England was using a quarter million pounds of tea a year, and by the end of the century annual imports *averaged* twenty-four million pounds! We can readily translate this latter figure into something over twenty-four ship loads a year, since John Company ships were generally 499-ton vessels. This was to get around a law that ships of 500 tons or more must carry a chaplain. The Company's directors, some of

---

*Singlo was a Green Tea that a tea buyer's guide of a little later period defined as follows: "The leaf is small and light curled at the end. The smell is very refreshing and it is a good and wholesome tea. . . . It will bear three waters well." The same guide describes Imperial as "rolled green tea of a round, bold character made from older leaves after the 'gunpowder' leaves are sifted out." The only Black Tea imported at this time was Bohea, which our guide says "is of a black cast, and yields a deep yellowish infusion. The strength of Bohea is drawn out quickly." One notes the concern with how many times the leaves could be reused. Singlo was the most expensive, perhaps for this reason.

the most privileged and powerful people in Britain, were quick to get their relatives on the payroll, yet hiring unrelated parsons they saw as a different matter entirely. But we have gotten ahead of our story.

Tea was still "tay" in 1711, when Alexander Pope wrote *The Rape of the Lock,* with its often overlooked reference to Queen Anne presiding at Hampton Court:

> Here thou, great Anna, whom three realms obey,
> Dost sometimes counsel take and sometimes tea.

This could not be poetic license, for Pope never allowed himself any. The old pronunciation persisted in parts of those "three realms" down through the nineteenth century, as witness the Irish-American railroad workers' song, "So it's work all day for the sugar in your tay—drill, ye tarriers, drill!" But Queen Anne, to correct Pope, drank tea not just "sometimes" but regularly and in such quantities that she substituted a large, bell-shaped silver teapot for the tiny china pots then in fashion. Our earliest silver tea services date from her reign; so does the ascendancy of the English coffee house, an uncommonly interesting eighteenth-century social institution.

The coffee house was a place where a man was safe from his womenfolk (who were forbidden to enter), and although the ladies in their drawing rooms complained about this, in truth no gentlewoman would have cared to set foot inside such establishments. Smoke from the outsized fireplace mingled with tobacco smoke from the clay pipes and the aroma of coffee being roasted and brewed, the mélange heightened by the scents used by the fops present and the perfumed pomades almost all men of the day used as hair dressing. Since baths were by no means the commonplace they are now and most men rode horseback or drove carriages, body odors and the fragrance of barnyard and stable joined with the other smells to produce what a modern nose would consider a general stink. As twilight fell and the evening wore on, the light from the oil lamps and candles fought a losing battle with the thickening atmosphere until it was no longer possible to read the broadsides, newspapers, or Rules of the House thoughtfully provided by the proprietor. Besides much good fellowship, however, these noxious hangouts spawned a number of customs and institutions still in use today.

Our now-familiar ballot box made its first appearance in the Turk's Head, where it was known as "our wooden oracle" and used when discussions could only be settled by vote. When business was brisk, patrons would place money for waiters and serving wenches in boxes marked T.I.P., "to insure promptness." Commodities, property, and *objets d'art* were commonly sold at auction in salesrooms attached to coffee houses and the great auction houses of Sotheby's and Christie's owe their origins to this tradition. One of Thomas Garway's early competitors was Edward Lloyd, whose clientele was mainly seafarers and their associates. It was for their convenience that soon after opening his doors in 1688, Lloyd began keeping a roster of ships, their sailing dates, their cargoes, and which ones were in the market for insurance. Ship owners and captains, merchants and insurance underwriters made Lloyd's their headquarters from then on and by the time of Lloyd's death in 1713, the foundations were well laid for two important institutions—Lloyd's Register of Shipping and Lloyd's Insurance. The uniformed attendants in the insurance firm's offices are still called "waiters" today, just as in coffee-house times.

As I said before, the coffee house, established for the drinking of one beverage, was soon invaded by the other. Thomas Garway's was among the first ten or twelve in London. When very young, Pope was taken to meet the aged Poet Laureate John Dryden at Will's in Bow Street, where Dryden held court for years, his armchair in its "settled and prescriptive place" by the hearth in winter and out on a balcony in summer. Pepys, too, loved the coffee-house atmosphere where, as he put it, a man "could toss his mind." It was the one place where a bishop and a highwayman—both sure to be well-mannered—might enjoy one another's company unmolested. The democratic character of these establishments worried some members of the government enough that in 1675, they persuaded Charles II to suppress them as centers of sedition. A remarkable thing happened. Men of all parties set up such an outcry at being denied their favorite haunts that the king cancelled his proclamation only eleven days after issuing it. By the time of Queen Anne, there were some five hundred of these "nurseries of idleness" in London.

It is not too much to claim that the coffee houses produced and polished the wit of the eighteenth century, that without them *Tom Jones, Tristram Shandy,* or *Gulliver's Travels* would make much poorer reading. This is why they were called "penny universities," a reference both to the conversation they bred and the penny admittance fee. A cup of tea or coffee cost twopence, usually, and chocolate a halfpenny more. A pipe of tobacco cost a penny, and newspapers were free. According to Richard Steele, all a man who wished to join a group of talkers did was to light his pipe from the candle on the table before them; this served as adequate introduction.

Steele and his friend Joseph Addison had become the first Englishmen to earn a livelihood as writers. The coffee houses not only read their periodicals, the *Tatler* and the *Spectator,* but provided much of the material for them—and a refuge for the authors as well. What Will's was to Dryden, Button's on Russel Street was to Addison. There, safe from his high-born wife, he enjoyed his friends and wrote his regular columns, like the one in 1711, advising his fellow citizens that "all well-regulated households" served tea in the morning, taking care that a copy of his *Spectator* should "invariably be part of the tea equippage." Addison's "citizen" visits the coffee house daily, there to drink tea. His "fine lady," modeled on his wife no doubt, drinks tea every morning and before going out to the opera at night. Jonathan Swift had his beloved niece Stella send her letters to his preferred St. James Coffee House, where he was familiarly known as "the mad parson." The list is endless.

TEA & THE LEXICOGRAPHER

The old philosopher is still among us in the brown coat with the metal buttons and the shirt which ought to be at the wash, blinking, puffing, rolling his head, drumming with his fingers, tearing his meat like a tiger, and swallowing his tea in oceans.
> —*Thomas Babington Macauley (1800–59)*
> THE LIFE OF JOHNSON

Even so brief a history as this one, however, must linger a little over the story of the age's greatest devotee of tea and coffee-house talk, Dr. Samuel Johnson. Although revered for his *Dictionary,* he can scarcely be considered an original thinker or even a first-rate writer: It is rather as the tireless talker of Boswell's *Life of Johnson* that he is remembered. Ensconced in his favorite chair at the Turk's Head, he would hold forth for hours in conversation with friends like Sir Joshua Reynolds, the portrait painter, the playwright Sheridan, Edmund Burke, the rising young politician, Garrick, the Olivier of the day, and fellow writers like Goldsmith, Boswell all the while taking notes.

Johnson was a man of kind heart and great common sense, but he never allowed these to get in the way of his outspoken prejudices. He hated America and Americans

and Scots almost as much. "Let me tell you," the Scottish Boswell dutifully records his saying, "the noblest prospect a Scotchman ever sees is the high road that leads him to England." Johnson loved strong drink like port and brandy and hated wine, saying "any man excepting Boswell could be drowned in it before it made him drunk." He took a glass once only, to toast Sir Joshua when the great painter was knighted. But he could nowise afford alcohol, being of necessity a worker—a reluctant but for many years an incredibly hard worker who knew alcohol to be work's deadly enemy. Before his monumental *Dictionary* finally appeared in 1755, a visitor to his quarters found "five or six Greek folios, a deal writing desk and a chair and a half," plus two small spoons he'd inherited from his mother, a huge and handsome Chinese teapot, and a retinue of cups and saucers. Johnson politely seated his guest in the whole chair and balanced his own huge frame on its three-legged companion, tenderly steadying it, like a wounded friend, against the wall. And thus the two men passed the night in talk and tea drinking.

Dr. Johnson's life, like Boswell's book, is punctuated with tea. A certain lady who once poured him sixteen cups in swift succession urbanely asked if a small basin "would not save him trouble." With more truth than politeness, Johnson answered "Madam, all the ladies put such questions to me. It is to save themselves the trouble, not me." Soon after his *Dictionary* had made the great tea drinker famous—and more comfortably off—a puritan-minded writer published an attack on tea, lamenting that sixteen ships and five hundred seamen were employed each year in bringing it to England. Even beggars cadged an occasional cup, he complained, servants clamored for it, and he knew but a single lady right-minded enough to confine this luxury to her immediate family! In words that resounded throughout the kingdom, Johnson rose to the defense, avowing himself "a hardened and shameless tea-drinker, who has for many years diluted his meals with only the infusion of this fascinating plant; whose kettle has scarcely time to cool; who with tea amuses the evening, with tea solaces the midnight, and with tea welcomes the morning." Boswell gravely records the whole affair, concluding with masterful understatement, "I suppose no person ever enjoyed with more relish the infusion of that fragrant leaf than did Johnson." That is still a safe supposition.

THE CUSTOMS OF TEA TIME

There are few hours in life more agreeable than the hour dedicated to the ceremony known as afternoon tea.

—Henry James (1843–1916)
THE PORTRAIT OF A LADY

After Dr. Johnson went to his reward and his century began drawing to its close, the coffee house entered a decline. Every profession, trade, class, and party had had its favorite, giving each coffee house a different character. By imperceptible degrees, these cliques converted the democratic coffee house into the exclusive clubhouse. It is estimated that by 1800, there were as many private clubs in London as there had been coffee houses a hundred years before. But the "pursuit of happiness," an eighteenth-century phrase that did not originate with our President Jefferson of blessed memory, had never been confined to men in coffee houses. Over this selfsame century there had evolved the custom of "tea time," which Johnson defined in his *Dictionary* as "any time tea is served." So it apparently was at first, for a laureate before Johnson's heyday had called it "the universal pretext for bringing the wicked of both sexes together in the morning," a description that must have amused the wicked of either sex who read it. It was the custom of the time for high-born ladies as far distant as the formidable Swiss Mme. de Stael to receive callers with their morning tea while abed and bare breasted.

Afternoon tea in the drawing room came some few years later, and for this custom we have Anna, the seventh Duchess of Bedford, to thank. Among the English aristocrats of the later 1700s it was customary to eat a huge breakfast, make do with a piddling lunch, and only sit down to a substantial dinner around eight or after. Not surprisingly, the duchess used to get what she described as "a sinking feeling" by five in the afternoon. To allay this discomfort she would order tea and cakes served and promptly started a fashion amongst her acquaintance, a fashion that also satisfied a need. Snacking on sandwiches and pastries followed by tea quickly became a habit among the aristocracy and soon developed into a ritual—usually the pleasantest ritual of the day. "Nowhere is the English genius for domesticity more notably evidenced than in the festival of afternoon tea," observes George Gissing in *The Private Papers of Henry Ryecroft,* his masterpiece. As it began, so it remained essentially a female ritual; gradually, however, two distinct "teas" evolved.

"Low tea" in aristocratic homes featured gourmet tidbits rather than solid nutrition and the emphasis was on the presentation. "High tea" (or "meat tea") became a bourgeois custom, serving as the evening meal and consisting mostly of leftovers from a huge lunch that were served with tea. High tea or low, it was sure to be a cozy interlude. William Cowper, a fine poet of the period who is unjustly neglected today, summed up all it stood for:

> Now stir the fire, and close the shutters fast,
> Let fall the curtains, wheel the sofa round,
> And while the bubbling and loud-hissing urn
> Throws up a steamy column, and the cups
> That cheer but not inebriate, wait on each,
> So let us welcome peaceful evening in.

It is impossible to say how widespread the custom of tea time became over the course of the eighteenth century, but it is certain that another peculiar institution called the "tea garden" flourished. The whole idea was for ladies and gentlemen to take their tea together out of doors and surrounded by entertainments, or at least temptations: a great ballroom with orchestra, hidden arbors, flowered walks, bowling greens, sometimes concerts, gambling, racing, or fireworks at night. These gardens, usually extensive, lovely, and filled with good cheer, became more and more numerous toward 1750. They attracted everybody "that loves eating, drinking, staring, or crowding," as Horace Walpole said of the 1742 opening of Ranelagh Gardens. Everybody from the royal family down was there, and everybody—Henry Fielding and Dr. Johnson included—returned often. It was at another similar garden that Lord Nelson met his beloved Emma, later Lady Hamilton. But Vauxhall, Marylebone, and the others were "tea" gardens thanks only to tea's fashionability. They made the drink more fashionable still, admittedly, but mainly they were important as places the men and women of this "most amusing and attractive society" could meet and consort freely. The gardens disappeared along with the coffee houses once they, too, had served their purpose.

BOOTLEG TEA

I like a smuggler. He is the only honest thief. He robs nothing but the revenue—an abstraction I never cared greatly about. I could go out with him in his mackerel boat, or about his less ostensible business, with some satisfaction.
—*John Company clerk Charles Lamb (1775–1834)*
essay on WITCHES AND OTHER NIGHT FEARS

It is undeniable that by 1800, tea had become England's national drink and she was importing an average of twenty-four million pounds of it a year. It is also time for me to admit that all figures relating to earlier tea consumption in England are merely official, which is to say, misleading as a Viet Cong body count. The English drank vastly more tea than any John Company records before 1784 reveal, thanks to a nationwide network of "free traders" or—from the government's viewpoint—smugglers.

About a decade after the Company began importing tea on a regular basis, the Crown slapped a duty of five shillings on each pound irrespective of quality. This did not much affect the price of the most expensive teas, but it served to knock the cheap right out of the market, or rather, to create a black market for it. The cheapest sort one could legally buy then cost seven shillings a pound—almost a laborer's whole week's wages—while just across the Channel or across the North Sea in Holland tea of this same quality could be had for two shillings. With a 350 percent profit to play with, "free traders" were not long in multiplying along the whole length of England's coastline. Mr. J. M. Scott, to whose grand book *The Great Tea Venture* these pages are much indebted, has written: "The trouble and talk which resulted publicized tea as nothing else could have done, and as the illegal industry spread and prospered it carried the new commodity to every door. It was calculated that at the height of this illegal campaign two-thirds of the tea drunk in England had been smuggled."

Many a fine old home near the English coast was built on the proceeds of a venturer, one who put up the smuggling capital but kept well in the background, leaving the risks to the captain and the lander. The captain purchased his goods quite legally abroad and then waited for a dark night to run them across to one of several spots the lander might arrange. The lander arranged with the local farmhands for transport, with the local parson, perhaps, for storage in the church, and for eventual sales. Besides the venturer, very often the only principal in the whole business who could read and write was the quill driver, the man who kept the accounts. Eternal vigilance is, to be sure, the price of law breaking if it is to be successful for long, and this is but one of the ways tea smuggling was carried on from 1680, the year of the tax, till 1784, the year of its repeal. In 1733, no less than fifty-four thousand pounds of bootleg tea were seized; present-day American consumption of illegally imported marijuana can give us an idea of how much was not.

The smugglers succeeded mainly because they had the sympathy of the whole countryside. On the Isle of Man they often unloaded as much tea and brandy as a hundred horses could carry, and stored their contraband in large caves no revenue man ever managed to discover because, as a pious old Manxman said, "Who'd ever be so wicked as to tell them?" The free traders knew every time a coast guard craft went into drydock, or when a riding officer had the gout or planned a raid. The country folks dealt with the smugglers less for the sake of getting luxuries cheap than of getting them at all. But the larger the band, the more contraband, and the more overawed the revenuers and the populace. The day of the small-scale free trader had passed well before the mid-1700s. And as the business grew, as rich men found it profitable to own three or four sloops engaged in illegal traffic, it became the part of wisdom to know nothing of what went on, as a ballad of the day recommends:

> Five and twenty ponies
> Trotting through the dark;
> Brandy for the Parson,
> 'Baccy for the Clerk,*
> Laces for a lady, letters for a spy,
> And watch the wall, my darling,
> While the gentlemen go by.

Without regard for secrecy, smugglers boldly stole their cargoes back from government customs houses more than once. Long cavalcades of horses loaded with tea were led quite openly through Kent; it is said six tons a week were run from France through Sussex. "The best that can be said of this period," observes J. M. Scott, "is that it was

*"Clark" was and remains the English pronunciation of clerk.

the beginning of yacht racing—revenue cutters chasing smugglers who almost invariably won the cup of tea."

There were, of course, occasional casualties on both sides. One of the famous "Wiltshire Moonrakers," who used the old church in Kingstone as their hiding place, is buried in its churchyard under this epitaph: "To the memory of Robert Trotman, late of Rowd, in the county of Wilts, who was barbarously murdered on the shore near Poole, the 24th of March, 1765."

> A little tea; one leaf I did not steal.
> For guiltless bloodshed I to God appeal.
> Put tea in one scale, human blood in t'other,
> And think what 'tis to slay a harmless brother.

Stripped of their glamor, most smuggling gangs must have been rather like the one Daphne du Maurier depicted in her novel *Jamaica Inn*: bloodthirsty and wholly out for themselves. Still, in a time when inland communications were unimaginably bad, when most roads were tracks, dangerous at night and unusable part of the year, when most of the populace was illiterate, living and dying within ten or twenty miles of their birthplaces, smugglers undertook a nationwide sales campaign of an expensive novelty—and succeeded. They were only put out of business entirely after Waterloo, when the country finally had spare troops enough to enforce the laws. But tea smuggling had ended in 1784, when the government finally repealed the tea tax, at the same time compelling the East India Company to import enough to satisfy demand without raising prices. For most Britishers, it was the first intelligent act of government in living memory, coming as it did three years after their American colonists had ended another dispute over tea by compelling the surrender of Lord Cornwallis at Yorktown.

TEA IN COLONIAL AMERICA

O! Could the smooth, the emblematic song
Flow like thy genial juices o'er my tongue...
—American poet Joel Barlow (1754–1812)
THE HASTY PUDDING

As expected of good colonists everywhere, the American colonists did their damnedest to ape the fashions of their mother countries. Thus when the English relieved the Dutch of Nieuw Amsterdam and rechristened it New York in 1674, they found themselves in possession of a colony that probably drank more tea than all England put together at the time. The directors of the John Company must have delighted to watch as the demand grew in America over the following decades. The sober Quakers created a new market for "the cups that cheer but not inebriate" when, under the patronage of William Penn, they founded Philadelphia in 1682. In 1712, a year after Mr. Addison prescribed tea for "all well-regulated households" in London, a Boston apothecary named Zabdiel Boylston hastened to advertise "Green and ordinary tees" for sale.

In imitation of London, New York City came to support numerous coffee houses and tea gardens. Over the course of the century there were three Vauxhalls alone, one Ranelagh, and several others. Present-day New Yorkers would be hard-pressed to imagine pleasure gardens on the Lower East Side, but there was at least one on the Bowery and another where the *Jewish Daily Forward* is now published near the intersection of Mulberry and Grand. Then as now, however, they could commiserate over the lack of decent drinking water in Manhattan. The city was forced to establish special "Tea Water Pumps," one of them where Christopher Street meets Greenwich and Sixth Avenue. Demand for the water the pumps and springs provided was, by 1757, such that the city fathers had to enact "a law for the Tea Water Men in the City of New York."

Not only in the cities but also throughout the countryside, tea was a long-established part of the American Way by the time of the revolution it helped spark. Trevelyan, an English historian, described its pre-revolutionary popularity:

The most portable, as well as the most easily prepared of beverages, it was drunk in the backwoods of America as it is drunk today in the Australian bush. In more settled districts, the quantity absorbed on all occasions of ceremony is incredible to a generation which has ceased to mourn in large companies and at great expense. Whatever the gentlemen, who rode or drove into a funeral from thirty miles around, were in the habit of drinking, the ladies drank tea. The very Indians, in default of something stronger, drank it twice a day.

But regardless of "the quantity absorbed," John Company revenues began to shrink during this period on account of a mere three penny per pound tax Parliament had specially imposed on tea and other goods America imported.

TAXATION WITHOUT REPRESENTATION

Lord North, purblind to the rights of a
continent, eye on a few London merchants...
— *Ezra Pound (1885–1972)*
CANTO LXII

The duty was voted at a time when the English at home were charged a tea tax amounting to over 100 percent of its value, but the amount was not the issue to the colonists. They were willing to pay the same taxes as any other British subjects, but were determined to resist any tax specifically levied on them as colonists, especially since they weren't consulted in the matter. Reacting in true British fashion, they boycotted the articles specially taxed and, in the case of tea at least, resorted to smuggling it in from Holland. Thomas Hancock, the uncle of John and a staunch Loyalist, amassed a considerable fortune smuggling in Dutch tea and selling it to the British army and navy outfits stationed in America. By 1769, British exports to America had fallen by one-half.

"The Cabinet was not seriously apprehensive, but perturbed," to quote Sir Winston Churchill. "It agreed to drop the duties, except on tea. By a majority of one, this was carried. Parliament proclaimed its sovereignty over the colonies by retaining a tax on tea of threepence a pound." The Americans were not amused, and certainly saw no reason not to go on importing ever larger quantities of the cheaper Dutch teas. Finding its colonial market ever more rapidly eroding and itself sitting on an unprecedented eighty-five hundred-ton surplus of tea in England, the Honorable

Company engineered the passage of the Tea Act of 1773. I return to Sir Winston's *A History of the English-Speaking Peoples*:

> An Act was passed through Parliament, attracting little notice among the Members, authorising the Company to ship tea, of which it had an enormous surplus, direct to the colonies, without paying import duties, and to sell it through its own agents America. Thus in effect the Company was granted a monopoly. The outcry across the Atlantic was instantaneous. The extremists denounced it as an invasion of their liberties, and the merchants were threatened with ruin. American shippers who brought tea from the British custom-houses and their middle-men who sold it would all be thrown out of business. The Act succeeded where [Samuel] Adams had failed: it united colonial opinion against the British.

By eliminating the tax of over 100 percent, the Company directors were sure to undersell the Dutch in America. The three-penny colonial tax seemed to them a silly issue—even a Dr. Johnson living in Charleston or Philadelphia and paying the maximum could trim his tea budget enormously. For the colonists, however, the issue remained the same: Taxation without representation was illegal under the British Constitution. "They have no idea," wrote another great tea lover of the time, Dr. Benjamin Franklin, "that any people can act from any other principle but that of interest; and they believe that threepence on a pound of tea, of which one does not perhaps drink ten pounds in a year [!!!], is sufficient to overcome the patriotism of an American." As a point at issue, it *was* silly—a saving to American tea drinkers and of no appreciable value to the British treasury. But as a cause, tea, "far-fetched and dear bought," assumed an enormous importance to both sides. And even thus, our harmless, necessary tea was dragged into the conflict, all for an expected annual income of a mere million dollars to the Crown.

THE BOSTON, GREENWICH, CHARLESTON, PHILADELPHIA, NEW YORK, ANNAPOLIS, & EDENTON TEA PARTIES

No! Ne'er was mingled such a draught
In palace, hall or arbor,
As freemen brewed and tyrants quaffed
That night in Boston Harbor.
— *Oliver Wendell Holmes (1809–94)*
BALLAD OF THE BOSTON TEA PARTY

Having appointed agents in Charleston, Philadelphia, New York, and Boston, the Company sent its first tea consignments on their way in the autumn of 1773, despite a warning from the New York consignee that "there will be no such thing as selling it, as the people would rather buy so much poison." In fact, at mass meetings first in Philadelphia, then in New York and Boston, the people resolved not even to let it land. The first of three ships bringing the tea to Boston made port on 28 November. The citizenry allowed the captain to unload everything except the tea and kept watch around the clock to make sure he did not. According to law, the cargo would be subject to seizure and sale by the customs for unpaid duty at the end of twenty days after entering port. This was what the consignees confidently waited for, since the customs men would be backed by British troops. On 16 December, the day before the scheduled seizure and landing, all business was suspended in Boston and people by the hundreds flocked in from surrounding towns. It was the greatest gathering the city had ever seen. Speeches were given and negotiations were carried on with the ship's captain, the customs men, and the governor, but by nightfall no progress had been made. "Who knows," a prominent merchant named John Rowe asked just before the meeting adjourned, "how tea will mix with salt water?"

Whether this was a prearranged signal or not, it was answered by war whoops from a party of men, variously estimated from twenty to ninety, disguised as Mohawk Indians. Followed by throngs of patriots, they proceeded with businesslike directness to the ship, warned the customs officers and crew to keep out of their way, brought the chests of tea on deck, and emptied them over the side. They repeated this process on two other ships that had arrived carrying tea. The account of this action in the *Massachusetts Gazette* of 23 December 1773 concludes:

> They applied themselves so dextrously to the destruction of this commodity, that in the space of three hours they broke up three hundred and forty-two chests, which was the whole number in these vessels, and discharged their contents into the dock. When the tide rose it floated the broken chests and tea insomuch that the surface of the water was filled therewith a considerable way from the south part of the town to Dorchester Neck, and lodged on the shores.

The fame of the Boston Tea Party has obscured the other tea protests, but others there were aplenty. Patriots disguised themselves as Indians on another occasion when tea meant for Philadelphia was actually unloaded in nearby Greenwich, then the largest town in New Jersey. Despite the efforts at secrecy, it was discovered. W. H. Ukers' *All About Tea* tells what happened next:

> Citizens of the quiet Jersey village hurried to their doors on that night, December 22, 1773, as shrill war whoops sounded and a lurid glow lit the low-lying clouds. The hated tea, together with the chests that contained it, was burning in the middle of Market Square, and none there were who dared to stay the weird figures in paint and feathers who burned it.

The Charleston consignees had a sudden change of heart about their arrangement with the Company, finding it much more in their interest not to accept delivery or pay duty on the tea. Working under armed guard, the customs men, at the end of twenty days, duly seized and unloaded the tea on the last day of 1773, and promptly stored it in the dampest available cellar to rot. Almost a year later, a great crowd demonstrated in front of the docked ship *Britannia* that had arrived with seven more chests aboard. Fearing that the ship and its entire cargo might be burned, the owners rounded up the Company's consignees and forced them to help chop the chests open and dump their contents overboard in full view of the protestors.

Many a protest meeting had already been held in Philadelphia by the time Captain Ayres of the *Polly* reached there on 26 December 1773. He was met by a committee of citizens who demanded he accompany them to what proved the largest public meeting the city had yet seen. The city knew about the events in Greenwich already; it was in

an outside square that Philadelphians first learned of the Boston Tea Party and unanimously passed a resolution which provided, among other things, "that the tea on board the ship *Polly,* Captain Ayres, shall not be landed. . . . That Captain Ayres shall carry the tea back immediately. . . . That the Captain shall be allowed to stay in town til tomorrow, to provide necessaries for his voyage. . . . That a committee of gentlemen be appointed to see these resolutions carried into execution." No doubt Captain Ayres was also impressed by the prominent posters demanding he be publicly tarred and feathered, for he wisely assured Philadelphia he would comply with the public wishes and next day set out on the long voyage back to London with his tea. The Company consignees were reasonable men who knew a stone wall when they saw one. They resigned.

A scene much the same was played in New York the following April. Captain Lockyear had left London for that port in September 1773, but storms drove his ship, the *Nancy,* to the West Indies and he only reached New York on 18 April 1774. No pilot would steer him nearer than Sandy Hook and there the *Nancy* lay, besieged, while her master went to consult the Company agent in town. A man with good reason to worry, he adjured Lockyear to carry his own resignation and absolute refusal to accept delivery of any tea back to London along with the cargo. The captain was lodged in a local coffee house and given every assistance in procuring supplies for the return voyage.

Meanwhile, the good ship *London* arrived and, upon her captain's oath that she carried no tea, was allowed to dock. The local Sons of Liberty, having been informed otherwise, commenced a search of the *London*'s cargo which turned up eighteen chests of tea belonging to the captain himself. The crowd on the wharf took matters into their own hands, breaking the chests open and dumping them into the sea. The captain fled their indignation, slipping off to the *Nancy* under cover of darkness. Next morning, having publicly thanked the citizens and the Sons of Liberty for the consideration shown him under awkward circumstances, Captain Lockyear was escorted to the foot of Wall Street and given a gala sendoff with all the bells of New York pealing forth. He set sail for England with all the tea he'd started out with some seven months before and with Captain Chambers of the *London* as his passenger.

The brig *Peggy Steward* landed at Annapolis, Maryland, the following October with a ton of tea consigned to the ship's owner, a Scottish merchant of the town. He got as far as paying the duty on the tea before his fellow citizens assembled and offered him the choice of being hanged on the spot or setting fire to his ship, cargo and all. He made the obvious choice and left the country soon after for his health's sake.

A less militant but no less patriotic demonstration occurred one week later in the then-important town of Edenton, North Carolina. Under the leadership of a thrice-married and thrice-widowed ancestor of mine named Penelope Barker, whose tea service is presently in a cousin's safekeeping, fifty-one ladies of Edenton bound themselves not "to Conform to the Pernicious Custom of Drinking Tea, until such time as all Acts which tend to enslave our Native Country shall be repealed . . . and we do therefore accordingly subscribe this Page, as witness of our fixed Intention and Solemn Determination. . . ." They not only signed "this Page," but also sent their document to a London paper for publication, knowing it would (as it did) create a sensation in England where many of the signers had family or social connections. A North Carolina historian records that the ladies substituted for tea "the balsamic 'Hyperion,' which was nothing more than the dried leaves of the raspberry vine, a drink, in the writer's opinion, more vile even than the vaunted Yupon." (Yupon is a Carolina plant found in few or no herbals; Hyperion was, if not enjoyed, at least known in other colonies as "Liberty Tea.") The declaration of the ladies of Edenton was published in England a scant few months before some anonymous New Englander fired "the shot heard round the world." The home government had taken an equally determined stand that its tea tax on America must be enforced.

"WE HAVE RENOUNCED TEA. . . ."

There is a great deal of poetry and fine sentiment in a chest of tea.
—Ralph Waldo Emerson (1803–83)
LETTERS AND SOCIAL AIMS

Amidst the roar of cannon and musketry, therefore, this great Republic was born—with a prenatal disinclination for tea. The colonists had given it up, abruptly but completely. En route to sign the Declaration of Independence, John Adams wrote his wife Abigail how he asked at a tavern, "Is it lawful for a weary traveler to refresh himself with a dish of tea, provided it has been honestly smuggled and has paid no duty?" The landlord's daughter answered sternly: "No sir! We have renounced tea under this roof. But, if you desire it, I will make you some coffee."

When the Reverend Joseph McKean celebrated his ordination in Massachusetts in 1785—presumably an austere occasion—the eighty-odd guests for both lunch and dinner consumed, according to the tavern bill, seventy-four bowls of a very alcoholic punch, twenty-eight bottles of wine, eight bowls of brandy and a shilling's worth of cherry rum. At the bottom of this formidable bill appears this modest item: "Six people drank tea—9d." Only six out of eighty-odd Americans drank tea in a year when England, having just repealed her tea taxes the year before, consumed thirty-two million pounds! It was also 1784, the year before the Reverend McKean's party, that Americans first traded directly with the Chinese. To comprehend what such trade involved, we must return to the Orient and attempt to understand politics and business practices there.

THE CHINA TRADE: FOREIGN DEVILS & PIDGIN ENGLISH

> *Je suis l'Empire à la fin de sa décadence.*
> *—Paul Verlaine (1844–96)*
> *I forget which poem*

The Ming Dynasty had come to power in China in 1368, and for a time ruled well. The later Ming emperors had ruled China in name only, however, leaving the daily business of government in the hands of the eunuchs of the palace. Corruption, extravagance, and economic distress were the predictable results. Several generations of misrule by rapacious and irresponsible eunuchs finally provoked popular uprisings against the dynasty. Faced with a rebellion that was getting out of hand in the north, a Chinese general sought help from the warlike Manchurians on the other side of the Great Wall. But once having let them through the Wall in 1644, the general found himself following *their* orders, instead of vice versa. The Mings were speedily deposed and within a couple decades the Manchurian, or Manchu, Dynasty had subdued the whole of China.

In the confusion, the English, along with the Dutch and Portuguese, had managed to trade in a number of ports for various and sundry goods, tea included, and the Portuguese had found it in their interests to permit other Europeans to do business at Macao. In 1684, the John Company finally was allowed a "factory" of its own just outside Canton, and within a year the Manchu emperor was powerful enough to restrict trade with Europeans to Canton alone. And there, officially at least, it remained for one hundred sixty years. Despite the admittance of Portuguese from Macao, Spaniards from Manila, Dutch from Formosa, Danes, Swedes, French, and, after 1784, Americans, no British subject was allowed to land at Canton without permission from the East India Company and only British ships licensed by the Company could trade there.

The emperor was after the maximum profit and the minimum trouble from the "foreign devils." Considering the imperial objectives, it's hard to imagine a more logical system than the one established. The emperor appointed an official to remit to his treasury a sum computed upon the tonnage of foreign ships entering port. Under the Chinese system whereby the employee pays the employer, this official received no salary but rather paid for his appointment; his gain came chiefly from the merchants whom he in turn appointed to carry on the trade. The English and other Europeans at Canton were to be governed by the "Eight Regulations." Among other provisos, they were only allowed to stay there from August through March—the sailing season—and could not have wives or other women with them. The rest of the year they spent—with wives—at Macao. They could not mix with the native Chinese, but had to conduct all business through the appointed merchants who were, in turn, responsible for their conduct. Not that the Chinese merchants could exercise any direct authority over the Europeans, but they could be much more safely punished than their foreign customers and, besides, knowing an innocent man would suffer for their offenses seemed for some reason to keep the "foreign devils" in order. Miraculously, the system worked. More miraculous still, everybody involved made money.

The Chinese merchants, or so-called hong members, forged links of friendship with the Europeans and depended on charm and tact to keep their often unruly charges from getting them into trouble. The official, or hoppo, relied on inaccessibility to get his way, i.e., money. This was more a matter of exactions than trading duties. On arrival, a ship was expected to dispense presents of large sums of money all around, then pay a tax gauged by her length and beam, another of up to 15 percent of the cargo's value, and finally contribute to a sort of insurance fund to guard against the embarrassing possibility of a hong member's going bankrupt and being unable to meet his commitments. These were just the basic charges before trade could begin; if the ship required anything unusual or anything at all in a hurry, further grease was necessary. An

insufficiently lubricated hoppo would often put off measuring a ship indefinitely, as if there were all the time in the world, knowing the captain had to conclude his trading and get away with the New Year's monsoon or waste a season.

If the "foreign devils" were taxed, so were the merchants. By the late 1700s, according to J. M. Scott,

> their *minimum* yearly payments for the privilege of being thus employed were calculated by Dr. Morrison, the East India Company's interpreter, to be as follows: presents for the Emperor on his birthday and on other occasions—£56,000; presents direct to the Hoppo—£14,000; tips to other officials—£14,000; the Yellow River Fund [officially a charity, but one which not only began but ended in the Hoppo's home]—£10,000; compulsory purchase of ginseng [a medicinal root]—£46,000. This adds up to £140,000 which these eight men had to pay their employer yearly. Occasionally... a Hong merchant was squeezed to bankruptcy by the Hoppo, and the Consoo [insurance] Fund had to be used to liquidate his debts. But one Hong merchant at least was said to be worth £5,000,000 sterling. The Hoppo must have been proportionately richer. This suggests fantastic fortunes. And yet the barbarians from whom all this money ultimately came also grew richer.... That gives an idea of the value of the China trade.

The East India Company's agents had to be remarkable men. In a country full of silk experts, they had to be able at a glance to appraise any sample offered; they had to know all about the numerous types of tea and their value. (Since the tea gardens were far from Canton in the prohibited interior, however, they knew little or nothing about the growing of the bushes or the manufacture of the finished product.) But to do business at all, they had to be able to talk face to face with their Chinese counterparts and for this a *lingua franca* had evolved. The word "pidgin," I am told, is a Chinese corruption of the word "business"—at least it sounds thoroughly corrupted—and business was done in pidgin English. The language was grammarless and consisted of English in equal parts with Portuguese and Indian words, all pronounced as the Chinese heard them.

Much pidgin has found a permanent place in English. "Mandarin," for instance, which comes from the Portuguese word *mandar,* meaning "to order," was used for any official who could give orders. The English word "cash" derives from the Portuguese *caixa,* meaning "case," which the Chinese sellers saw purely in terms of their coins with square holes in the center. *Dios* became "joss," as in joss house—temple—or joss stick. The Chinese word for their pound, catty, is preserved in our tea "caddy," or container. "Hoppo" is the English corruption of *haikwan.* "Chow," our slang word for food, and "chow chow," which today designates any condiment consisting of mixed fruits, vegetables, heavy syrup, and whatever, began as the pidgin term for "cargo." Ships' captains returning from China with cargoes that included a little of everything would simply label such cargo "chow chow" to avoid itemizing. The dogs they brought back wound up called by this name also, for in the eyes of the old tars they, too, were merely "chow" or "chow chow"—just that much more cargo. "Chin-chin" became the Chinese greeting between equals, being short for *chin-te-le-mun.* "Chop" or "chop-chop" could mean almost anything, depending on context. Like "dandy," "coolie," and "chit," it is of Indian origin.

The list is a long one. The xenophobic Chinese government considered even their language a state secret and learning Chinese proper was made none the less difficult in that Chinese teachers were subject to decapitation upon discovery. This comic sort of baby talk somehow sufficed.

TEA DRINKING & OPIUM WARS

What a jovial and merry world would this be, may it please your worships, but for that inextricable labyrinth of debts, cares, woes, wants, grief, discontent, melancholy, large jointures, impositions and lies.

—*Lawrence Sterne (1713–68)*
LIFE AND OPINIONS OF TRISTRAM SHANDY, GENT.

Language was not the major obstacle to doing business with the Chinese—currency was. The goods the British had to offer in trade were mainly English broadcloths, not much wanted in semitropical Canton and not allowed for sale in bitterly cold north China, where woolen cloth might have been welcome. For the difference between what they bought and what they sold, the Chinese required payment in silver. At first, of course, the amounts were not very large, but toward 1800, with the British buying twenty-four million pounds of tea a year, on average, they were having to pay for two-thirds of it with silver coin or bullion. Yet despite what would appear to be a rerun of the old Roman gold story, the Company continued to thrive. The secret of its success? Opium.

It is instructive to reflect that the beverage John Wesley, the Methodist evangelist, was urging on his flock in the name of temperance in England was purchased at the price of drug addiction on the other side of the world. Having addicted the greater part of the English-speaking world to tea, the Honorable Company proceeded to addict its Chinese tea suppliers to another of its commodities—Indian-grown opium. Until introduced to opium on the now classic free-samples-till-you're-hooked basis, the drug was all but unknown in China. It was only a matter of time, however, before the Chinese customers, predictably, wanted more and more of it and that, eventually, at any cost. And having seized control of India, the John Company had a monopoly on it.

The Company sold the opium crop yearly at auction in Calcutta, and there, they were careful to point out, their responsibility ended. It was bought by what were called the "country firms," British and Persian outfits that traded Indian goods with China by arrangement with the East India Company. The Company's only proviso was that the country firms sell their opium for silver. This being before the days of electronic banking, these firms were happy to let the Company apply against their bills in London as much of their silver in Canton as it liked, thereby sparing themselves the perilous necessity of transporting bullion. Thus the Company was able to collect silver in payment for its opium in China, only to turn around and pay for its tea with the same silver. The silver circulated, to be sure, but it also stayed where it was. Sluggishly, the emperor responded to the debauching of his people and in 1800 forbade the importing of opium under the severest penalties. The only result was that the emperor was henceforth defrauded of his rightful duty on it. Opium was no longer brought to the Canton anchorage but to an island in the middle of Canton Bay. There it was stored on hulks lying at anchor for collection by the many-oared Chinese galleys—called centipedes or scrambling dragons—which smuggled it ashore.

Any fair-minded student of imperialism is compelled to admit that the British constantly sought to open up a more regular form of commerce with China. Their diplomatic efforts were unflagging, but the Chinese viewed them only as outside "barbarians" bearing tribute. In 1792, for instance, the Lord MaCartney (perhaps a kinsman of the great McCartney of our day) was carried up river on a boat with the inscription

"Tribute-bearer to the Emperor." Once having reached the imperial court, he was refused an audience unless he would "kow-tow"—more pidgin, and a bitter pill for a proud British peer. He was finally allowed to compromise by merely bending his knee, but came away with no trade concessions. Lord Amherst a few years later was not even granted an audience.

The concession the British wanted most was for the emperor to legalize opium and this one emperor after another steadfastly refused to do. The British response was to corrupt the Imperial Customs by cutting its officials in on their constantly more profitable drug traffic. In the late 1820s, the Company connived at exporting an average of less than ten thousand cases of opium annually to China; fifty years later it was almost one hundred thousand. In a book published in 1882, an American businessman named W. C. Hunter recollected how opium smuggling on such a scale could be carried on from an island in Canton Bay:

> So perfect a system of bribery existed (with which foreigners had nothing whatever to do [?]) that the business was carried on with ease and regularity. Temporary interruptions occurred, as for instance on the installation of newly arrived magistrates. Then the question of fees arose; but was soon settled unless the new-comer was exorbitant in his demands or, as the broker would express it, "too muchee foolo." In good time, however, it would be arranged satisfactorily, the brokers re-appeared with beaming faces, and peace and immunity reigned in the land. . . . The Canton officials rarely made any reference to the Lintin [Island] station; but sometimes, compelled by force to do so, would issue a proclamation ordering vessels "loitering at the outer anchorage" either to come into port or sail away to their own countries lest the "dragons of war" should be opened, and with fiery discharges annihilate all who opposed this, a "special edict."

Occasionally there were "fiery discharges," about as dangerous as ritual Chinese firecrackers. Once an opium ship had finished her business at Lintin Island and set sail on the return voyage, mandarin junks would sometimes set out in hot pursuit. Your more mischievous "country firm" captain would slow down at once, compelling the junks to shorten sail as well, for the last thing they wanted was to come up with the "enemy." But out of sight of land—though not out of hearing—a furious bombardment would begin and in due course Peking received a report of a "barbarian" smuggler sunk or driven off. Thus the Chinese perfected the arts of self-deception, while their every official was in on the racket, from the meanest mandarin to the hoppo and the emperor's viceroy. Tens of thousands of chests of opium passed through their hands each season. "But," to quote J. M. Scott again, "the point here is this: Of the tea being drunk in the West—at Methodist and anti-slavery meetings, in fine drawing rooms and poor cottages—nearly all of it was bought with opium."

Since this is a book about tea, we must leave the fascinating story of opium veiled in a decent obscurity and return to our subject. Suffice it that all sides knew a major crisis was inevitable, but the British were not worried because they despised China's weakness, while on their part the Chinese were not worried because they believed themselves invincible. The Opium War, when it finally came, dispelled Chinese illusions. It was speedily concluded with the Treaty of Nanking in 1842, dictated at the point of a few thousand British bayonets. China was forced to accept free trade, dismantling forever the cumbersome hoppo-hong system, recognizing foreign consuls, and setting a single low tariff on all imports whatsoever. Four more Chinese ports were opened up to foreigners and the island of Hong Kong, across Canton Bay from Macao, was ceded to the British, who still hold it. Other Western powers soon exacted similar privileges for themselves. If European imperialism prevailed against the loudly decried "Yellow Peril," it awakened Asians to a cruel sense of the "White Disaster." British troops invaded a second time, burned a summer palace in Peking, and forced imperial legalization of opium in 1857. The shipments of tea and the opium that paid for it had continued without interruptions even during the hostilities. And by this time Britain was importing over twice as much tea as she had at the beginning of the century—more than fifty thousand pounds of it a year.

The demand for opium, which is to say number of addicts, increased almost 100 percent in the decade following legalization, just as the Honorable Company and the British government expected. If India was acquired in a British "fit of absence of mind," as Sir Winston Churchill would have it, it was cynically premeditated British policy that made ever more millions upon millions of Chinese opium addicts—and kept them that way. One must consider the opium business the most protractedly sordid aspect of all British imperial history. It proves that where money is concerned, a government can be just as greedy, unscrupulous, and suicidally stupid as any private enterprise. The British saw to it that Indian opium remained a legitimate article of commerce in China until 1908, and the scourge of opium and heroin has now spread around the world, all thanks to the British government's making it a big business in the first place.

THE ERA OF THE CLIPPER SHIP

The ship, a fragment detached from the earth, went on lonely and swift like a small planet.
—Joseph Conrad (1857–1924)
THE NIGGER OF THE NARCISSUS

The 1840s saw the beginning of the last and most exciting chapter in the history of the China tea trade. The *Rainbow,* the first "extreme" clipper ship, was launched in New York in 1845. Her maiden voyage was to China and she made the round trip in under eight months, paying back her cost of forty-five thousand dollars and an equal amount in profit. Her second round trip was faster than any other ship could sail one way—ninety-two days out and back in eighty-eight.

Almost from the beginning, Americans had realized the value of trade with China and, despite the limited American market for tea, our first three millionaires, T. H. Perkins of Boston, Stephen Girard of Philadelphia, and New York's John Jacob Astor, made their fortunes in the China trade. The ships they used had evolved from the swift privateers that were built, with a certain indebtedness to the design of British smugglers, for the War of 1812. Now that trade with China was greatly increased, American merchants soon brought out a whole fleet of clippers and captured such a large proportion of that trade that the British were forced to imitate them. This was doubly the case by the close of the 1840s when the English Navigation Laws, passed so long before against Dutch shipping, were finally repealed and ships of any nationality could carry cargoes from anywhere direct to England. The Navigation Laws could never have been repealed, except that after 234 years our corporate hero, the Honorable East India Company, had finally lost its monopoly on trade with China, overcome by a couple hundred would-be competitors finally strong enough to sway Parliament and acquire a piece of the action. When India eventually passed from being a corporate fiefdom to being a dominion of the British Crown and the John Company's monopoly gave way to

competitive trade, these were the men and these the firms that replaced the stately old East Indiamen, or "tea wagons," with clipper ships.

The master, though not the originator, of clipper-ship design was Donald McKay, an American of Scottish extraction. His first ship, the *Stag Hound,* was the largest merchant ship ever built at the time of her launching in 1850. She was 1,534 tons and made the run from Canton to New York in eighty-five days. His second ship, *Flying Cloud,* made the run around Cape Horn to San Francisco in eighty-nine days, twenty-one hours. Three years later she excelled her own record by thirteen hours. These sailing records have never been equaled. The clipper *Lightning* once made 436 nautical miles in twenty-four hours, a still unbeaten record for a sailing ship. Clippers were faster ships because they were much slimmer and carried acres more sail. What had seemed impossible before they accomplished, voyaging quickly enough from China to England or America not to have to put in anywhere en route for stores or water.

"The whole art of sailing was rapidly improving," says J. M. Scott. It would be a shame to paraphrase this passage of his from *The Great Tea Venture:*

> The ships were not everything, of course. Designs can be copied. Whether they were a success or failure rested with the officers and crew who had not only to force their vessel to the limit, and keep her at that pitch for three months or more—a sufficient strain in itself—but also maintain spars and rigging in racing trim. What sort of men were these? . . . They were experts at their craft, but simple souls. To them, the land was a place to get drunk and make love on. The sea was their profession. They were warmhearted, impulsive, superstitious, brave, unruly . . . qualities . . . accentuated by a life that seemed to prevent them from growing up as far as responsibility was concerned. They were constricted like boys at school, with no feminine influence—except the ship. Their days and nights were governed by certain rules which, being concerned only with the efficient running of the ship, had no moral basis. . . . Their masters were by no means always models of morality and sobriety. But in the better ships at least both officers and men loved their ship with a fanatical loyalty. You might more safely insult a sailor's woman than his ship. In the race of 1866 one clipper crew to a man backed their ship with a month's pay to beat their chief rival.

THE GREAT TEA RACE

Oh Susanna, darling take your ease,
For we have beat the clipper fleet,
The Sovereign of the Seas.
— *Victory song of the crew of the* SOVEREIGN OF THE SEAS *when she*
won the New York to San Francisco race around the Horn, 1852

"The race of 1866" is the most famous of all the great tea clipper races, the natural consequence of the meeting between clipper ships and free markets. The first tea on the market in England each year sold for the most money. Regardless of the tea's real quality, everybody who was anybody in England wanted to offer their guests a sample from the cargo of the year's fastest and most famous ship. Its crew might divide a bonus of as much as five hundred pounds. China's first picking of the year—very small and high quality, two leaves and a bud—was made in mid-April. By mid-June the first tea would reach one of the treaty ports, usually Foochow, five hundred miles north of Canton and that far south of Shanghai. The tea was bought and stowed with great care, not only because it is one of the easiest cargoes to damage but also because the clippers with their fine lines were easily put out of trim. Quickly but carefully loaded, ships as much as a thousand miles apart made off, knowing nothing (unless by chance encounter on the high seas) of where they stood in the race until they docked in London, distant at least sixteen thousand miles by the log. The landsmen in London spent the months in hope and conjecture, odds-making in clubs and bets-taking everywhere. To the public at large, the excitement of the tea clipper races was rivaled only by the Derby.

Finally the news would arrive by semaphore that one or three or four clippers were beating up the English Channel. Then, as W. H. Ukers describes it,

swarms of sampling clerks would descend upon the docks to draw samples for brokers and wholesalers as soon as the news came that the racers had passed Gravesend [the mouth of the Thames]. Some spent the night at near-by hotels; others slept at the docks. By 9 A.M., the samples were being tasted in Mincing Lane.* Then the bids were made by the large dealers; duty was paid on the gross weight, and by the

---

*Mincing Lane was to the English tea trade what Fleet Street was to English journalism or what Wall Street is to American finance.

following morning the new season's Congous* would be on sale in Liverpool and Manchester.

A weak analogue would be the present-day French (and Francophile) passion for each year's Beaujolais nouveau.

The race of 1866 saw forty-odd ships—all British and none American, as it happened—sail from Chinese ports with that season's tea. Of these, five left the Foochow anchorage within three days of one another and these were the real contenders. The *Ariel,* Captain Keay, was the favorite. Launched the year before, she was 852 tons and could pile on over twenty-five thousand square feet of sail, about the area of ten tennis courts. The *Fiery Cross,* Captain Robinson, was the ship the *Ariel* had to beat, it was thought. Of 695 tons, she had won the race in 1861, 1862, 1863, and 1865, losing by only one day in 1864 to the *Serica.* Her best time on the Foochow to London run had been 101 days. The *Serica,* 708 tons, had a master with a reputation as a hard driver, Captain Innes. The *Taeping,* 767 tons, was built, like the *Ariel,* to excel in light winds. Her captain had died on the outward voyage and she was commanded by First Mate Dowdy. The fifth ship was the 815-ton *Taitsing,* newer than the *Ariel* even and commanded by another hard driver, Captain Nutsford.

Let me admit the story of the race itself is a digression of perhaps minor historical value, but I'd have to be cold as a Boston romance to consider omitting it. I must acknowledge myself too poor a sailorman, however, to improve on the classic account in Mr. Basil Lubbock's 1914 book, *The China Clippers.* "The struggle," he writes,

> began in the offices of the ships' agents and in the hongs of the Chinese merchants, fortunes in money being dependent on the winning ship. Thus the favorites for the race got the first chests, and were therefore the first to finish loading. The tea . . . was slung aboard the ships, and stowed in every nook and cranny, even to the Captain's cabin, by clever Chinese stevedores who worked in shifts day and night. *Ariel* was made the favorite in the betting on the race. *Taeping* had made the fastest passage in 1865, and the first ships in that year were *Serica* and *Fiery Cross,* the latter having the luck to fall in with a tugboat off Beachy Head when *Serica* was leading her by two

*"Congou" is a general term used to describe all China Black Teas regardless of their district of origin.

miles. But, as regards speed, there was only a slight difference between first and last, and the race depended quite as much upon the skill and nerve of their captains as upon the ships themselves.

The *Ariel* was the first to finish loading but she made an unfortunate start, and had to anchor before the tide had fallen [28 May 1866, at Foochow anchorage]. *Fiery Cross* passed her and put out to sea ahead, getting a day's lead. *Taeping* and *Serica* crossed the bar of the Min River together with *Ariel; Taitsing* the following day. In a race of one hundred days across three-quarters of the globe, one would imagine that a few days start would have made little or no difference in the result, but as a matter of fact these racing tea ships were as closely matched as a one-design class of racing yachts, and every hour was of value. Each of the tea ships carried a picked crew; *Ariel*'s numbered thirty-two all told, all A.B.'s [Able Bodied Seamen], two more than her normal—non-racing—crew.

On 18 June, *Fiery Cross,* twenty-one days out, left the China Sea and entered the Indian Ocean by the narrow strait between Sumatra and Java. *Ariel* followed forty-three hours later, six hours ahead of *Taeping* and eleven hours ahead of *Serica.* Crossing the Indian Ocean, the *Ariel* logged a record 330 miles in one day's sailing time. Lubbock resumes:

By the time the Cape was reached, *Ariel* had nearly wiped off her lost twenty-four hours, being only two or three hours behind *Fiery Cross* on July 15th, when both ships rounded. *Taeping* was twelve hours astern, while *Serica* and *Taitsing* still lagged behind. In the passage up the Atlantic all five ships got closer and closer to one another without knowing it. At St. Helena two and half days covered the first four ships. . . . *Taeping, Fiery Cross* and *Ariel* all crossed the Line [Equator] on the same day, August 4. *Serica* had dropped a couple of days, and *Taeping* and *Fiery Cross* were within sight of each other in doldrum weather, *Ariel* further to the westward having better winds and running into the lead. On August 17, *Fiery Cross* saw *Taeping* pick up the breeze and run out of sight ahead in a few hours. . . . Nonetheless, the first four ships passed Flores in the Azores on the same day, August 29, while by brilliant sailing the *Taitsing* had made up lost time and passed on September 1st. At 1:30 A.M., September 5, *Ariel,* the leading ship, picked up the St. Agnes lights [off Cornwall's Land's End, the mouth of the English Channel]. In the skipper's private log, the next entry reads: "A ship, since daylight, has been in company on starboard quarter—

Taeping, probably." After racing up the Channel neck and neck at fourteen knots, the *Ariel*'s Captain noted at 5:55 A.M. September 6: "Rounded to close to pilot cutter and got first pilot. Were saluted as first ship from China this season. I replied, ' Yes, and what is that to the westward? We have not room to boast yet.' " *Ariel* cleared the Strait of Dover ten minutes ahead of *Taeping* that day, *Serica* four hours later.

One may imagine the excitement, both aboard the two ships and ashore, where the news that two tea ships were racing up Channel spread like wildfire. From each headland the report of their positions was rushed to the nearest post office and, though they had not our facilities in those days, the owners of both ships and their agents in London soon learned the two vessels were neck and neck. The race was not finished until the sample boxes of tea were hurled ashore in the London Docks; but, so scared were the owners of *Ariel* and *Taeping* of losing the 10 s. extra per ton on a quibble as to which ship really won that they agreed privately to divide the premium. . . . The Captains knew nothing of this arrangement [of course] and the excitement aboard both ships was still at fever heat. The air all around the *Ariel* must have been blue when *Taeping*'s tug proved much better and soon towed her past. The yarn goes also that half a dozen great burly seamen, headed by *Ariel*'s bos'n, offered to board the tug by way of the tow rope in order to supplement the stokers and sit on the safety valve. However, there was no help for it. . . .

Ariel did reach her dock first, having a shorter distance to go, but because of the tide could not enter it until exactly twenty minutes after *Taeping* had managed to dock and, technically speaking, win the race, ninety-nine days after it began. Lubbock concludes his account: "*Serica* managed to haul inside the West India Dock at 11:30 P.M.. . . . Thus *Ariel, Taeping* and *Serica,* after crossing the bar of the Min River on the same tide, all docked in the Thames on the same tide."

The 1867 race was won by a newer ship, *Sir Lancelot,* in a ninety-nine day run from Shanghai, with *Ariel* arriving from Foochow second. *Ariel* lost by six hours in 1868. In 1869, *Sir Lancelot* beat five competitors in an incredible eighty-nine day run, a record that still stands today. The truth is that, in a close race, the winner was the clipper that got the first good steam tug, a clear portent steam must soon replace sails even on the high seas. On his way to locate Dr. Livingston in Africa in 1869, the journalist Henry Stanley stopped off to cover the opening of the Suez Canal. Verdi's "Egyptian" opera *Aida* had been commissioned for the occasion and all the speechmakers agreed it opened a new era in world commerce. And so it was to be: China's tea crop of 1870 was mainly carried in awkwardly adolescent steamships and 1871 marked the last of the tea clipper races. But the cultivation of tea in India and elsewhere by this time had already doomed the Chinese tea trade to insignificance.

THE DISCOVERY OF TEA IN INDIA

Then felt I like some watcher of the skies
When a new planet swims into his ken;
Or like stout Cortez when with eagle eyes
He stared at the Pacific—and all his men
Looked at each other with a wild surmise—
Silent, upon a peak in Darien.

—John Keats (1795–1821)
ON FIRST LOOKING INTO CHAPMAN'S HOMER

For almost three hundred years, China and China alone supplied the West with its tea. Before we trace the story of tea in other lands, we should try to understand how China managed to maintain her monopoly on tea for so long. The Arabs, after all, had endeavored to monopolize coffee cultivation, but failed. Why didn't the Chinese?

The coffee plant is thought to be a native of Ethiopia. Its berries were first used as a food, but the Arabs discovered how to roast and powder them and make a drink they called *qahveh.* By the end of the Crusades, coffee was widely cultivated in Arabia and its use had spread throughout the Islamic world. It was introduced to Europe (through Venice, naturally) about the same time as tea; it caught on faster because the source of supply was so much nearer. After being hulled, coffee beans were shipped green and unground to keep them from losing their freshness. It was the user who had to know how to process them by roasting and grinding. And the constant intercourse between Christian and Moslem enabled Europeans to procure and grow plants of their own as soon, almost, as they developed a taste for the drink. The Dutch were growing coffee in Java as early as 1696; the French planted it on Martinique in the New World in 1715.

Tea, by contrast, had to be prepared by withering, rolling, and firing at its point of origin or it would spoil. The consumer only had to add boiling water. The Chinese, isolated both by culture and by great distance from the West, liked it that way, each dynasty doing its best to minimize contact between the two. The Chinese always have been reluctant to share their secrets, and since their customers didn't *need* to know anything about tea cultivation and manufacture, they figured, why tell them? Imperial edicts made tea production a state secret, which it was worth a man's life to reveal.

Though not quite at hand, the First Opium War and the end of the East India Company's monopoly of the China trade were already in sight in the early 1830s, when some anonymous Company official wrote in a memo to higher-ups: "At no very distant period and from some apparently accidental event, not only the British Nation but other foreigners might be prohibited entering the Chinese territories. . . . Some better guarantee should be provided for the supply of this Article [tea] than that already furnished by the toleration of the Chinese Government." The writer goes on to propose the Honorable Company should "resolutely undertake" the cultivation of tea in its Indian territories, such as Nepal or any other place that might be congenial to it. Once the Company was stripped of its tea monopoly in 1834, a Tea Committee was appointed for this purpose and, in best committee fashion, circulated a questionnaire to all Company officials in India asking if there were any places with the climate and altitude they believed tea required. The questionnaire did not ask if anybody had seen a tea plant.

The history of tea abounds with Scotsmen. One named Robert Bruce had participated in the conquest of Assam a decade before the Company appointed its Tea Committee. This adventurer had lived with the native tribes of this remote province of India and discovered they drank tea that they themselves produced from indigenous plants. After he died, his brother Charles had sent specimen branches to the director of the Company botanical gardens at Calcutta. Because they came from the last place he expected tea to flourish, a low-lying jungle valley, it couldn't possibly be tea, the director said, but just another form of camellia.* There the matter rested until this same botanist was named secretary of the Tea Committee and circulated his questionnaire.

---

*Tea, *Camellia sinensis,* is one of the four-hundred-odd members of the *Camellia* genus; our commonest garden variety is *Camellia japonica.* The genus *Camellia* takes its name from its Western discoverer, the German Jesuit (and botanist) Kamel, who was a missionary in Japan in the 1600s.

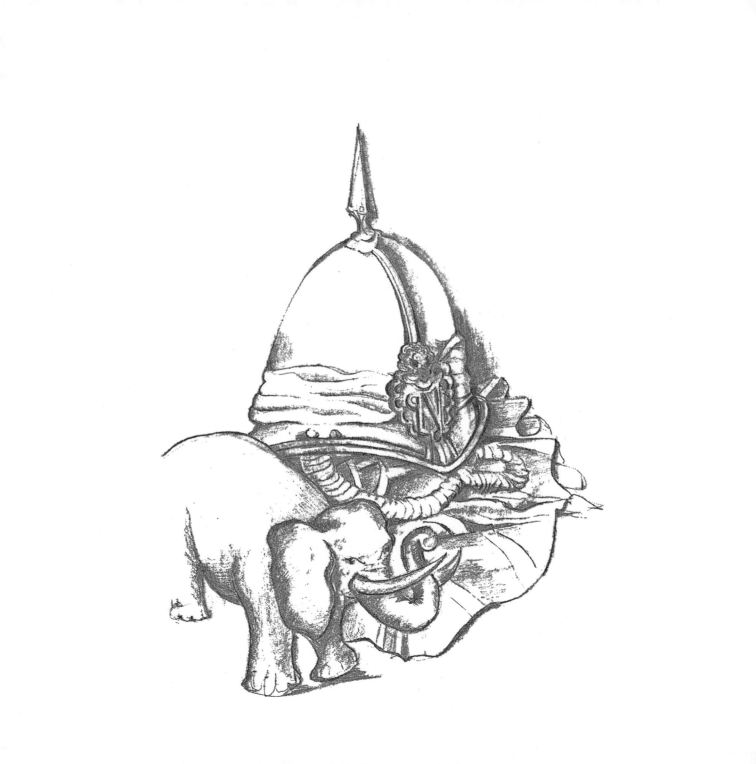

By way of reply, Charles Bruce this time sent actual tea seeds, plants, and "manufactured" leaves from Assam. Even the botanist was forced to the obvious conclusion and the committee soon reported: "We have no hesitation in declaring this discovery . . . to be far the most important and valuable that has ever been made on matters connected with the agricultural or commercial resources of the Empire."

Brave words, but it would stagger the Tea Committee, even in its wildest enthusiasm, to imagine India the world's largest tea producer, which she is today. Her all-time record crop of 1978 exceeded one billion pounds, over half of which she drank herself, having also become the world's leading tea consumer. India now boasts some thirteen thousand tea estates or "gardens" with a combined acreage of about one million, all but a fifth of it in north India. It has been estimated the industry provides employment for one and a quarter million people. The recent decades' marked increase in production has been achieved with only slight expansion of acreage. Virtually the entire Indian tea agribusiness of today was created by the British in the three generations between the Tea Committee's report and India's independence from Great Britain after World War II. It is now time to ask how Britain gained control of India in the first place.

THE JOHN COMPANY CONQUERS INDIA

As Alexander had unleashed the hoarded gold of Persia, and the Roman proconsuls had seized upon the spoil of Greece and Pontus, and the Conquistadores the silver of Peru, so now did the English nabobs, merchant princes and adventurers . . . unthaw the frozen treasure of Hindustan and pour it into England.

—*Major-General J.F.C. Fuller (1878–1966)*
A MILITARY HISTORY OF THE WESTERN WORLD

The British and French followed the Portuguese and Dutch into the Orient. When England's Charles II married the Portuguese princess Catherine of Braganza, he received as part of her dowry the Portuguese-held port of Bombay, which he promptly leased to the East India Company for the kingly sum of ten pounds Sterling per year. On the other side of the subcontinent the cities of Calcutta and Madras grew up around the Company's two other chief "factories," and that was about as far as British interests went until the outbreak of what Sir Winston Churchill has justifiably called "the first world war." In Europe it was the War of the Austrian Succession. We in America know it as the French and Indian War, but it was Indian in more ways than one, being fought in India also. In league with Indian allies, their French business rivals attacked the Company's "factories." The Company men had to fight or die, and by 1757, they and their Indian allies ended the affair with a complete triumph over the French and *theirs* at the Battle of Plassey. The Company's general was a former clerk named Robert Clive. The opposing Indian potentates had for untold generations simply accumulated and sat on their annual tribute and taxes. Clive's victory won not only territory for Britain, but also the largest supply of uncirculated wealth the world had seen since Alexander conquered the Persians. This was the capital that produced our Industrial Revolution. It was also the end of peaceful trading, or what would nowadays be called nonintervention in Indian affairs. By the time the Company's Indian monopoly ended one hundred years later, virtually the whole of India was under its control.

In his *A History of the English-Speaking Peoples,* Sir Winston comments:

Modern generations should not mistake the character of the British expansion in India. The Government was never involved as a principal in the Indian conflict. . . . Faced with the difficulties of communication, the distance, and the complexities of the scene, [Prime Minister] Pitt left Clive a free hand, contenting himself with advice and support. The East India Company was a trading organization. Its Directors were men of business. They wanted dividends, not wars, and grudged every penny spent on troops and annexations. But the turmoil in the great sub-continent compelled them against their will and against their judgment to take control of more and more territory, til in the end, and almost by accident, they established an empire no less solid and certainly more peaceful than that of their Mogul predecessors. To call this process "Imperialist expansion" is nonsense, if by that is meant the deliberate expansion of political power. Of India it has well been said that the British Empire was acquired in a fit of absence of mind.

Churchill notwithstanding, it was the profits accruing to "a handful of adventurers from an island in the Atlantic," as the historian Macauley described the Company to Parliament, that made possible "the subjugation of a country divided from the place of their birth by half the globe." Macauley led the fight against the Company in Parliament and in 1834, it was stripped of its monopoly of the China tea trade (and hastily appointed its Tea Committee). The Honorable Company was permitted to continue its administration of India, along with its monopoly of the Indian and, of course, opium trade. How India was ruled the Company neither knew nor cared, so long as peace was maintained and trade prospered.

The Company did much good also. Not even the meanest of its employees was ever allowed to experience the pinch of poverty, and first-rate artists, writers, and intellectuals (of proper family, to be sure) were among the many Englishmen who found a sinecure with the John Company over its long history. One good example is the brilliant and now all-but-unread satirist Thomas Love Peacock. Another is Charles Lamb, a great essayist best known today for a book he wrote in collaboration with his sister Mary, *Tales from Shakespeare*. But the Company's eloquent, yet futile, valedictory was composed by the best of them, the philosopher John Stuart Mill. He solemnly reminded the nation that her magnificent empire in the East had been acquired for her by the John Company and had been governed and defended without the slightest cost to the British Exchequer. The empire to the East was secured, he said, ". . . at the same period at which a succession of administrations under the control of Parliament were losing to the Crown of Great Britain another great empire on the opposite side of the Atlantic."

The author of *On Liberty* somehow leaves the Company's starring role in provoking the American Revolution unmentioned, but despite his plea Parliament voted against extending its Indian monopoly. On 2 August 1858, possession of India was formally transferred to the British Crown, marking the effective end of the greatest of all multinational corporations the world has ever seen.

THE STRUGGLES OF CHARLES BRUCE

If I had a lower IQ
I could enjoy this interview.
   —*Muhammad Ali to Tom Snyder, NBC TV, 1980*

Returning, as it is high time we should, to the history of tea per se, we left the Tea Committee of 1834 assuring the Company tea not only could be but actually was grown in India. That this news took the directors by surprise illustrates how keen of hearing and swift to respond multinational corporations are. Mr. William H. Ukers's exhaustive *All About Tea* cites one Company scientist who'd already submitted five reports on the subject by this time. According to Ukers, tea had been successfully grown as early as the 1780s and by half a dozen different people since, while the wild native tea of Assam had first been reported in 1815. The past was prologue: If the committee's first act was to admit, somewhat grudgingly, that the tea plant was indigenous to Assam, its second act was to import the first commercial lot of China tea seeds, which a later historian called "the curse of the India tea industry."*

Commissioners were dispatched to Assam with Charles Bruce as guide. One of them sniffed that Bruce "was brought up to a sea-faring life and his long residence in Assam had been devoted entirely to mercantile pursuits and the command of gunboats on the Brahmaputra." Bruce was, admittedly, neither a scientist nor even a very good businessman, but he knew how to pioneer a jungle and how to win and keep the friendship of Assam's native tribes. Ingenious as Robinson Crusoe and hearty as a hog, his entire adult life was spent in a malarious wilderness where few white men survived their first year. He explored as far as the borders of Burma and China, mapping a chain of one hundred twenty tracts of wild tea. In his memoirs he tells of finding one tea shrub that had grown into a tree forty-three feet high and three feet around, "though very few attain that size." Bruce was positive that this was the tea to propagate in Assam and he patiently did so, creating gardens with young plants brought from the jungle.

The commissioners would have none of it. Reasoning that "a wild plant is not likely to give as good produce as one that has been cultivated for centuries," they decided "the China plant and not the degraded [sic] Assam plant" should be used in the government-backed experimental gardens. A pioneer, by definition, cares little or

---

*They also set about the translation and study of Lu Yu's *Ch'a Ching,* the only existing book on the subject of growing, harvesting, and manufacturing tea. Though with minimal success, the Dutch had already resorted to it as a guide to their tea experiments on Java and Sumatra. The *Ch'a Ching* was to prove extremely useful to the first British cultivators. In what other subject could one imagine a textbook over a thousand years old that was still of practical value?

nothing for learned opinions that it cannot be done. Bruce continued growing the Assam plants on his own while the Company went about importing more and more Chinese tea seeds each year.

THE ADVENTURES OF ROBERT FORTUNE, ESQ.

When you appeal to force, there's one thing you must never do—lose.
—*Dwight David Eisenhower (1890–1969)*
obiter dictum

It was difficult, even with Chinese law enforcement breaking down, to obtain tea seeds of good quality. Even when you found a merchant willing to wink at the law and sell you some, the chances were he'd boil the seeds first to prevent their germinating. Seeds and plants sold in good condition would arrive mysteriously moldy, diseased, or dead. The only solution was for somebody sufficiently daring and intelligent to penetrate China's forbidden interior and procure the goods himself. Far the most remarkable of all these remarkable men was Robert Fortune, who made his first journey through China the year after the First Opium War. Fortune's Chinese was hardly good enough to pass unnoticed; he allayed suspicion by claiming to be a traveler from a distant province of the Empire, "beyond the Great Wall."

Although Fortune was always aware of being on an adventure, the most striking thing his books reveal is that for him the adventure was discovering and collecting things. He might have written almost as well if he had lived a more conventional life, for the difficulties and dangers he endured were incidental to him. One gradually realizes that he found it perfectly natural to be touring China's forbidden interior or coastline disguised as a Chinese. He was an educated Victorian gentleman absorbed in his collecting who was occasionally forced by "tiresome difficulties" to put "a bold face on it," and for him, that was that.

These "tiresome difficulties" are so liberally sprinkled throughout Fortune's accounts that it's hard to choose just one as an illustration. He describes in his *Wanderings Through China*, published in 1843, how he came down with fever and arranged to be carried, along with his most valuable specimens, to a treaty port down the coast in a small passenger vessel. It was attacked and fired on by pirates, five junkfuls of them. The captain and other passengers hid their valuables in the ship's ballast and put on their very worst clothes, so as not to look like they were worth much ransom. Roused from his bed of pain by the commotion, Fortune appeared on deck armed with a pair of pistols and a ferocious blunderbuss. "The pilot, an intelligent old man, now came up to me and said that he thought resistance was of no use; I might manage to beat off one junk, or even two, but I had no chance with five of them. Being at the time in no mood to take advice or be dictated to by anyone I ordered him off to look after his own duty."

The nearest pirate junk fired a broadside that fell short but cleared the deck of everyone except the helmsmen, whom Fortune kept at their post by threatening them with his pistol. A second broadside was followed by a third from about thirty yards range; it splintered the wood around the men left on deck. "The pirates now seemed quite sure of their prize and came down upon us looking and yelling like demons," writes Fortune. "This was a moment of intense interest. . . . I raised myself above the high stern of our junk and while the pirates were not more than twenty yards from us, hooting and yelling, I raked their decks fore and aft with shot and ball from my double-barrelled gun. . . . They could not have been more surprised. Doubtless many were wounded and probably some killed. At all events the whole crew, not fewer than forty or fifty men, disappeared in a marvelous manner." He dealt with the second junk in the same fashion and all five of them turned away. "The fever which I had scarcely felt during all this excitement now returned with greater violence and I was heartily glad to go below and turn into my own bed," Fortune remarked after a similar set-to against *six* junks the following afternoon. Here was a man.

Occasionally even Robert Fortune enjoyed moments of serenity. His second visit to China was at the behest of the East India Company. He was to bring back seeds, plants, and experienced hands from the finest tea districts of northern China. In disguise and in and out of "tiresome difficulties" as usual, he became the first Westerner to learn that Green Tea comes from the same plant as Black and is only prepared differently. He learned the secret of keeping seed alive through the winter in baskets filled with damp sand. And at last he reached the heart of the Bohea district, "considered by the Chinese to be one of the most wonderful as well as one of the most sacred spots in the Empire" and home of the best Pekoes and Souchongs in the world.

He went up to a temple atop a thousand-foot peak and, as with all he met in peace, made friends with the monks. To quote his *Visit to the Tea Districts of China*: "The High Priest . . . drew out of his tobacco pouch a small quantity of Chinese tobacco, rolled it for a moment between his fingers and thumb and then presented it to me. I lighted my pipe and began to smoke. . . . He called the boy and ordered him to bring us some tea. And now I drank the fragrant herb, pure and unadulterated on its native hills." That must have been one of the finest moments of Robert Fortune's life. He arrived back in India in 1851, with quantities of seeds and tools, a highly skilled team of Chinese workmen, and twelve thousand plants.

THE ASSAM COMPANY COMES OF AGE

The time will come when a single original carrot will be pregnant with revolution.
—Paul Cezanne (1839–1906)
speaking of painting

Charles Bruce was the first to prove you didn't have to be Chinese to grow and manufacture tea. Because of him, in 1839, the world had its first small sip of tea that had *not* come from China. Due to its novelty value, it brought unheard of prices. The second lot of his Assam tea—ninety-five chests—again brought high prices in London in 1840. It moved the venerable firm of R. Twining & Co., Ltd. to pronounce a cautiously understated bit of prophecy: "There seems no reason to doubt but that increased experience in the culture and manufacture of tea in Assam may eventually approximate a portion of its produce to the finer descriptions which China has hitherto furnished." It also moved a number of investors to set up the Assam Company. This was duly approved by the directors of the East India Company, who directed their government of India to turn over practically all its experimental gardens in Assam to the new enterprise free of charge for the first ten years. Bruce was appointed as a superintendant.

The comedy of errors that ensued was compounded of poor soil one place, insufficient labor another, bad cultivation elsewhere, and rampant ignorance from top to bottom. It was in part a battle of vegetables in the jungle, which reclaimed its space with magical rapidity. It was likewise a battle with disease, even the Assam Company doctors dying in their tracks. The directors of the John Company—"a corporation of

men with long heads and deep purposes " Macauley had called them—saw the writing on the wall by 1845. In an effort to forestall further losses, they sought to force the Assam Company to buy their holdings outright, deceitfully writing their Indian government that since ". . . the article may under proper management be cultivated at a real remunerative price . . . we accede to your proposal that the Government should withdraw from any further connection with . . . tea in Assam."

Alas, the Assam Company was in no position to buy, being already insolvent. Less than two years after the Honorable Company had told the world India's tea industry was an established success, Assam Company shares bought at twenty pounds were being hawked on the market at half a crown. A scapegoat had to be found and Charles Bruce was sacked. He left the Company the same way he'd entered it, calling the directors fools for not propagating the indigenous Assam plant as he had done. He was right.

In 1852, a year after Robert Fortune's return from China, the Assam Company finally declared its first earned dividend, 2½ percent, largely a result of the sale of Fortune's seeds. By 1853, there was little doubt the Company was on the high road to success, especially since that same year Charles Bruce's old job was taken over by one George Williamson, who is considered the greatest figure in the development of the Assam tea industry. By his day, most other problems had been set right. Williamson's "greatness" lay in admitting that Bruce had been right about the Assam plant all along. Williamson quickly recognized the advantage, as he put it, "in having no China plant, the inferior yielding of which in respect to quantity is now a well established fact." His successor was later to write of the one experimental garden of China tea that thrived: "It is a matter of profound regret that this experiment did not share the fate of its predecessors, for it proved the chief means of disseminating the pest of Assam—the miserable China variety—all over the province."

Today, Indian tea made from China *jat,* a Hindi word for "type" as applied to tea, or from China-Assam hybrids is of no commercial value whatever. Gradually, yet energetically, Williamson saw to it that the native Indian *jat* succeeded to its birthright. Present-day planters in all the tea-producing countries outside China and Japan raise Assam *jat* exclusively and virtually no China plants remain in the land for whose sake Robert Fortune had struggled so heroically to outwit the China tea jinx.

I must allow the fanciful Mr. J. M. Scott the last word on this matter:

You have read the romantic story of how the Indian Princess Camellia [her other name as yet unknown] was found blushing, unscientifically recognized, in the wild jungles of Assam, of how emissaries went forth and searched through China for a prince of the highest lineage who would share her modest realm and thus raise her in the eyes of the world. Prince after prince languished after leaving China, died and had to be replaced. But the ultimate survivors perked up most surprisingly and impregnated all the native plants within reach. There is no cure for hybridization except extermination. And the experts are now convinced that the simple Indian plant was of much the better class. The Chinese princeling, no good away from home, weakened her pure, strong blood. She could travel, but not he. The couple will certainly live happily ever after in their vegetable way. No one can stop them. But those financially interested continue even now to describe this marriage arranged with such difficulty and final triumph as the curse of the Tea Industry.

TEA MANIA & MODERN MACHINES

So hear it then, my Rennie dear,
  Nor hear it with a frown;
You cannot make the tea so fast
  As I can gulp it down.
I therefore pray thee, Rennie dear,
  That thou wilt give to me
With cream and sugar softened well,
  Another dish of tea!

—*Dr. Samuel Johnson (1709–84)*
untitled lines Boswell reports his extemporizing
to ridicule the ballad form of poetry

It was an industry off and running by the time George Williamson retired from Assam in 1859. His success had taught scores of private entrepreneurs the best tea to plant and the right way to grow and harvest it. The Honorable East India Company had surrendered its Indian perquisites to the Crown the year before, forcing all manner of subalterns and junior officials to look for something better than poverty or an office job back in England. Many decided tea planting would be the simplest, pleasantest, most lucrative and gentlemanly possible alternative. One such wrote at the time: "To those (and the class is numerous in England), who, possessing but a moderate sum of money, wish nevertheless to maintain the position in life to which they have been educated, to whom trade and the professions are obnoxious, who having no military tastes or nautical tendencies are still anxious to use the energy and enterprise which are said to belong to the British—to such tea-planting offers particular inducements."

Inducement enough that vast new acreage was planted, especially around Darjeeling and elsewhere in the foothills of the Himalayas. Everyone was sure of getting rich—the estate managers who didn't know a tea plant from a cabbage, the highly paid boards of directors in Calcutta and London with their still more highly paid secretaries, and, of course, all the investors—rich as Croesus! As a doctor in Assam was later to diagnose the mania: "Although tea has the reputation of furnishing a beverage that cheers but does not inebriate, its cultivation in new districts exercises the most strangely intoxicating influences on those engaged in it, equalled only by the sanguine dreams of gold explorers." Greed and tea had met once again. The outcome was a repetition of the youthful follies of the Assam Company, but on a vastly greater scale. Millions of pounds Sterling were squandered in the name of tea and by 1865 the very word had become a stench in the nostrils of the investing public. It took another five years for the young industry to recover from the tea mania and the resulting financial disasters. By then the tea men who survived had learned their business and the old established estates that had escaped the speculative blight were flourishing. The future was, in fact, rosier than any of them suspected.

One day in 1871, a side-paddle riverboat steaming lazily down the Brahmaputra slid to a stop in mid-stream. It had run aground on one of the shifting sandbars for which the river is notorious, forcing the captain to tell his passengers it would be some little while before they could go farther, as the boat would require rather extensive repairs. Why didn't they explore the surrounding countryside while they waited—and stay out of his way? Two of the passengers who clambered ashore were the brothers John and William Jackson, who were on their way home to England from a tea estate in Upper Assam. Somewhere in the vicinity they came across a portable steam engine that still showed no signs of breaking down after ten years' nonstop performance. William, who had a head for machinery, liked the design so well he made a note of the maker's address. The English firm of Marshall Sons & Company, Ltd. owes its extensive tea machinery business to this happy accident.

The brothers Jackson—for they worked together at first—finally got off the sandbar and, once home, asked the steam engine firm to produce a tea-rolling machine of their design. It was the first to do the job better and faster than it could be done by hand. Up until then the leaf was hand-rolled, dried over charcoal fires, and trampled into the chests by barefoot workers. Eventually William Jackson was to invent and patent machines for every one of these procedures. He and his competitors introduced scientific preparation of the leaf under hygienic conditions.

In 1872, when Jackson began inventing, the cost of tea production in India was elevenpence a pound, but by 1913, improved machinery had reduced the cost to about threepence a pound. Eight thousand rolling machines did the work once done by one and a half million people. Formerly, eight pounds of good-quality wood turned into charcoal were required to dry a pound of tea. The Jackson machines produced the same results with any wood, grass, or anything else that could be burned. Where coal was used, the amount required was only one-quarter pound of Assam coal per pound of finished dry tea. The Jacksons revolutionized the manufacture of tea to the same extent that Williamson had its cultivation.

The Jackson brothers had returned to England the year of the last tea clipper race. In a short time their machines were to multiply India's tea output manyfold, just as steamships using the Suez Canal made its transport many times cheaper. The speculators of earlier days had been foolish but not wrong: India was on the way to capturing the giant's share of the world tea market. Ceylon, to the south, was doing the same with coffee just then when suddenly disaster struck.

God's mysterious ways cannot but amaze, yet I still wonder how two of the most devastating scourges in agricultural history could occur in the exact same decade. In the late 1860s, a microscopic organism unheard of before started killing the roots of all the grapevines in Europe. Europe would not produce an ounce of wine today if someone hadn't finally learned to graft the vines onto native American rootstock, which was impervious to the disease. Over this identical period a similarly noxious life form was attacking the leaves of Ceylon's coffee plants, only this time no cure was found for it. All the coffee died and all the planters were ruined. What followed could be called either "true grit" or "the rush into tea." Ceylon, formerly the Isle of Serendip, now called Sri Lanka, had a total of 1,080 acres of tea in 1875. By 1895, the figure was 305,000 acres; another 100,000 were added over the next twenty years. The Assam *jat* had proved conclusively that *it* could travel, take root elsewhere, and flourish.

THE TRIUMPH OF THE ASSAM *JAT*

Consider the Passion Flower:
Who'd ever think a plant would go to
so much trouble
just to get fucked
by a Bee.
> —*Lew Welch (1926–71)*
> *lines from* BOTANY

Thanks, yet again, to novelty's perennial value, the first lot of Ceylon tea sold in Mincing Lane in 1891 for £25 10s. per pound. Since then Assam *jat* has blossomed around the world. It is extensively cultivated in Kenya, Tanzania, Uganda, and other unhappy African countries. Tea has long been a mainstay of the Indonesian economy. New Guinea, Equador, Brazil, and Argentina produce it in ever-growing amounts. William Jackson's brother John even induced the United States government to experiment with it in South Carolina. This experiment was discontinued in 1912, after twenty-five years, not because the tea didn't thrive, but because costs were too high and it did not pay. As it was in the beginning, tea must still be plucked by hand, after all, and Third World hands remain much less expensive than those of Americans.

All of these teas are from the same single variety of plant, *Camellia sinensis*, yet all are different. Everybody is bound to have his own likes and dislikes. One of my heroes, a great snob even in a snobbish era but a man of superlative attainments besides, the author and occultist Aleister Crowley studied Buddhism in Ceylon in 1906. "There seems to be something in the climate"—he remarks in his *Confessions*—"that stupefies the finer parts of a man if he lives there too long. The flavor of the tea seemed to me somehow symbolic. I remember one day pleading with the local shopkeeper to find me some Chinese tea. It chanced that the owner of a neighboring plantation was in the shop.

He butted in, remarking superciliously that he could put in the China flavor for me. 'Yes,' I said, 'but can you take the Ceylon flavor out?' "

As the blessed Aleister must have known, he could not. And this is why, in due course, we shall examine in detail the characteristics of the different kinds of tea.

TEA MERCHANTS & TEA MERCHANDISING

It seems in some cases kind nature hath planned
That names with their callings agree,
For Twining the tea-man that lives in the Strand
Would be "wining" deprived of his "T."
—Thomas Hook (1778–1841)
famous witticism

The first decade of the twentieth century saw two innovations that have revolutionized tea habits and the tea industry. The first may be traced to the St. Louis World's Fair of 1904, the one the song "Meet Me in St. Louis" was written for. Most of the tea drunk in America at that time came from China, and in the Midwest, for reasons that have never been entirely clear to me, people drank mostly Green Teas. (In fact, Liptons markets its only Green Tea there to this day.) To popularize Indian tea, therefore, an association of India tea producers established a special pavilion at the fair, staffed with exquisitely mannered turbaned Indian servants under the supervision of an Englishman named Richard Blechynden. What the promoters had not reckoned with was the scorching Midwestern summer, which can give New Delhi's competition in the Fahrenheit category. Blechynden's exotic, steaming brew was the last thing the sweltering fair goers felt like sampling. Finally, Blechynden himself began sweating, for there was no unemployment compensation at the time, and in his desperation began pouring his tea into glasses crammed with ice just to get people to drink it. People drank it. They came back for more and carried the liking for it back home with them. Thus a new American drink was born.

Though uncommon in other countries, as of the early 1980s, the United States was drinking thirty-six billion glasses of iced tea a year as compared to ten billion cups of hot. It takes almost two hundred million pounds of tea to fill those cups and glasses each year. That only about 3 percent of this amount is still sold as loose tea these days is thanks to that second accidental innovation, the tea bag.

In 1908, a New York City tea importer named Thomas Sullivan made an effort to economize on his operating costs by sending samples out to his retail dealers and private customers in little silk bags sewn closed by hand. He was perplexed but delighted when virtually everybody placed orders. Only when they all complained that the tea he delivered wasn't packaged in those bags for convenience in brewing did he get the idea to substitute gauze for the silk and rake in sizable profits producing the first tea bags. Expensive and elaborate machines and specially treated fiber papers are used today, but this development, like instant tea, has more to do with business administration and international finance than with the present history.

The oldest extant tea firm in the English-speaking world is so old it was founded eight years before tea was even introduced. That was 1650, when a friend of Sam Pepys named Rawlinson opened the Mitre Tavern. By 1750, it had become a tea business and belonged to Sir Thomas Rawlinson, the Lord Mayor of London. Since his death, the firm has been known as Davison, Newman & Company. Of almost equally venerable descent is John Travers & Sons, which traces itself under various names to 1666, the year of

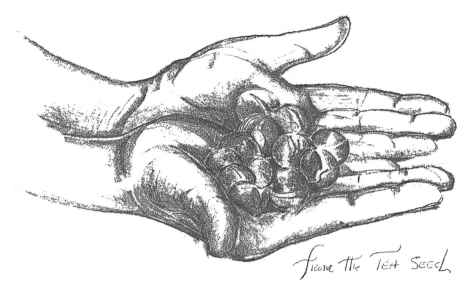

from the Tea Seed

London's Great Fire, and one other firm I forget. It was to give grocers like these some competition that William Fortnum and Hugh Mason quit their positions as servants in Queen Anne's court and formed a partnership early in the 1700s.

Tea was but a sideline with all these houses at first, of course, and one they shared with apothecaries and coffee houses at that. By 1717, however, the proprietor of Tom's, one of London's newer coffee houses, found that his retail coffee and tea business had outgrown its premises. He acquired the building next door and established the first retail outlet for Twinings teas where, unlike the coffee house, women were also welcome. In those days of no street numbers, tradesmen identified their places of business as at or near one or another sign and Twining chose the sign of the Golden Lion for his, a singularly fortunate choice. The ninth generation of his family is still doing business in the Strand at this same location. Before he died, old Tom Twining was rich enough to afford a portrait by Hogarth and a fine country home to hang it in.

Maria Tewk (or Tuke), a single woman of thirty, founded the only comparable tea dynasty when she set up a tea business in York in 1725. Although she died a spinster, she left the firm to a nephew who handed it down even unto the seventh generation. The male world of the eighteenth century also saw Twinings single-handedly run by a woman for some seventeen years until widow Mary Little Twining was succeeded by her son Richard. It was in his capacity as "Chairman of the Dealers in Tea"—all thirty thousand of them legally dependent upon the Honorable East India Company for supplies—that Richard succeeded in persuading the Crown to reduce tea taxes in 1784, and thereby put an effective end to the picturesque industry of tea smuggling.

Once free of the John Company, the Americans lost no time in establishing trade with China and by 1789 seven American ships had made the voyage to Canton and back. In 1800, a young New York merchant accepted delivery of a wagon load of kegs containing fifty-five thousand silver dollars. It was John Jacob Astor's half of the proceeds from his first China venture. Success dogged the footsteps of the boy from Waldorf, Germany, from then on as for the next twenty-seven years Astor carried on an immensely profitable trade with China. He regarded a 50 percent profit per voyage as only fair and often made 100 percent or more. He was one of America's first three millionaires, and it is interesting to note that all three were involved in the China trade and with tea.

The most likeable of these three was Stephen Girard of Philadelphia, whose loans to the United States government were crucial in "winning" the War of 1812 and whose admirable orphanage perpetuates his good works still. The least known is Thomas Handasyd Perkins of one of Boston's old sailing families. In 1789, he was in Canton as a twenty-six-year-old ship's supercargo and concluded his business with the even younger Houqua, who had just become one of the thirteen hong merchants who alone were authorized to deal with the foreign devils. These two transacted business deals on an enormous scale for the next half century and never put a word in writing. But though Astor, Girard, and Perkins dealt in tea, the American market remained quite limited and the great tea merchants continued to be British.

Tea consumption not only kept up with the enormous growth in Britain's population during the 1800s, but actually trebled per capita. At the beginning of the century you incurred a two-hundred-pound fine if you sold tea and were not a registered tea dealer or the John Company itself. With an annual consumption of two pounds per capita, tea was the most profitable item the English grocer stocked. Up until this period Green had always been far more popular than Black Teas, but over time this preference was gradually changed by the cunning manufacture of elder buds into a product called "Smooch," which the unwary might mistake for Green Tea. It was with Smooch very much in mind that honest Quaker John Horniman introduced the sealed packet containing a guaranteed net weight of unadulterated tea. He began by having peddlers distribute his packets in 1826, and ended by amassing a fortune. Ironically, the firm that was eventually to buy Hornimans out was founded in 1837 by two orphaned teenage brothers, the Tetleys, who were supporting themselves by peddling tea to remote Yorkshire villages.

Ridgways Ltd. and Robert Jackson & Company (Jacksons of Piccadilly) also date from the 1830s, almost, indeed, from the very year Victoria soberly mounted the throne and established the fashion of rarely touching anything stronger than the strongest tea. As the decade that saw the last of the John Company's China monopoly and the first shipment of India-grown tea, the 1830s discovered tea quality and abundance both. The fledgling Victorian tea companies throve and made room for newcomers in their ranks—Kardomah, Brooke Bond—and eventually for the Lyons phenomenon.

The last of London's old tea gardens had succumbed to urban sprawl by 1850, and nothing arose to take their place. The tea garden, like the coffee house before it, had always been relatively free of class distinctions. Whether you were male or female, it was always a place where you could get into a little trouble if you liked. And then for thirty-odd years—the span of a generation—there was no place to go out to tea except other people's houses. This goes far toward explaining the stuffiness of the period, just as the popularity of Oscar Wilde's comedies condemns the taste of the age. "You have filled my tea with lumps of sugar, and though I asked most distinctly for bread and butter, you have given me cake!" exclaims indignant Lady Windemere.

It's hard to understand why nobody, not even naughty Oscar, thought of the tea shop before 1884, but nobody did. That first one was a space in a bakery near London Bridge, and the idea caught on. There are several things Englishmen like to do without their womenfolk (though through no lack of love, to be sure), but drinking tea is not one of those things. This accounts for the phenomenal success of the Lyons chain, which quickly sprouted two hundred fifty tea shops staffed by uniformed waitresses called "nippies." Lyons became a national institution overnight, and ever since the British have found it impossible to imagine a time when the tea shop did not exist. But let us now praise justly famous old Sir Tea himself—Sir Thomas Lipton.

SIR TEA

T stands for Tommy, and also for tea,
It is well known on shore,
He is quite to the fore,
But a little bit backward at sea.
—Caption of a kindly 1913 caricature of Lipton
before his fourth attempt to win yachting's America's Cup

Thomas Lipton was the only son of Irish parents who fled the Great Potato Famine to Glasgow, Scotland, the year before Thomas was born there in 1850. As a teenager Lipton went to America and found jobs in Virginia and New Orleans and at length found his true vocation in New York working in a fancy grocery store. He returned to Glasgow with one hundred pounds in savings, a sack of flour, and a rocking chair for his mother, arriving on a Saturday and going to work the next Monday in the grocery his father'd acquired. On his twenty-first birthday he opened one of his own, waiting on his customers in an always crisp white apron and often sleeping under the counter at night.

Advertising was in its infancy, but everybody in Glasgow soon knew about Lipton's. The young grocer's first front-page achievement was to hire two Irishmen to parade two of the largest hogs in captivity through the streets bearing signs proclaiming, "I'm going to Lipton's. The best shop in town for Irish bacon!" The resulting bedlam, complete with traffic jams and policemen, assured newspaper coverage. A series of such stunts soon had everybody going to Lipton's. Within a decade there were twenty Lipton's shops and more coming.

By 1890, Lipton was forty, already a millionaire, and his many shops—seventy odd in London alone by then—famous for their hams and cheeses; he needed new challenges. He had always lived with his parents and had lost first his mother and now suddenly his father. Within a few months after his father's death he announced that he was at last taking a vacation, a cruise to Australia. He did not announce that he had sent one of his business associates on ahead to Ceylon, but when his ship stopped over for refueling at Colombo, the agent was ready with his report.

The early kings of Ceylon had traded with the Roman Empire, their ships following the monsoon to and fro across the Indian Ocean. During Europe's Dark Ages, Ceylon's cities were great and her vast rice croplands fed by irrigation channels from reservoirs of up to thirty miles in circumference. Then malaria-bearing mosquitoes, invaders from India and finally European Christians had laid the land low. The British deposed the 186th and last Sinhalese king in 1815, and Ceylon became a fully occupied Crown Colony. Coffee, which the Arabs had introduced long, long before, became the island's economic mainstay and by 1875, enterprising Englishmen had over a quarter of a million acres of coffee under cultivation. Things had never looked better and suddenly a natural disaster struck—not an earthquake, hurricane, or tidal wave, but a blight (*Hemeleia vastatrix*) that appeared out of nowhere and destroyed the coffee and left the English planters ruined. The ones who could afford to planted chinchona until quinine prices fell and it was no longer worth taking the bark off the trees. By the time the planters thought of trying tea, few of them had the price of seeds, but those who made the experiment proved Ceylon could grow quality tea.

The situation Lipton found in Ceylon was rather as he'd imagined it would be. (It was not until a full year later, in 1891, that the first lot of Ceylon tea would reach

Mincing Lane.) Lipton made an excursion into the high country and bought plantations left and right. Bankrupt landowners were so plentiful he paid out only half the three hundred thousand dollars that he'd brought to spend. "He was seized with the possibilities of Ceylon tea for the masses," wrote Gervas Huxley, a cousin of Aldous's and a man who knew Lipton personally. "He would have his own Ceylon tea estates. He would sell all over the world a blend of good quality Ceylon tea in attractive standardised packets at the lowest possible price. 'Direct from the tea garden to the tea pot' would be his slogan, and publicity and advertising would tell the world about Lipton's tea and Ceylon."

The Ceylon tea estates were publicized in every way. When his initial twenty thousand chests reached Glasgow, Lipton had fifty dray loads hauled through the streets escorted by brass bands and bagpipers. Tea at the time was generally priced at three shillings the pound and not to be found as low as two. Lipton opened his campaign by selling his tea at one shilling sevenpence per pound while advertising it as "The Finest the World Can Produce." He very soon captured a very large share of the retail market. While his estates were soon supplying only a small fraction of his huge volume, Lipton's advertising somehow left the distinct impression he grew all the tea he sold. Orange Pekoe, likewise, was only an obscure bit of tea jargon denoting the size of the leaf until Thomas Lipton first heard the term and perceived more romantic overtones. Using every package and available billboard, he convinced the world Orange Pekoe was a superior type of tea. "It's brisk," his advertisements said, "brisk," in this case, being tasters' jargon meaning only that the tea isn't plain flat tasting. He was a showman, new to the trade, showing off the new terms he'd learned. He succeeded grandly and the millionaire grocer became a multimillionaire tea merchant.

When Lipton moved to London in 1894, he was once more in need of a challenge and with his usual enthusiasm took up social climbing. With his unusual good luck, he soon became a friend of the Prince of Wales. When he found himself conveyed in the royal yacht to the Isle of Wight to kneel before his new friend Edward's mama and be dubbed Sir Thomas, he was not entirely forgetful of the publicity value to Liptons Tea, but it was probably in gratitude to the prince for the honor that Sir Thomas made the grandest gesture of his life. Since Edward liked racing in sailing yachts, Lipton decided to commission the world's fastest racing yacht and win the America's Cup for England.

HRH was properly impressed and appreciative and responded to Sir Thomas's gesture by proposing him for membership in the Royal Yacht Squadron at Cowes. This tightly held bastion of the aristocracy affected horror. One member, the prince's nephew Wilhelm II of Germany, was in England at this time and was asked while strolling the Squadron grounds if he had seen his uncle. Replied the kaiser: "They tell me he has gone boating with his grocer." To avoid the embarrassment of having a royally sponsored candidate blackballed, Edward quietly withdrew Sir Thomas's name; Lipton was, or pretended to be, merely amused and quite content with his membership in the Royal Ulster Yacht Club at Belfast. Flying its ensign, his *Shamrock* challenged the *Columbia* of New York for the America's Cup in 1899, and was soundly beaten. "I am not discouraged," Sir Thomas said, and raced *Shamrocks* II and III with the same sad results. "No man was ever more confident of winning anything than I was when I came over," he admitted in 1903. "What can I do? I have tried my best." It was to be years before Lipton returned to the challenge.

His royal friend and patron died in the meantime and Sir Thomas seemed to lose interest in social acceptability; he acted as he damn well pleased. The steamer carrying him to visit his estates in Ceylon ran aground in the Red Sea, and seeing the captain had ordered some cargo jettisoned, the passengers took to the lifeboats in panic. Sir Thomas calmly occupied himself stenciling Drink Liptons Tea on every bale or box likely to float. He bought a huge warehouse in Hoboken, New Jersey, and erected a Liptons Tea sign large enough to read from any point in New York harbor. He had his building's elevator enlarged to accommodate his limousine so that he could alight from it inside his twelfth-floor office. And at last he admitted he still wanted to win the Cup... and in 1920, *Shamrock IV* brought him the closest he had come to his ambition.

The challenge of taking the America's Cup, "to lift the ould mug" as he put it, left the old man no peace. The summer of 1930, he was back with *Shamrock V.* Americans had long since taken the game old Sir Tea to their hearts, and spectators came by special trains from as far away as Chicago to cheer the octogenarian challenger. Sir Thomas returned the affection, saying he regretted that in America "my only blood relatives are some New Jersey mosquitoes." The letdown of the old man's defeat was felt as a national disappointment, even the winner, a Vanderbilt, finding his victory "so tempered with sadness that it was almost hollow." In a letter to the *New York Times* Will

Rogers suggested, "Let every one send a dollar apiece for a fund to buy a loving cup for Sir Thomas Lipton bigger than the one he would have got if he had won." Ten days and sixteen thousand Depression dollars later, Tiffany & Company began the two-month job of creating the cup. It stood eighteen inches high and was eighteen-karat gold, with a sterling-silver base contributed by some miners in Utah. The inscription read: "In the name of hundreds and thousands of Americans and well-wishers of Sir Thomas Johnstone Lipton, Bart., K.C.V.O."

Among the presents on his eighty-first birthday the following year was a letter from the Royal Yacht Squadron informing him of his unanimous election to its sacred membership: "In recognition of his great services to yacht racing." That summer of 1931 he went down to Cowes to watch his fifth and last *Shamrock* win the Squadron's main event, the King's Cup, but though he flew the Squadron's white ensign he did not enter the clubhouse even for the dinner celebrating his victory. A few months later he was dead. ❧

TEA THINGS

Where Did That Come From?

AN INTRODUCTION TO POTTERY, CHINA, & SILVER

This is a subject which I could no doubt handle much better were I a profound scholar in any of several fields. But I am not writing for scholars, but for people like myself; some defects may be compensated by some advantages; and what one must be judged by, scholar or no, is not particularised knowledge but one's total harvest of thinking, feeling, living and observing human beings.

—T. S. Eliot
THE IDEA OF A CHRISTIAN SOCIETY

HE BASIS of civilization is the pot in any of its various forms. God obviously decided to tell the first archeologist "by their pots ye shall know them," for pottery has always been the principal means of identifying and dating the cultures of the past, and the future, if there is one, will just as certainly describe the teapot as *the* characteristic artifact of the last several centuries. British expansion during the Victorian era and before coincided exactly with tea's increasing popularity in this world, and wherever Englishmen settled and wherever they went, from British Guiana to British North Borneo, the teapot went with them. Almost all other cultures have by now produced variations of their own.

The teapot has not always been the undisputed lord of the tea service; historically the teacup comes first. The Chinese both before and after Lu Yu's day appear to have crumbled their tea bricks into kettles that they set boiling. Practices changed and by the Ming Dynasty boiling water was poured directly onto loose tea leaves in tiny cups. According to the best authorities, the first teapots of which positive records exist only appear around the year 1500. This is hard for me to accept: Ewers with spouts that look very like teapots go back centuries earlier and it strains credulity to believe so inventive a people as the Chinese never thought to brew tea in their so-called wine ewers.

Let us agree, nonetheless, that the official history of the teapot begins around 1500 with the pots of Yi-Xing, just up the Yangtze from Shanghai and the main Ming pottery. Yi-Xing teapots of unglazed red or brown stoneware quickly became popular all over over China and were exported in large quantities to Japan, where native potters paid them their sincerest compliment by making imitations and, eventually, an improvement. They relocated the handle, removing it from the side and arching it over the *top* of the pot. This is customary even in China today, but the next time your eye lingers on your grandmother's outsized silver teapot, put aside larcenous thoughts and reflect that if only some earlier Commodore Perry had opened Japan to international commerce, perhaps we should never have accustomed ourselves for over three hundred years to teapots with handles on the side, Ming style.

By the time the Dutch became the first to import tea into Europe in 1610, the teapots they brought along with it were approaching perfection in design. They were broad based, not to say squatty, because long experience had proved the wisdom of minimizing the chance for a vessel full of scalding liquid to tip over in your lap. The spouts were made too big to clog up with tea leaves, and opposite the spout was a handle shaped to fit fingers and hand and provide easy handling. These pots were small, not as has often been suggested because tea was expensive (which it was not in China), but so that everybody might have a pot to himself. Small likewise were the cups that accompanied such pots, holding little more than several thimblefuls. We should bear this in mind when recalling Dr. Cornelius Bontekoe's judgment that even one or two hundred cups of tea a day did not seem excessive to him. We might also reflect that it was these imported accessories that made tea drinking even possible in Holland; their own Delft earthenware could not stand up to boiling water.

At the beginning of the China trade, the highest achievement of the potter's art in Europe was a kind of earthenware that was fired, then coated with an opaque enamellike glaze and fired again, fixing the colors with which it had been painted. It was known as majolica, a name first used in Italy during the 1400s for Spanish pottery imported in ships from Majorca. Mistakenly supposing that the wares came from the same place the ships bringing them did, the Italians called such goods majolica and the name stuck even after it began to be produced all over Europe. By the 1500s, the French were calling a variety of majolica faience, named for the city of Faenza in Italy where it had been developed. The products of Delft and other European pottery centers were basically further variations on the majolica theme.

The heat-resistant, nondissolving Chinese pottery that Europe saw for the first time in the late 1500s, let us say, was not earthenware but stoneware, made by firing the kiln beyond a certain temperature so that the clay becomes vitrified and impervious to liquids, boiling or not. It was only in the 1670s that Dutch potters first managed to duplicate unglazed Chinese stoneware, though by no means equal in substance and finish to the original models. We may be reasonably confident that no European before this date ever made tea—for long—in European-made vessels. The premier potters of their day—the brothers John and Philip Elers—were almost certainly among the followers of William and Mary of Orange when they left Holland to assume joint tenancy of the British throne in 1688. After finally locating the clays they were seeking, the Elers settled in Staffordshire in 1693, and founded England's most important pottery industry there. This is worth mentioning for the "school of pottery" they established was to culminate a century later with Josiah Wedgwood (1730–17), son of one Staffordshire potter, apprentice to another, and himself arguably the most important ceramicist in European history.

Second only to tea, perhaps the most important contribution China made to European life was "china" itself—the hard, translucent glazed pottery the Chinese had invented under the T'ang Dynasty and which we also know as porcelain. Majolica, faience, Delft, and stoneware aside, what really had European potters and their patrons and customers amazed from the late 1500s onward was this altogether different Oriental something—the nonopaque pottery they called china. If you held a piece up to the light you could see the outline of your fingers, so unbelievably thin and translucent was it. Even so wise a man as Sir Francis Bacon considered it to be a kind of plaster that was buried in the earth where, after a long lapse of time, it "congealed and glazed itself into that fine substance."

For years before the advent of tea it had been the dream of all European potters to produce china themselves. The Elers brothers mastered stoneware, but their efforts to reproduce china proved unavailing, and so did the efforts of all the other first-rate potters in Europe. The potters of St. Cloud in France developed a substitute now known as soft-paste porcelain, but nobody came near approximating the real thing until an apothecary's apprentice named Johann-Friederich Böttger bumbled onto the scene.

When he was nineteen, Böttger met the mysterious alchemist Lascaris in Berlin and received a present of some two ounces of transmutation powder from him. If you refuse to believe in alchemists and transmutation, you may as well assume that Mr. Lascaris stepped out of a UFO for the stories of his—and Böttger's—careers are entirely too well documented to dismiss. As Lascaris no doubt intended, Böttger couldn't resist showing off the powder's powers. Unfortunately, he also claimed to have made it himself with the predictable result that he soon had all the crowned heads of Germany in his pursuit. He finally reached safety, so he thought, in Dresden, under the protection of Augustus II, "the Strong," Elector of Saxony and King of Poland. But with extravagant gifts and riotous living, his stock of powder was exhausted rather sooner than later and his "protector" proved not to be the disinterested well-wisher he had seemed. Poor Böttger found himself confined in the castle of Königstein where he was given a laboratory for his researches and a clear understanding of the fate reserved for him should he fail.

He finally convinced his jailer, a certain Count Tschirnhaus, that he was not an Adept in the spagyric arts but merely a demonstrator. The count proposed that in that case he should put the laboratory to use in quest of the secret of making china, since next to gold and power, collecting Japanese and Chinese porcelains was Augustus's ruling passion. (He had filled a palace with his collection—some twenty thousand pieces and still growing—by the time of his death.) Fortunately for the prisoner-researcher, Saxony abounds with the two main ingredients for the manufacture of porcelain—china clay or kaolin and the so-called china stone, a type of rock made up mostly of silica and alumina that serves as a flux and gives the ware its translucency. Böttger first produced stoneware and then, after numerous false starts, finally obtained a hard-paste red porcelain in 1703. The kiln had been kept burning for five days and five nights and in anticipation of success his royal patron had been invited to see it opened. It is reported that the first product Böttger took out and presented to Augustus was a fine red teapot. The long-sought secret had been discovered at last! After a few more years Böttger managed to come up with genuine hard-paste white porcelain.

Completely restored to favor, the young man admitted he had never possessed the secret of transmutation; he was formally forgiven and promptly appointed director of Europe's first china factory. It was established near Dresden in a little village called Meissen and proved to be worth almost as much to Augustus as the Philosopher's Stone would have been. Soon after full production got underway in 1713, the export market for Meissen figurines alone ran into the millions. In a letter of 1746, Horace Walpole grumbled about the new fashion in table decorations at the banquets of the English nobility: "Jellies, biscuits, sugar, plums, and cream have long since given way to harlequins, gondoliers, Turks, Chinese, and shepherdesses of Saxon China." Teapots and teacups were also produced in ever increasing quantities.

Having resumed his riotous living, Böttger died a victim of his habits in 1719, aged thirty-seven. Lascaris vanishes from history between the years 1730 and 1740. The most readable recent account of his career and his connection with J.-F. Böttger is in Jacques Sadoul's *Alchemists & Gold* (New York: Putnam, 1972). It goes without saying that the transmutation of elements is today a commonplace of nuclear physics.

Industrial espionage spread the secret of porcelain manufacture beyond the Germanies during the 1740s and in 1751, fifteen English entrepreneurs joined together

to found the Worchester Royal Porcelain Works. To the chagrin of every prince and duke in France lavishing patronage on a little porcelain works of his own, the king's beloved Madame de Pompadour decided to bestow hers on a little factory located near Versailles at Sèvres. Louis XV bought it to please her in 1759 and, just to make sure it would prosper, ordered the royal chinaware made there. When in need of money the king sometimes forced the courtiers at Versailles to buy quantities of Sèvres at extortionate prices.

The contrast between French and English porcelains is predictable, for the English nobility of the day were far too busy riding to hounds and improving their estates to bother much about porcelain tea sets. That they left to the bourgeoisie and as a result most English china is doggedly middle class. Worchester tried to emulate Sèvres,

God knows, but a certain earthiness kept getting in the way and the results were as unmistakably English as a cricket bat. They did manage to copy some of the Sèvres colors—a Pompadour pink and a *bleu celeste,* for instance—and they did attract an occasional "prestige" customer. Admiral Lord Nelson, for one, ordered a breakfast, dinner, and dessert service of a pattern so excruciatingly ornate that only the breakfast set had been completed by the time of his death at Trafalgar. Lady Hamilton then sent word that she did not fancy the pattern and canceled the order. Some pieces of Nelson's set are still in Worchester today in the Dyson Perrins Museum, founded by an early collector of Worchester porcelain who is better known for his invention of Worchestershire sauce.

The English porcelain firms of the eighteenth century kept experimenting with the formulae filched from the Continent and it would be interesting indeed to know how Mr. J. Spode first hit upon the idea of using the ingredient that distinguishes English from all other porcelains—the ashes of burned bones. Yes, Virginia, bone china is rightly so-called. It comes only from England and may consist of over 50 percent bone ash. Porcelain's ingredients, whatever they may be, must be combined into a medium about the consistency of toothpaste and then "jollyed," "jiggered," and "chummed" into shape for firing. The terms are craft slang handed down from the eighteenth century; one who makes handles and attaches them to casseroles, for example, is an "oval jollyer sticker-up." And from the beginning, the mainstay of the production at Worchester, Chelsea, Spode, Limoges, and all the other centers of china making in Europe was the "tea equippage."

We still use at least one china pattern that originated in those days and that most of us would recognize: the traditionally Chinese blue-and-white willow pattern. The best is produced in England by Johnson Brothers today; it is thought to have originated at a porcelain works in Shropshire about 1780, and the pattern was soon being reproduced by numerous others. Look closely at the next willowware plate you see and you should be able to make out the illustrations of the legend of Koong-tse and Chang. Details of the legend differ with each telling, but all agree that willowware tells a love story.

Koong-tse, a rich man's beautiful daughter, lived with her father in the two-storied house in the center of the pattern. There's an orange tree behind the house and a footbridge with a willow tree overhanging it in front. To the annoyance of her father,

Koong-tse fell in love with his poor clerk, Chang. In time-honored fashion, her rich daddy fired Chang and speedily betrothed Koong-tse to a wealthy old mandarin. Across the foreground of the pattern is the fence or palisade the angry father built to keep the lovers apart. Koong-tse was restricted to the garden and tea house one sees encircled by a stream, but Chang floated messages down this stream to her and outlined a plan of escape. The three figures shown running across the footbridge are Koong-tse, who holds the distaff as symbol of virginity; Chang, who carries the box of jewels the old mandarin had given her; and the enraged father brandishing a whip. The boat in the design bore the lovers far downstream to the island shown in the upper left portion of the pattern. Here they built a house and, as the furrows show, took up farming. But Chang was also a writer and at length his fame reached the old mandarin, who had him tracked down and killed. Koong-tse then committed suicide in despair but Kuan Yin and the other gods, out of regard for their great love, transformed the souls of the lovers into two immortal doves, the emblems of constancy, which we see floating above the whole design.

As we have seen, the teacups originally imported from China were dainty little things, usually less than two inches high, only slightly wider across and innocent of handles. The teacup handle is a distinctly Western improvement, an idea the English borrowed from their "posset cup." The posset cup was also intended for hot beverages, a posset being heated milk with wine or spirits in it.* Why the descendant of the posset cup came to be called the tea "dish" history does not tell us, but "dish of tea" it was in English parlance well into the nineteenth century. The English teacup also grew to approximate the size of the posset cup and by the time tea had become Britain's national beverage, the teacupful had become a standard of measurement for the nation's cooks. A standard of measurement of similar origin is the teaspoonful, and with it we come to the story of silver ware.

---

*Sir Walter Raleigh's recipe for "sack posset" is as follows: Boil together half a pint of sherry (sack) and half a pint of ale and add gradually a quart of boiling cream or milk. Sweeten the mixture well and flavor with grated nutmeg. Put it into a heated dish, cover it, and let it stand by the fire two or three hours.

In striking contrast to their attitude toward early porcelain and pottery wares, the English nobility—like people in all countries and every age—have always coveted silver. The metal has been known since the Stone Age, though it is rarely mined as such, but rather is extracted from lead, copper, and other ores. It has almost always been regarded as so much cash on hand or money in the bank, regardless of the beauty and workmanship of the articles made from it. England has probably produced more fine silver wares than the rest of the world combined, and the enormous influence of her silversmiths is obvious from the international acceptance of the English "sterling silver" standard.

The word sterling owes its origin to a band of immigrant German silversmiths whom King John of Magna Carta fame summoned to England in 1300 to refine silver for coinage purposes. For some reason lost to history, these medieval artisans were known as Easterlings. The standard of purity that they introduced was subsequently recognized by law, but the statute that applied their name to silver for all time inexplicably misspelled it, dropping the first two letters to give us "sterling." In 1560, Elizabeth the Great reestablished the sterling standard at 92.5 percent pure silver and, except for the first couple decades of the eighteenth century, this definition has remained in force down to the present day.

Today the only enemy of silver, English or otherwise, is too heavy a hand with the silver polish; indeed, virtually every piece of *old* silver, large or small, with or without historic or even aesthetic appeal, is safely in the clutches of some collector. One of these is my esteemed friend Mr. Simpson Hemphill of Paloma Plantation in the Mississippi Delta, and these pages are much indebted to his expertise. Like most, his collection centers on English silver and contains no example earlier than about 1650.

During England's civil war between Cromwell's Puritans and the Cavaliers supporting King Charles I, both sides looted their own and their opponents' troves of silver to melt it down for bullion. This is why there is very little pre-1648 English silver around. In the absence of many earlier examples, connoisseurs consider the greatest years of English silver wares to be roughly 1660–1830, or from the restoration of King Charles II almost up to the accession of Queen Victoria. In America over this same period we have records and examples of over fifteen hundred hallmarks of different silversmiths—something like one hundred fifty silversmiths had been established in

Boston alone by 1800—yet early American silver is a rarity. The English obviously employed many, many times more silver craftsmen and artists. For one thing, they were far richer and needed more prestige ware, "special" silver for gifts, for the courts, the great ancestral homes, and ambassadors traveling abroad, not to mention the breakfast, tea, and dinner tables of the recently rich.

But both the English silversmiths and their provincial American colleagues developed the same chief stock-in-trade—tea things. Though not the least of them, teapots and teaspoons were only the beginning. There were "mote skimmers" and "caddy ladles," there were trivets and trays and kettles and slop jars, strainers and urns and scoops. There was a special pot for chocolate, another for coffee and, of course, the creamer and sugar bowl. As its wares attest, the great age of English silver corresponds exactly with the time it took for tea to become an institutionalized part of the British way of life.

Even the not-too-serious student of the silver produced over this 170-year stretch begins to spot and appreciate changing styles. On the whole, the periods and styles of silver are the same as those of architecture and furniture, for silver design—like architecture or furniture or music for that matter—followed the great cultural trends and developments. One of the most interesting and rewarding things about silver is that these changing styles can be read like a history book of taste. They are easily datable thanks to a simple system of hallmarking silver objects.

Only rarely is anything known of the makers of these beautifully shaped and gleaming silver pieces except the articles themselves, mute records of their makers' skills, and the odd date or two—the year of an apprenticeship perhaps, or an obituary notice—but almost all English silversmiths can be identified by the hallmarks on their work. Each mark has a reason and results from a law passed on a given date. This makes it possible for a beginner with an average memory to date a piece at a glance—within certain broad limits, of course—even before he has mastered the stylistic changes. But to a practiced and Hemphillian eye, the hallmark will identify not only the maker and the year the piece was made, but also the place of making and the standard of silver used. The knife Chaucer refers to in his *Canterbury Tales* as a "Sheffield whittle" probably bore a hallmark on its silver hilt, for the system had already been in effect one hundred years when the poet died in 1400.

The earliest known "Silver Tea-Pott," as it's called in the inscription it bears, was presented to the Directors of "ye East India Cumpany" by Lord Berkeley, "A Member of that Honorable and Worthy Society and a True and Hearty Lover* of Them 1670." Although certainly cumbersome enough to hold tea for an entire board of directors, this vessel is of merely historic interest, being perfectly plain and practically identical with the earliest coffeepots. Silver teapots were not made in great numbers until the reign of Queen Anne (1702–14) and even then they were executed only to special order of the nobility and in small sizes, since the tea of those days was only a little less expensive than the silver. One of the advantages to being queen that Anne enjoyed most was that she could have as much tea as she liked and consequently her teapot was the biggest in the land and of the latest style. It was shaped like a pear, broadest at the bottom with a curved spout and the stem end hinged to create a domed lid. The first American-made teapots are of this type and it has never gone entirely out of style.

That this style was known as Queen Anne, however, is not to imply that Anne deserves any credit whatever for the accomplishments of her reign. Her mind, as the Duke of Marlborough complained, was "slow as a lowland river," while her husband was either "too stupid or too shrewd" to lend a hand. The Georgian style, to which the Queen Anne gradually gave way, had little to do with the Georges either.

Had Anne died some months sooner, she would have been followed by another queen, a lively octogenarian named Sophia, dowager electress of Hanover and the granddaughter of England's James I. As it fell out, however, by the time the news of Anne's death reached Hanover late one night, it was Sophia's son and heir whom the British minister was directed to awaken and salute as King of Great Britain. It is said George I merely grunted and rolled over. Torpid, stodgy, and colorless Germans, the Georges were to rule England in succession from 1714 until 1830. George III (king, 1760–1820) was the only one among them to take an interest in government, helping as he did to touch off the American Revolution. He then went harmlessly insane, returning to his senses only when periodic efforts were made to depose him. His son ruled for him

---

*This formal use of the word "lover" was not unusual. Throughout its history the John Company clung to the practice of ending all letters, even letters of stinging rebuke, with the phrase "Your loving friend."

as regent during the last nine of the old madman's sixty years on the throne and succeeded him as George IV, unquestionably the coarsest of England's monarchs despite his interest in fashion and applied arts. In 1830, George IV was followed by his dimwitted and boring brother William IV, whose reign was a mercifully short prelude to the accession of his niece, Queen Victoria, in 1837. Keeping these people's names and order of appearance in mind makes styles and periods of silver, architecture, furniture, and so forth somewhat easier to remember.

Many consider the Queen Anne period to include the reign of George I (1714–27), because the baroque tastes of her day persisted and Early Georgian pieces reflected them. Less plain and differently shaped silver only gradually came into vogue, but it did. Most generations like to have things in a different style from those of their fathers and grandfathers, and in silver these changes seem to appear at intervals of about twenty years. Perhaps this was mainly due to the long apprenticeships, for only after working ten or fifteen years for another could a silversmith become his own master and develop his own style. By the time George II came to the throne in 1727, few pieces of silver were uninfluenced by one or another new taste for decoration, and the ensuing Mid-Georgian period may be said to last through the first decade of George III's reign. What had been simple and symmetrical gradually became complicated and covered with shells and scrolls, foliage and flowers. Tea-table silver retained its simplicity longer than most, but by the 1740s it too fell under the spell of this rococo style.

Something of the grace of the Mid-Georgian tea-table ritual is caught in a painting of the Walpole family by the great William Hogarth (who had begun his artistic career as a silversmith's apprentice). He depicts Sir Robert Walpole, prime minister at the time, at tea with his wife and lay-about son Horace, later to be known as the century's foremost letter writer, gossip, and art patron and the inventor of the gothic or horror-story genre, among much else. The tea equippage receives detailed attention: the small mahogany tea table, a tray set with porcelain cups and saucers and silver teapot and sugar bowl. On the floor is a shagreen tea caddy enriched with silver mounts and inlay work in which to lock away the precious tea; its open lid reveals a vase-shaped silver tea cannister, mate to the one Lady Walpole is seen measuring dry leaves from. (Caddies almost always had compartments or held cannisters for both Green and Black Tea.) In the center of the picture a servant waits with a steaming kettle; behind him a low tripod supports the silver kettle stand and spirit lamp. Queen Anne's pear and the Early Georgian globular pot have given way to a more decorative, inverted pear shape, broad at the shoulders and narrowing toward the foot; the globular kettle is obviously a holdover from the preceding style, especially since it is not, like the pot, embellished and encrusted with ornament. (Matching tea services will not appear until the end of the century.)

The rococo movement produced no English equivalent to Continental practitioners like Watteau, Fragonard, Boucher, and Tiepolo and remained a rather "un-English" phenomenon. It was certainly a successful attempt at enlivening silver design, however, and covered a multitude of sins. Horace Walpole, for instance, was to carry rococo into the realm of complete fantasy, reviving what he imagined to be medieval or Gothic design. At the same time, tea's Oriental origins sparked other fantasies and brought in a fashion for *chinoiserie,* or Chinese-inspired motifs—pagodas, strange trees, coolie-inhabited landscapes, and exotic maidens surrounded by swirls of scrollwork. Even the chaste designs of Thomas Chippendale revealed this influence when they were published in 1755 under the title *The Gentleman and Cabinet Maker's Director.* By this time even the most ardent lovers of rococo had begun to crave greater simplicity in place of extravagant and disorderly decoration, and Chippendale's sense of proportion influenced silver design toward a return to the Grand Manner. The excavation of Pompeii began the same year his book appeared.

In retrospect, the rise of neoclassicism seems inevitable. Within living memory, taste in silver and the applied arts generally had moved from the severely simple to the grand baroque, and thence through the rococo and "the gaudy gout of the Chinese." For a decade or so at midcentury, all these styles coexisted, and then about the time George III came to the throne in 1760, people knew just what they wanted again. They wanted classicism. Although its triumph was not complete until around 1770, the Late Georgian or Neoclassic Revival may be said to have begun. It is also sometimes called the Adam style because it largely owed its existence to the Scottish architect Robert Adam and his brother James. They designed not only buildings, but also their furnishings—from ceilings and carpets and color schemes right down to the furniture and silver ware, always seeking to emulate "the most elegant ornaments of the most refined Grecian articles." In this identical spirit, Josiah Wedgwood founded his Etruria

Paul Revere after Copley

Pottery Works in 1760, and began producing earthenware of the most formal charm possible, for which he was soon named potter to Queen Charlotte. The effort in everything that was made was to follow classical shapes and lines and ornaments.

Candlesticks proved easy enough to produce in the shape of a classical column, but there simply was no classic precedent for the teapot, and this led to many experiments. The oval-bodied teapot, usually with a straight spout, dates from this period. American craftsmen stayed well behind the times in this as in all other styles and fashions of the mother country. Paul Revere, certainly our most acclaimed early silversmith, posed for John Singleton Copley to paint his portrait around 1770.* The piece of silver old Paul chose to be shown proudly holding is an Early Georgian globular teapot. Yet when imported neoclassicism finally did reach him in later life, Revere was as content as his contemporaries to imitate it. He was a political, not an artistic, revolutionary.

Then as now, the possession of silver was an expression of wealth. It both reassured the gentry and nobility of their privileged position and also affirmed the self-made man's arrival in society or success in business. All silversmiths prospered since they always had more work than they could handle and charged accordingly. The Paul Revere Copley shows us is already very successful at age thirty-five. Yet throughout this entire age when demand greatly exceeded the supply of fine pieces of silver, the craftsmen never sacrificed the quality of their wares. And for a long time after silver goods were no longer produced one at a time by a master's hand, this continued to be true.

Horace Walpole, writing his friend Mrs. Montague in 1760, tells of passing through Sheffield, "which is one of the foulest towns in England," and remarks, "One man there has discovered the art of plating copper with silver." What we call Sheffield plate was known to the Romans and others before them, but the secret of fusing a thin layer of silver to a copper core had been lost in the sad collapse of the classical world. A Sheffield cutler, one Thomas Boulsover, is credited with rediscovering this process by accident around 1742, but his trade secret was soon out and it was others who subsequently grew rich on it. A plate was developed that could be rolled, hammered, or stamped by machine into any shape desired without losing its coating of silver. And by

---

*This now famous painting was later given by the Revere family to the Boston Museum of Fine Arts where it hangs today and where some of Revere's finest silver may also be seen.

the late 1760s, the finest-quality Sheffield plate wares the world has ever seen were being produced by a Birmingham industrialist, the brilliantly gifted Matthew Boulton.

Boulton was an outstanding silversmith in his own right and a collaborator of the brothers Adam at the height of their fame. He became the first manufacturer to employ the steam engine, which his friend James Watt had just developed. Watt always claimed his invention would have been a failure without Boulton, who was also fast friends with the likes of Josiah Wedgwood and Dr. Benjamin Franklin. If one of Boulton's larger accomplishments was transforming the crafts of silver into the silver industry, he also set it an unsurpassed standard in quality. No Sheffield plate was required to bear either hallmarks or the heavy taxes imposed on solid plate. Suddenly it was no longer necessary to belong to the well-to-do classes to own silver.

The tea service was just as important in English cottages as it was in English mansions, but it was the houses (and classes) in between that welcomed the flood of mass-produced silver tea things. Matched sets had come into fashion—and have never gone out since—by 1800, about the time neoclassicism seemed to be gasping and dying. Walpole had long before castigated Adam designs as "snippets of embroidery," too neat and pretty, and the truth is after thirty years or so the style had simply bored itself to death. So many different teapots and sets to match were made from this point on that no one type or style has ever predominated since. Between 1800 and 1830, silversmiths and potters ran through a whole gamut of styles—Greek, Roman, Egyptian, Turkish—spiced with *chinoiserie* here and romanticism there and liberally mixed with imitation rococo. This mishmash period has been named Regency, though in fact it overlapped the whole last half of George IV's life, and the Victorian era that followed makes it look good. Victorian design reflects a perfect horror of undecorated space.

My friend and mentor Mr. Hemphill is fond of saying that the nineteenth century, with its limitless energy, its often marked absence of good taste, its appreciation of fine craftsmanship and its inability to apply that same fine craftsmanship to the creation of everyday things, did foster one new genus—the collector of antique silver. Granny's old teapot is more than likely electroplate, but it's descended from a noble line and the family resemblance is there if you can see it.

TEA TYPES

What Do You Call This?

A SHORT SURVEY OF THE WORLD OF TEA

Hyson, Congou, Bohea, and a few lesser divinities. . . .
            —Ezra Pound
                    CANTO LXX

The naming of teas is a difficult matter,
It isn't just one of your everyday games—
Some might think you as mad as a hatter
Should you tell them each one goes by several names.
For starters each tea in this world must belong
To the families Black or Green or Oolong;
Then look more closely at these family trees—
Some include Indians along with Chinese . . .

ND SO FORTH, with apologies to T. S. Eliot's *The Naming of Cats*. The subject of tea names and types, I have decided, is best broken down as follows: Trade Name Teas; Black Teas—& Oolong; Green Teas; China Teas; Scented, Flavored, & Decaffeinated Teas; and Barks, Tonics, Decoctions, Infusions, & Tisanes. And this is how I have arranged the present chapter. Because it is a rather serious chapter, moreover, you should read no more of it than you need to know.

TRADE NAME TEAS

We [English] are surely the least quarrelsome of all the nations of the earth, and in this the tea-table has undoubtedly played its part. We should, therefore, regard as public benefactors those who have made it possible for us to refine our passions, steady our nerves, and promote whatever degree of civilization we may be supposed to have reached by the aid of "a nice cup of tea."

—the late Stephen H. Twining

ENGLISH BREAKFAST With the naming of teas—as with so much else in this life—it seems best to begin with breakfast. Over a hundred years ago in Scotland a man named Drysdale went into the specialty tea business within sight of the castle of Edinburgh and offered a tea called Breakfast. The firm is still there and still so Scottish they sell refills for their tins. And they still sell the only tea on the market called simply Breakfast and nothing more, probably reasoning that Scots have little need of English or Irish breakfasts, after all, and at that time of day want to be told nothing more than which blend of teas makes a good eye-opener.

Almost every tea dealer in existence offers a tea designed to accomplish just this and almost every one of these is called English Breakfast, a designation brimming with quite as much meaning as California Burgundy. One authority has seriously suggested that the classic English Breakfast is a particular China Black Tea, Keemun, because its fragrance is brought out by the addition of milk and this bouquet reminds people of "toast hot from the oven." If Keemun is indeed the classic, one wonders why Britain's biggest specialty tea firms market blends of Indian and Ceylon teas as English Breakfast: Look at the labels on Jacksons of Piccadilly, Melroses, Ridgways, and Twinings. Ridgways also markets an Imperial Breakfast Blend, presumably to the Englishman for whom it is not enough just to wake up each morning a raving nationalist.

These and all the other teas I'll be mentioning in this chapter are procurable in the United States and Canada. On this side of the water, the American firm of John Wagner & Sons sells a light-bodied Formosa Black Tea under the name English Breakfast, while Mark T. Wendell's is made from Indias and Ceylons again. Your tea dealer is almost certain to have an English Breakfast blend of his own—as long as it's Black it can be any tea in the world he likes in the morning. Nobody seems to know how long this meaningless name has been in use.

OTHER BREAKFASTS Occasionally you see other Breakfast Teas like John Wagner & Sons Ceylon Breakfast, which speaks for itself, or Twinings Irish Breakfast, which is a strong, thick Assam. The Irish Tea M.F.K. Fisher remembers with such respect definitely deserved its reputation for quality, according to W. H. Ukers. "The Irish Free State," he wrote, "particularly the South and West, always secures the choicest teas." There must have been a distinct preference for Assam in Ireland at one time, but not even McGraths, the only Irish company whose teas are available in this country, seems to know why. Their Irish Breakfast is mostly Assam all the same, but their best seller is McGraths Original Irish Blend, which they describe as "a blend of fine Indian, African, and Indonesian teas." It sounds more Original than Irish, perhaps, but it tastes very good. Wagners Irish Tea is an Assam and so mostly are the Irish Blends offered by most tea merchants. Anyhow, there is certainly nothing imaginary about different tea-drinking countries having distinctly different tastes. It would make perfect sense to have Dutch Breakfast Teas, for instance, and it would be more interesting if we did. We don't only because Holland's tea has long come largely from Java and Sumatra, formerly the Dutch East Indies, and for obvious historical reasons English-speaking peoples never got much of it. On the other hand, "historical reasons" have not prevented our enjoying Russian Tea, so-called.

RUSSIAN-STYLE TEAS Our Russian Tea, to be sure, belongs to our fantasy Russia, all onion domes and samovars with tea to match the caviar packed across Siberia on camel caravans. This fantasy creates such wonderful watering holes as The Russian Tea Room in New York City and, regrettably, also maintains such monuments to pretension as Alexis on San Francisco's Nob Hill, a place dark as the moods of Ivan the Terrible with food you wouldn't serve serfs. In point of fact, very few Russians know what tea tastes like out of a samovar these days, and no one at all remembers the he-man scent of hot camel that old Russian Tea quite often had: The last camel caravan carrying tea for Russia left Peking in 1900.

Our fantasy, quite rightly, pays fact no mind and we go right on asking for Russian Caravan Tea. You may find Wagners or Twinings on the shelf, or you may order one from Mark T. Wendell or nearly any tea merchant. The name is all they have in common, not surprisingly: Twinings is a blend of China and Formosa Oolong teas, Wendell and Wagner use Blacks of unspecified origins, and so it goes. Some tea men swear the best formula is Keemun, with a fraction as much Lapsang Souchong. A striking aroma seems to be the one thing all Russian Caravans set out for, which is more than I can say for genuinely Russian tea. (See Russian tea, page 145.)

O'CLOCK TEAS Before we leave generically named teas like the Breakfasts, I may as well point out a number of blends that are designed for other hours of the day. There's only one French tea I know of available in this country. It is an excellent and indescribable blend packed at Enghien-les-Bains, France, and sold as Indar Boudoir Tea. Jacksons sells its Afternoon Tea and Evening Tea in Victorian caddies. Five O'Clock is the blend Ridgways obviously thinks every Briton should be drinking at that hour. It turns out to be a surprisingly delicate Ceylon. This veddy Brit thing of naming teas by the clock reaches its utterly logical conclusion with The Tea Planters & Importers Company, London, which has never sold but six teas, each distinct and specially blended: Morning Tea, Lunchtime Tea, Afternoon Tea, After-Dinner Tea, Evening Tea, and Drawing Room Tea.

EARL GREY sounds like a stock-car driver from Appalachia, but of course he was not. His given name was Charles, actually, and he was the second Grey to bear the title of earl, which is a rank in the English peerage above that of viscount and below that of marquess—in other words (in any other language) a count. Charles Earl Grey was a humane and energetic fellow in his day (1764–1845), the scion of a wealthy Whig family and something of a political reformer who bested the arch-Tory Duke of Wellington to become prime minister for a time under William IV (king, 1830–37). According to one story, the earl was already drinking the tea that's named after him by the time he became prime minister, having been given the recipe by a mandarin while doing a stint as a diplomat in China. Others claim he got it from a returning envoy after he was already in office. Either way it might appear the Chinese were trying to tell the earl something, for they themselves are not now and have never been Earl Grey Tea drinkers. But this is only the first part of the mystery.

There is a not unrelated puzzle, the discussion of which degenerated into open antagonism and contention among tea men generations ago. It is, which firm has rightful claim to the original Earl Grey formula? The serious contenders are Twinings and Jacksons of Piccadilly, which produce noticeably different Earl Greys. The present generation continues to disagree and their opposing views of the matter are on record. The Honorable Georgina Stonor, whose family bought Jacksons in 1931 from the descendants of the founder, has written: "This [secret recipe] was entrusted by Lord Grey to George Charlton in 1830—who was a partner of Robert Jackson and Company. . . . Jacksons remain sole proprietors of this original formula which remains unaltered today. There are many imitations but none match Jacksons original blend." Samuel H. G. Twining, O.B.E., has replied in his turn by emblazoning his Earl Grey packages with a message from the present Earl Grey. The earl's message reads: "Legend has it that my ancestor, the second Earl Grey, was presented with this exquisite recipe by an envoy on

his return from China. Generations of my family have enjoyed Earl Grey tea and, today, I am proud to continue this tradition with the tea celebrated throughout the world known as Twining's Earl Grey Tea."

On rereading, the earl sounds like a press secretary for Richard Nixon to me, but Twinings conclusively kills its case by disclosing *its* original formula calls for "long leaf China and Darjeeling teas." Even the most inscrutable of mandarins on his best day could not have blended a tea with Darjeeling before any was planted, which was only eleven years after the good earl had died. One is also at a loss to know what the Grace Tea Company of New York means with its sales material that describes its Original Earl Grey Mixture as ". . . not a corrupt version, but the original of this fine blend."

To me, however, the real mystery about Earl Grey is why everybody seems to like it. Not that I actively dislike the stuff, mind you—it has its place and gives its pleasure too—but I find it exactly analogous to Lancer's Crackling Rosé wine from Portugal: Nice enough now and then but how'd it get to be the best-selling imported wine in America? That's the same status Earl Grey enjoys among specialty teas. As long ago as 1937, Jacksons announced it was selling a ton of its Earl Grey blend a week. Worldwide, Twinings Earl Grey is the best selling of the company's nineteen different blends and shares, they say, first place with its English Breakfast in the United States. And like English Breakfast, it's one of those teas your own and every other dealer is sure to have some version of on hand.

Regardless of the source or sort of tea used, what makes Earl Grey taste the way it does is the oil of bergamot with which it is scented, even though a few rascally tradesmen even try substitutes for this, the one agreed-upon essential ingredient. Earl Grey was the first Scented Tea known in the West. Bergamot, no matter what you're thinking, does not come from the Italian town of Bergamo. The name is actually derived from the Turkish for "prince's pear" and designates a pear-shaped citrus (*Citrus bergamia*) that is grown around the Mediterranean for the oil that can be pressed out of its rind for use in perfumery and, of course, Earl Grey. This oil is very powerful. Too much of it will produce a tea with the reek of cheap perfumed soap and the ability to anaesthetize the roof of your mouth and the back of your throat. Just the right amount, however, gives you a well-mannered, mild-flavored tea with a very distinctive, yet delicate scent. Everybody produces an Earl Grey, as I've said, and everybody has his own idea as to what constitutes just the right amount of scent, so suit yourself.

HU-KWA TEA keeps alive the memory of a Chinese peasant born in 1769—the same year as Napoleon and Wellington—who became the greatest merchant prince in the world of his day and a household name in America for half a century. The Astors, Perkins, Peabodys, and Girards grew rich importing silks and porcelains and teas bearing Hu-kwa's label (which they spelled Houqua those days). From the 1820s on, Hu-kwa controlled all the business transacted at Canton between the Celestial Empire and the foreign devils with their cursed opium to trade. He was already rich and weary, but the imperial administration would not allow him to retire from his position and Hu-kwa, thanks to his magic gift for winning cooperation and good will, made genuine friends of the foreign devils. He did business with them on a handshake (he signed only one slip of paper in his life, it's said) and managed the difficult feat of keeping his foreign-devil friends within the legal limits of the emperor's edicts, for the emperor held him personally responsible for all their social activities as well as business dealings in China. Apparently the most troublesome rule was the one forbidding female foreign devils in Canton, but recalcitrant visitors could always eventually be brought to obey it because, as one of them wrote, "It is unfortunately the case here that there is no man to be relied upon but Houqua and he has too much business."

To the hungry market abroad, the stamp of Hu-kwa's name became a sure mark of the excellent and genuine. Hu-kwa meanwhile, with melancholy resignation, lived to behold the ruin he had foreseen for his homeland and himself as a result of the opium trade that he could not control and was helpless to prevent. The inevitable Opium War had barely concluded when America launched her first commercial clipper ship in 1843. It was called the *Houqua* and a model of it was sent to the venerable merchant in Canton as a gift. Hu-kwa died before it reached him.

From that day to this, one company or another has continued to offer a Houqua Tea of some sort. For example, the man who bought up the entirety of the first shipments of Assam tea to London, a certain Captain Pidding, was also the proprietor of a Howqua Mixture. The only one of which I'm presently aware is offered by the old Boston firm Mark T. Wendell and is called Hu-kwa Tea. I understand it's the same one they've carried since 1904, and that it currently makes up around half of all their mail-order business. Taste it and you'll understand why—that is, if you like Lapsang Souchong, a type of smoked tea which I'll discuss when we come to it as, in due course, we shall.

CHIN CHU ORIENTAL BLEND was created in the 1950s by the late Bert Hauser, the founder of Servit Foods, to provide an alternative on the supermarket shelves for consumers looking for a change from run-of-the-mill tea blends. Packed only in tea bags, this blend contains closely guarded proportions of fine Black Teas and really top-quality Keemun, Oolong, and Pouchong teas, yet it sells for little more than regular tea bags. It is handsomely packaged in Chinese red and black and gold foil and seems to be gaining wider distribution around the country each year. Some markets put it in their Oriental foods sections.

LADY LONDONDERRY TEA is an interesting blend of Ceylon, India, and Formosa teas that Lady Londonderry was especially fond of and that she had Jacksons of Piccadilly prepare for her. The old-timey custom old established tea dealers still follow today is to keep a file of their regular customers' personal blends—exactly which teas and what proportions. In milady's day, anybody could go to the merchant and ask for her blend and the merchant would happily make some up and sell it to him, but the recipe itself he would—and does still—keep in strictest confidence. Tea merchants have always named such blends after the customer to whose specifications they were concocted, naturally, and some few of these have been widely popularized when the customer in question happened to have as many friends or envious enemies as Earl Grey or her ladyship. Doctor Milton's, for instance, was another Jacksons tea, now discontinued. Not only individuals, but also clubs and hotels wanted their own private blends—my own dealer makes an excellent Colonial Dames Tea, to cite a contemporary example. Then, too, there were blends the merchant aimed at specific markets, like the Dowager Tea Fortnum & Mason still sells—no kidding. There used to be such a thing as Nursery Tea, and the fact that Invalid Tea is also nowhere to be found says something, for it was ubiquitous in the Victorian era. (Ty-phoo originated as an Invalid Tea.)

Getting back to Lady Londonderry, Mr. Eustace Crawley, Jacksons managing director, writes: "The Marquis and Marchioness of Londonderry were huge landowners of enormous wealth who kept a great house in London and for many years in the first quarter of this century were London's most famous social and political hosts. . . . We were fortunate enough to get her permission to use her name, and this we still do." Her taste in tea was quite good, by the way.

J. P. MORGAN TEA was the favorite blend of another lover of fine tea, the financier Pierpont Morgan. It consists of I know not what and is still sold today by the firm that always blended it for Mr. Morgan, Simpson & Vail, late of New York City. Although downtown rents have driven the company to Westchester, they swear their J. P. Morgan Tea has remained unchanged since 1929, and add that there are former associates of the great banker still extant who can prove it.

There's a great story about Mr. Morgan and his tea I read somewhere in Ukers and have heard tea men repeat gleefully in different versions. There was a tea company near Morgan's offices and every day he would pass the windows behind which the tea tasters could be seen at their work—"sipping, spitting and looking wise" as someone has put it. Morgan prized fine tea and prided himself on his connoisseurship, wherefore one day he ventured inside the tasting room for a professional appraisal of his favorite blend. He left visibly agitated and shouting, "You can't possibly understand tea—I don't know what's kept you in the business!" The magisterial oldest tea taster just shook his head in reply and maintained his look of mild authority until Morgan disappeared, then broke out laughing. "I may be the only man alive who's ever tricked him! That tea was the best money can buy and I told him it was the worst I'd ever tasted! He's going to wonder about that tea for years!" I'm looking forward to trying some.

PROPRIETARY TEAS There are two Connoisseur blends, which are just that—Drysdales and that of Grace Rare Tea. They are markedly dissimilar but both are harmonious master blends of superb teas, no doubt of many origins. In a class with them is Boston Harbour Tea from Davison, Newman & Co., Ltd., London. It is sold in the United States through Melroses and importers like Mark T. Wendell and perhaps others. Davison, Newman is considered the oldest tea dealer in England, having been founded eight years before tea was even introduced. It seems some of the tea tipped into Boston Harbor was theirs and they petitioned George III for compensation. This petition is reproduced on the one-half and one-pound tins, which also carry the notation "Bawstonaba Registered." The tea is a blend of exceptional Indias and Ceylons.

You will occasionally find other proprietary names for companies' unique or favorite teas. The Schapira Flavor Cup Tea is advertised as "served by our family for over 60 years." The Fortnum & Mason Fortmason is a China-India blend specially scented and sui generis. First Colony has an exciting blend of Black and Green Tea called London 77, though the idea is perhaps better than the tea itself. Sarum Teas, a small but top quality mail-order business, sells Countess of Salisbury, a unique creation of the late founder, Mr. Stanley H. Mason. As a boy Mr. Mason was apprenticed to the trade in 1913, in London. When he eventually settled in Salisbury, Connecticut, and set up a tea business of his own he named it Sarum, the Latin name for ancient Salisbury in England. His Countess of Salisbury is a Formosa Oolong Jasmine of elusive delicacy.

ROYALTIES Of all the proprietary brand names, far the most common and best known are those associated with the British monarchy. The British have a proven love for imprinting the dear though regrettably horsey features of members of their royal family on anything at any excuse and tea caddies head their list: The Prince of Wales peers pleasantly at me from my cannister of Drysdales Connoisseur Blend even as I write. Besides seeing royal faces on their tea tins, the British also like their teas to have names connecting them, however remotely, to the institution of the monarchy. This practice dates to the halcyon days of Victoria, who countenanced the use of her name and face in any connection with the national campaign to "buy Empire." The London *Evening News & Post* of Thursday, 6 July 1893—the wedding day of the duke of York (later George V) and Princess Mary of Teck—carried a full page ad picturing the aged queen handing the bride and bridegroom her wedding present—a packet of Mazawattee Ceylon Tea!

Hornimans ads of the same period depict the Prince of Wales (later Edward VII) in full dress uniform and decorations clasping (in an extremely peculiar-looking grip) a steaming cup of tea with "Hornimans" written boldly on the cup and a caption below that reads "A Right Royal Drink—Hornimans Pure Tea." Examples could be multiplied *ad infinitum,* and at least one reason the British still like to buy teas associated with royal personages is that they cannot forego a nostalgia for those days. It

is as the great novelist Ford Madox Ford wrote in 1935: "In my day we had King, Lords, Commons, the Book of Common Prayer, the London County Council, the Metropolitan Police, the Home Secretary—and Christ Jesus Who had died to make us and our vast Empire what we were."

In our own day we find Ridgways still selling Her Majesty's Blend (HMB), which they originally made for Victoria, while Melroses best Darjeeling goes by the name of Queen's Tea. Fortnum & Mason go all the way back to Queen Anne, their founders' patroness, for the name of their best Ceylon-Assam blend, probably a better tea than they ever supplied the old queen herself. F&M's Crown Tea is also very fine—a mixture of Darjeeling and China Keemun. Twinings markets a pure Keemun as Prince of Wales Tea, which was probably named for Edward VII before he became king. Twinings Queen Mary Tea is a special blend of Darjeeling that was supplied the wife of George V, apparently. Jacksons created a tolerable Coronation Tea blend of Ceylon and India teas in 1953 to commemorate the coronation of Elizabeth II. Curious as to exactly what the rules are for the use of the royal family's names on commercial products, I wrote Mr. Eustace Crawley of Jacksons:

> The rules are now very much stricter than they were at one time. If for instance we wanted to call a tea Princess of Wales blend, we would have to ask her permission through her private secretary. I am told that nowadays this would not be granted. . . . The Royal Family are very careful indeed not to link their names to commercial products and even if they asked for a particular blend, it is almost completely certain that they would not allow their name to be linked to it except through the Royal Warrant. If a trader regularly supplies the Royal Household with a product, e.g., Jacksons English Breakfast for a minimum of 3 years, the company can apply for the grant of a Royal Warrant. But if they cease to supply the Warrant after a period of a year or two may be withdrawn. . . .
>
> There is a story about King George V's butler which might amuse you. He had a number of teas in his pantry on a tray which got knocked off the table, and the teas were spilt on the floor. Being a lazy man, he swept them up and put them in a single box, and shortly afterwards made tea for the King. He said that it was the best tea he ever drank, and told the butler that he never wanted any other. He went off to a tea blender, and asked them to make up a matching blend and that company still supply

the Royal Household to this day. But they do not use the name of the butler or the King as a brand name!!

I have not yet tracked down this mystery royal tea. Other British examples abound, yet America's only one as far as I know is the First Colony Queen's Blend, which was originated by the company's Scottish immigrant founder in the 1870s and named, inevitably, in Victoria's honor.

BLACK TEAS—& OOLONG

This admirable drink reconciles men to sobriety.
—John Ovington, an eighteenth-century English parson

ASSAM is a district in northeastern India that lies along the Indian-Burmese border. It produces more Black Tea than any other area on earth, with the probable exception of a few in China, and is proof that not all high-quality tea has to be grown high in the mountains (Keemun and Formosa Oolong are also low grown). Assam's tea gardens cover some four hundred six thousand acres of the rolling plains on both sides of the mighty Brahmaputra River, and those who have seen it from the air say one gets the impression of a gigantic billiard table stretching as far as the eye can see. This rainy valley is the birthplace of Indian tea: Robert Bruce discovered the plant growing wild here in 1823, and the first commercial lot of tea ever produced outside China—eight chests in all—came from here in 1839.

The dormant bushes come to life and put out the first leaves of the new season in March; the plucking of this first flush goes on for eight to ten weeks. The second flush plucking begins in June. Thanks to heavy seasonal rains from August through October, the area's vegetation grows at a tremendous rate and about 75 percent of Assam tea is produced during this period, but the flavor is less concentrated. As the climate gradually turns dry and colder, the last or autumnal flush, said to be very like the second flush in character, is harvested; by December dormancy sets in once more.

I know not why but Assam, unlike Darjeeling, is almost never retailed as a first or second flush tea, leading one to assume that the Assam we generally buy is blended from both the poorer and the better harvests. Some Assam teas are indisputably better than others, nevertheless, and occasionally you run across a great one. Los Angeles's fifteen-store chain, The Coffee Bean & Tea Leaf, actually stocks first flush Assam, for instance, while the Pannikin stores in the San Diego area and Starbucks of Seattle wholesale and retail Fancy Golden Tip Assam as one of their most expensive and exotic teas. Drysdales is noticeably tippy and also excellent; likewise the Fortnum & Mason Assam Superb.

For the first time Indian tea is now being attractively packaged for the North American market by Indian companies. For fine Assams keep an especial eye out for Duncans, Maya, and Makhams Sindbad brands: all of them are wonderful. Assam is a traditional component of Irish Breakfast blends, as I've noted elsewhere, and it's extremely useful for adding weight to any other blend, as the mid- and high-grown Ceylons are for adding flavor. If you like it strong, Assam makes just your cup of tea. It is pungent, malty tasting, and full-bodied and looks unusually dark. If you add a few teaspoons of milk you'll notice it takes on a bright red-brown color, in contrast to the bright golden Ceylons turn. Milk gives Darjeelings a grayish cast.

CEYLON TEA is so-called because, as Mr. Reg Dennis of the Ceylon Tea Centre explained in a letter, "Although the Island reverted to its original [Sinhalese] name of Sri Lanka in 1972, it was decided to retain 'Ceylon' to describe its most famous product in order to avoid confusing consumers to whom the new name was unfamiliar and to save the cost of redesigning brand labels and advertising the change. There is also the point that in the major importing countries [Iraq, the United Kingdom, and the United States, in that order as of 1980] 'Ceylon' has the more euphonious sound."

Ceylon—or Sri Lanka—is a beautiful tropical island about the size of England that lies just twenty-two miles off the southern tip of India and supplies about one-quarter of all the tea the world imports today. Her nearly six hundred thousand acres of tea also provide well over half the island nation's overseas earnings. Ceylon grew no tea whatever until 1867, when one James Taylor, the Scottish manager of Loolecondera Estate, first planted some—and that just in time. In 1869, a fungus disease descended on the island's coffee estates and in a few disastrous years what had been Ceylon's leading industry was ruined. Those who could afford it turned to growing tea and after Sir Thomas Lipton became their most famous colleague and leading customer in the 1890s, the success of Ceylon tea was assured.

Ceylon tea is grown from sea level to altitudes exceeding seven thousand feet. It produces its greatest yield in the steaming wet plains and foothills, where the flush can be harvested every seven or eight days and is picked all year round. This low-grown leaf is generally bought to be used as filler in mass-market blends, being sound quality but neutral and without distinctive flavor. "Mid-country" teas are grown between two thousand and four thousand feet and these are often very good, but Ceylon's reputation for quality rests with the 40 percent of her tea estates that lie at altitudes of four thousand feet and over. Here the bushes grow more slowly and yield far less, not to mention being harder to harvest—most high-grown Ceylons come from gardens so steep the newly picked green leaves must be conveyed to the estate factory by means of aerial ropeways. While an experienced lowland plucker may gather up to sixty pounds of fresh leaf in a day, her upland sister is lucky to average half that.

The quality of high-grown Ceylon tea varies with the weather. The districts of Uva and Maturata on the eastern slopes of the island's central mountains (that is, facing Malaysia) produce their best in August and September, their dry months. During those months the districts of Dimbula and Nuwara Eliya situated on the western slopes of these mountains facing Africa are drenched by the southwest monsoon. These districts do their best during January and February when they are dry and the opposite side of the hill is getting rain from the northeast monsoon. When and wherever it's raining, the tea grows like crazy but loses its distinctive quality. At their best, these high-grown Ceylons have incomparable fragrance, fine flavor, and a rich golden color in the cup. The dry leaf has an attractive black color—usually blacker than Assam—often with a bluish tinge. Uva teas are grown between four thousand and six thousand feet and have a distinct and particularly mellow flavor: Twinings Ceylon Breakfast is a fair example. The Nuwara Eliyas are grown above six thousand feet and show a rather lighter color and more concentrated flavor.

The Ceylon tea industry is eager to assist you in drawing comparisons like these. You can get a package of Five Fine Ceylon Teas (a quarter pound of each) by writing the Ceylon Tea Promotion Bureau, P.O. Box 295, Colombo, Sri Lanka. They'll bill you.

Closer to home, the Pannikin shops and others carry excellent Dimbula and Uva. The very best Ceylon tea I can remember is the Mark T. Wendell Cheericup Ceylon. The company's president won't say where exactly it comes from, but does aver that it's the product of a single estate. For this reason the tea's character varies somewhat from year to year (MTW does no blending), but its excellence does not. Most Ceylons are blends of many gardens and several districts and pluckings. The brands vary in quality, but all aim at consistency.

In promoting his Ceylon tea almost a century ago, Sir Thomas Lipton popularized the technical term Orange Pekoe to the point that many people today still believe it's a special kind of tea plant instead of just the name for a size of leaf. Ceylon Orange Pekoe (OP) is a leaf grade denoting long, thin wiry leaves that sometimes contain tip, small golden particles that are the remains of tiny, just-opening shoots. Tip shows the tea has been carefully manufactured but it doesn't necessarily follow that the raw leaf was any better than it ought to be. Generally speaking, in fact, the most sought-after grade of Ceylon tea and the one that fetches the highest prices is not the leaf grade OP, but a broken grade, Broken Orange Pekoe (BOP). BOP is by definition a much smaller size and has correspondingly more uses in blends.

This matter of grades seems worth touching on in connection with Ceylon tea, because while Assam and all other Black Teas are also divided into the various leaf and broken grades, they are seldom advertised as such to the retail customer. Yet thanks to the market demand old Sir Tea did so much to create, Ridgways, Melroses, and First Colony market a Ceylon Orange Pekoe to this day and the Orange Pekoe Teas Twinings and Wagners and everybody else offers are also invariably Ceylons. The grade name Orange Pekoe is no particular recommendation of quality. Roughly the same grade names are used for all Black Teas from the finest to the poorest—cup quality is all that counts.

DARJEELING is a small resort town, as towns in India go, situated in northwest Bengal 400 miles due north of Calcutta in the little neck of Indian territory that separates Nepal and Bhutan. Its location at some sixty-five hundred feet above sea level provides a temperate if rainy climate and breathtaking views that allow the eye to travel from the scorching and insalubrious plains below upward over a succession of ranges that culminate in the Himalaya's mighty Kanchenjunga, almost as high as Everest. Because of this location, Darjeeling was the hot-weather headquarters of the Bengal government under the British raj and a vacation spot where, if we are to believe Kipling et al, officers' bored wives and daughters carried on Victorian affairs with subalterns only slightly less boring. To the world's Buddhists it is famous today as the place of exile of His Holiness the XIV Dalai Lama of Tibet. Only to the Western world is the name Darjeeling synonymous with superior tea. This is because the district's mere forty-two thousand acres under tea cultivation account for no more than 3 percent of all the tea India produces, yet its reputation for quality is so high India can't afford not to sell almost the entire crop abroad. Indeed, I've seen it said in print that four times as much Darjeeling as the district could possibly produce is marketed each year.

As in Assam, the Darjeeling tea bushes begin waking up from winter dormancy following the first light spring rains in March and the first flush is picked from then until the end of April. As in Ceylon, the higher it's grown the better it is in most cases. Darjeeling estates range from less than four thousand to almost ten thousand feet in elevation. The truly high-grown first flush tea has been known to go for as much as forty dollars the pound at auction (two to four weeks after manufacture, grading, and packing), but that's in exceptional years. Even at the typical price of around twenty-seven dollars the pound, it is easily the world's most expensive tea. It makes a noticeably puckery but light and lovely cup with an incredibly flowery bouquet, and it's all but unobtainable for most of us. Wealthy Indian connoisseurs compete for it with the tea dealers themselves, who like to buy it for presents to special customers and friends. Then there are certain European (including Russian) interests willing to pay whatever it costs for commercial quantities. It is so highly prized in Germany that the first consignment is flown directly from the Calcutta auction and parachuted into the country, a gesture that rather dwarfs the annual French enthusiasm for the Beaujolais nouveau. By way of contrast, it ordinarily takes at least eight weeks or more travel time for a Calcutta-bought tea to reach the United States.

The second flush is gathered during May and June, after which time the monsoon rains set in and last through September. As in Assam and Ceylon, rainy-season leaf is quick growing, abundant, and of little or no distinction. Since Darjeeling's rainfall is not evenly distributed, however, a few gardens do manage to produce outstanding tea during this period. October yields another superior flush, the autumnal, and the plants go back into hibernation for the dry, chilly winter.

Even from this short account it's easy to deduce that cheap and expensive Darjeeling are simply two different teas; nevertheless, it may be said to put an unmistakable stamp on any blend in which it's used and only the worst could be employed as neutral filler. A broker and importer friend of mine, Mr. Mike Spillane, likes to say, "The harder it is to explain what it tastes like, the better your Darjeeling is." Certainly you can't judge it by appearance. Fortnum & Mason used to market a handsome, large leaf Flowery Orange Pekoe (FOP)—flowery meaning it has tip, not flowers—but I've known coarse, unsightly Darjeeling to give me a cup just as beautifully flavored. "Goodness is a decision for the mouth to make," Lu Yu would remind us. Certainly many tea men prefer the second and autumnal flushes to the first. They boast significantly less bouquet and the cup is darker, with more weight and heavier character. The flavors, haltingly described as black-curranty sometimes or as resembling muscats, seem to be more concentrated and stand out. Tea professionals also claim the second and autumnal flushes "hold their value" twice as long as the first, giving them quite a bit more shelf life. These vintages, if one may so call them, have the added advantage of being available— sorta. I've heard it authoritatively estimated that there are never more than fifty chests of second flush Darjeeling in the United States in any given week.

I must confess to a little diluting and stretching of Darjeeling myself. Many connoisseurs swear by the Grace Superb Darjeeling 6000, a second flush from estates over six thousand feet. I find it so very astringent I blend it half and half with another like Wagners, which can use the boost. Having already mentioned FOP Darjeeling, I should go on to warn you that Darjeeling tea estates are prone to eloquence in grading their teas. Besides customary abbreviations like OP and BOP, you may encounter TGFOP (Tippy Golden Flowery Orange Pekoe) or even FTGFOP (Fancy Tippy Golden etc.). All this will assure you that the leaf is well made and looks good but not that the tea tastes any better. On the other hand, should your dealer invoke the name of Balasun, Mim, Thurbo, or Margaret's Hope—Darjeeling's most famous estates—ask no questions and buy the tea. Remember too, however, that quality will vary: Adverse weather conditions in 1981 rendered the entire first flush a disaster, for example.

As you will have gathered, the best Darjeeling takes some tracking down. One sure way of getting some is to write R. N. Agarwala & Son, Nehru Road, Darjeeling, India, and ask for their price list and air mail costs. (Even if you don't like Darjeeling, their half-kilo packet makes a never-to-be forgotten gift to those who do.) Los Angelenos can find first flush Darjeeling in The Coffee Bean & Tea Leaf shops, while tea merchants like mine in San Francisco, Freed Teller & Freed, or Milwaukee's Northwestern Coffee Mills sell first-rate second flush and there must be others. Along with Indian brands like Duncans, Chai, and Maya, Drysdales and Twinings FOP Vintage Darjeeling are the best I can think of available in tins off the shelf, but none of them are easy to find. This leaves you in the hands of the prestige mail-order tea dealers: Grace, O. H. Clapp, Mark T. Wendell, and friends. Good hunting.

FORMOSA OOLONG is rightly considered "the champagne of teas." It's called Formosa instead of Taiwan for the same reason Ceylon isn't called Sri Lankan, and the Latin name the Portuguese gave the island aptly applies to this tea, for Formosa translates "beautifully shaped, beautiful." It is not a Black Tea, like Assam, Ceylon or Darjeeling, but I put it here because it's not a Green Tea either. Tea leaves, like any others, wither once they're taken off the bush. If you "kill" the fresh leaf with heat before it has a chance to wither, you've got Green Tea. If you wait until it's just about to wither you've got Pouchong, which looks brownish and tastes interestingly nutty. If you make sure the leaf is well withered and goes through the attendant chemical changes you'll have Black Tea, which is 3 percent caffeine by weight as opposed to Green Tea's one. Should you let the leaf wither and ferment a little you come up with 2 percent caffeine and something altogether different: Oolong.

The mainland port of Amoy lies directly across the straits from Taiwan and merchants from there are credited with planting Taiwan's first tea around 1810. One wonders what took them so long. There was a population on the island from Fukien, the province where Amoy is situated and where Chinese Oolong had originated (*wu* = black, *lung* = dragon). Naturally they preferred tea made like the tea back home. No one seems sure when Formosa Oolong was first made or whether it satisfied the Fukienese, but it is certain that an Englishman named John Dodd was the first to export any, shipping a quarter million pounds to New York in 1869. It went over well: Within ten years the island was exporting ten million pounds annually. About this time the British tea planters in India began to feel the competition and sent a delegation to Taiwan to bring back the secret. They brought back the discouraging word that Formosa Oolong could not be duplicated. Same plant and no more nor less care in manufacture than in China, so it must be growing conditions, they said, and no one can duplicate those. I wish I knew more about how Formosa Oolong gets that way myself, but scholarship is not everything after all—it's the *je ne sais quoi* that counts.

Formosa Oolong may be the last tea grown in commercial quantities in the old Chinese way, by families on family farms, and although there are 120-odd tea factories on Taiwan, a number of these families still make the tea themselves. The farms with the best reputation are the ones with the most worthless soil, a yellow clay derived from decomposed rock that comprises the "teela" or broken land tailing off from over two hundred feet to sea level. The poorer the vine, the better the wine as vintners would say. The Oolong is not sold or identified by district or estate names, but according to the grade assigned it by the government Tea Inspection Office, and this is one case where the grade name actually denotes the quality of the tea. There are eight such grades altogether and of these the ones to remember are Fancy and Fanciest, though Extra Choice will do in a pinch.

Any Fancy Formosa Oolong is invariably a crisp open Souchong leaf, mostly reddish brown in color with a little greenish brown and a little brownish black intermixed—Oolong's a Black-Green in-between, remember? It will usually be liberally flecked with white tip. Souchong means large leaves largely intact and more curled up at the edges than twisted lengthwise. Examine infused Souchong leaves and you'll notice a good many unfurl sinsemillalike into full-sized tea leaves again: If the tea shows tippy white leaflets, these too are largely unfragmented. Why Oolong has to be Souchong and not, say, Flowery Orange Pekoe grade I do not know, but so it is. As with any large leaf tea, you steep it longer and five to six minutes seems about right for Fancy Formosa Oolong—longer and you detract from its freshness somehow. Then once you pour the first cup everybody around the table detects the ripe peach aroma and exclaims. Invite them to have some, too.

Formosa Oolong has none of Darjeeling's astringency. It has no astringency at all, in fact, and there's none of Black Tea's bitterness to the taste. No peaks, no bites is how tea tasters put it. It's more deliciously fruity than any other tea and of a sparkling character that makes lemon and sugar unnecessary even for those accustomed to them and makes milk unthinkable. Yet seldom in recent decades has this country imported as much as three-quarters of a million pounds of Formosa Oolong a year. It was not always thus. "Fifty years ago American tea drinkers were well acquainted with this wonderful tea," the tea merchant brothers Schapira wrote in 1975. "In those days black tea accounted for only 40 percent of the tea consumed here. Green tea accounted for an equal amount, while oolongs made up fully 20 percent of our tea diet. Today 98 percent of our tea is black. Fully 36 percent of the tea Americans drink is made from instants or 'instant' tea mixes. If you could but once savor the ambrosia that is a first rate Formosa Oolong, you could only share our horror at what constitutes tea in America today."

Most of us have made the acquaintance of an Oolong of some sort at Chinese restaurants, where it's universally esteemed as a perfect dinner-time tea, both for its flavor and its lesser caffeine content. Wagners commendable Ch'a Ching Chinese Restaurant Tea is an above average representation of this grade of Oolong, probably falling somewhere between the Superior and Fine grades. Nothing, however, can prepare you for the delight of Fancy or Fanciest Formosa Oolong. It's usually the second most expensive tea after Darjeeling, lately bringing an average of about twenty-five dollars the pound on the international tea brokers' market. Pay unflinchingly I say, but as to whose to buy I must disqualify myself. For some years now I've tasted other Oolongs only to see whether they measured up to Freed Teller & Freed's and the only one that ever had—very nearly—is the Grace Tea Formosa Oolong Supreme. Mr. Richard Sanders is president of Grace Tea and when the Mark T. Wendell company just recently brought in a seventy dollar a pound Fancy Formosa Oolong, I was jokingly told it was "to make Dick Sanders jealous." The MTW is certainly one of the most beautiful teas I've ever seen or tasted.

FORMOSA TEAS worth mentioning in the same breath with Formosa Oolong do not exist.* All Formosa tea comes from the north end of the island around Taipei and flushes five times between April and early December. It's never grown above a thousand feet or so and the best is always plucked between late May and mid-August. It makes the

*Wrong. See note on Ten Ren Teas on page 238.

perfect semifermented or Oolong Tea but peculiarly enough produces no comparable Blacks or Greens. Usually the only reason to drink a Formosa Keemun would be if real Keemun from the mainland was not available, which was, of course, why it was ever made in the first place. Occasionally it is quite fine. Japan was the leading buyer of Taiwan's tea until the late seventies when Morocco captured that distinction. Both import Green Tea almost exclusively. The United States is the third-ranking importer of Formosa tea but only about a fourth of what we buy is Oolong, the more fools we. Formosa Pouchong, not surprisingly, is very pleasant indeed when you can find it here, though most of it is shipped to Far Eastern markets. It's nutty tasting and flavorful, easy on the system, and has a rough peasanty quality I like. Some of the best Pouchongs are used as a base for Jasmines.

INDONESIA TEAS come from the world's fourth largest tea producer but like coffees from Angola, the world's fourth largest coffee producer, they are virtually unknown by name in this country. This is no great loss, I believe, even though the venerable Mr. W. H. Ukers long ago allowed "when traveling the Netherland Indies [I have] found Java teas most satisfying." All Indonesian tea comes from either Java or Sumatra and all of it is Black. The Dutch began experimental plantings of it there as long ago as the 1600s, but try as they might they could never make it flourish until they finally obtained seeds of the Assam *jat* from British India little more than a century ago. Holland's ex-colony continues to be her chief tea supplier and one supposes Dutch connoisseurs must have Javanese favorites that would rank with any Ceylon, but if so the secret is well guarded.

Tea flushes and is plucked throughout the year in Indonesia and is, they say, consistent in quality and appearance. The United States imports between ten and thirty million pounds of it a year for use in supermarket tea-bag blends, but even John Wagner & Sons, extensive as their tea list is, offers not a single Indonesian tea. If your tea merchant does, it probably means his wholesale supplier is the reputable Tiffiny Gourmet Coffee of Mt. Vernon, New York. I was interested to note that their latest catalog lists a Java OP Select and a rather pricey tea called Sumatra Bah Butong, something I'm eager to try if only for the sake of the name. I'm told on good authority that high-grown Indonesia teas have a flavor somewhat similar to correspondingly high-grown Ceylons. The only one I've ever had, however, is Mark T. Wendell Indonesian, an unusual tea with strong rich flavor that bore no resemblance to any Ceylon whatever.

KENYA TEA is sure to grow in commercial importance in this country and the world. During the late seventies United States imports averaged about twenty million pounds a year, all of it destined for anonymous blends and worse, but the more discerning tea companies have now begun offering a fraction of Kenya's finest under its own name. African tea was pioneered in Malawi in 1887, and has been grown in Kenya since 1903. The principal growing districts are in the Kenya Highlands, an extensive area covering both sides of the Rift Valley between Mount Kenya and Lake Victoria. These highlands range in altitude from five thousand to nine thousand feet and also enjoy that second essential for growing good tea, copious rainfall. The tea can be harvested most of the year and thanks to Kenya's Tea Development Authority, almost two-thirds of the country's tea acreage is farmed by small landholders. The quality is so high in part because British companies have poured capital into the industry, developing specially bred, higher-yielding plants and some of the world's most modern tea factories. With an annual production of over a hundred million pounds and growing, Kenya is likely to remain Africa's leading tea producer.

The Kenya teas I've seen look reddish black and unbelievably tippy. They make a strong, dark, and hearty brew, with a sort of sweetness to the fragrance and flavor you'll encounter in no others. Tiffiny Gourmet Coffee wholesales one; Portland's prestigious Country Spice Tea Company carries a Kenya Ragati High Grown BOP, and though I have no idea what "Ragati" means I recommend it highly. The Mark T. Wendell Mountain Kenya is described as "a blend of the finest teas grown on the African continent" and examples are bound to multiply from now on.

NILGIRI is a Tamil word that translates "Blue Mountains," a range at the southernmost tip of India overlooking the Indian Ocean toward Africa. It is a land of peaks and precipices, lush with vegetation and teeming with wildlife, most notably elephants by the herd. Almost fifty-seven thousand acres of tea grow on every slope, valley, and plateau that will support the crop, from elevations of twelve hundred to almost eight thousand feet. Unlike the heights of nearby Sri Lanka, however, the tea gardens here

are drenched by both monsoons—the southwest during August and September and the northeast during January and February. The closest the tea comes to suffering for moisture is during December and early January and that is when the best Nilgiri is harvested, though flush is produced and plucked throughout the year.

India has a number of commercially important and aesthetically distinctive tea districts, starting with the northernmost Darjeeling and Assam on the Calcutta side of the subcontinent. Also there are Dooars and Terai, both with hundreds of tea estates, while from the Bombay side comes Kangra, Mandi, and Dehra Dun. Dooars, nearer the central part of India, produces a Black Tea not quite as heavy as Assam, which is usually consigned to blends but also stands especially well on its own. Southern-grown teas, those of Kerala, Madras, and Mysore as well as the Nilgiris, are usually lumped together under the name Travancores by the trade. Men far wiser than I, members of the Tea Board of India, made a policy decision some years ago to promote none of these teas except Assam, Darjeeling, and Nilgiri as "self-drinkers," and it is for this reason alone that I single out Nilgiri here.

Judging from what little I've tasted, Nilgiri is relatively mild, combining the body and strength of an Indian tea with the flavor of a Ceylon. This makes it a blender's dream, of course, and when the tea packers packed better tea, so I'm told, Nilgiris were widely used. Nilgiri makes a well-rounded cup of tea in its own right, rather mellow tasting with a genuinely bright and brisk cup quality. But while I would never turn it down, I don't think I should seek it out again—and this despite a yearning to back the underdog—unless for curiosity's sake. Although the Indian companies I mentioned earlier generally include a high-grown Nilgiri in their lines, it remains a rarity in this country. Should you burn with curiosity to see if you agree, write Mr. Bedhi of the Tea Board of India, 445 Park Avenue, New York, New York 10022, and he will send you some and bill you. And after all, why not?

RUSSIAN TEA has been cultivated since 1848, in what is now the Republic of Georgia, where the largest and best known of the USSR's estates—the Chakve—was planted in 1892. Situated on the slopes of the Adjar Hills bordering the eastern shore of the Black Sea—a region where snow is not uncommon—it is the northernmost tea plantation, or in this case, collective farm. Some tea is also said to be cultivated in Russian

Transcaucasia and the Republic of Azerbaidzhan bordering Afghanistan, for a total approaching two hundred thousand acres. The thirtieth edition (1981–82) of *The International Tea & Coffee Buyers' Guide,* the bible of the trade, estimates that Soviet tea production now exceeds two hundred million pounds annually, a figure that has steadily increased since the Sino-Soviet split left Russians bereft of their beloved China Blacks. Despite this impressive production and imports—chiefly from India—sometimes amounting to over half again as much, returning travelers and tea industry observers report that there's barely enough tea in the Soviet Union for the commissars, and that the populace by and large does without, an especially bitter thing for a Russian. Part of the reason for this sad state of affairs is that the Soviet Union is estimated to export (and re-export) some forty million pounds of tea per annum to Poland and Outer Mongolia. The tiny fraction of her domestic production that shows up on the Western market deserves notice if only for its rarity.

The managing director of Jacksons of Piccadilly, Mr. Eustace Crawley, says in a letter, "We have sold our Russian Tea for about 10 years. I cannot honestly say that it has been particularly successful, but we sell small quantities in about 15 markets, including the U.S.A. and Canada." Jacksons Russian is beautiful to behold, long leafed, and closely resembling James Ashby & Sons Rose Brand Pure Russian. Very similar Russian teas may be had from First Colony and others in this country; all of them seem extremely tannic, but I find a certain communistic flatness in the flavor, to which lemon adds a welcome tartness. I am informed that new import regulations classify Russian with Turkish and Iranian tea in the lowest quality category, but remember: Most teas with the word "Russian" in the name have other origins and hew to no party line. (See Russian-style Teas of the type M.F.K. Fisher serves on page 122.)

OTHER BLACK TEAS, with few exceptions, exist because of glaring, grinding poverty in the so-called Third World countries. There's no perceptible need for them in the midst of the world's perennial tea glut. There's little hope any of them will achieve the greatness of, say, a Darjeeling. And there's no doubt tea will always be one of the poorest paying crops in the world. Yet the goad of a relentless poverty has driven one unlikely land after another into the overcrowded tea market, desperate for a share.

First among the numerous countries you'd never suspect of producing tea is the home of Yerba Maté, Argentina, which has over a hundred thousand acres under cultivation. She produces over sixty million pounds a year and the best of it, which is considered pretty fair, she sells to Chile, the United Kingdom, and the United States, in that order. Tea is raised throughout East Africa. Malawi has bushes over seventy years old—the oldest in Africa—and sells her crop at the London auctions to avoid any connection with Nairobi and her chief rival, Kenya. Facing Kenya across Lake Victoria, Uganda has—or did have—over fifty thousand acres in tea. Her exports are at or near zero today, but in 1972, the year before Idi Amin's takeover, she sold over sixty million pounds, almost two-thirds of it to the United States and Canada. Neighboring Tanzania produces about forty million pounds a year now; her tea is considered of fair quality except by the natives—Africans have never taken much of a liking to their chief products for foreign exchange and don't drink very much tea.

A former Food and Drug Administration tea examiner in San Francisco told me he saw more and more South American tea entering the country—sad proof that somebody can always make a cheaper tea bag. Besides Argentina, this comes from small plantings in Brazil, Bolivia, Ecuador, and Peru, the latter's tiny high-grown crop being the only one of any promise. Zaire, Papua New Guinea, and the Seychelles also produce teas of a sort.

Bangladesh has grown tea of good quality since the nineteenth century in the Cachar and Sylhet districts next door to Assam; most of it is for home consumption. Thankfully, this is also the case with Malaysia and Vietnam—one taste of Vietnamese tea and you regret it wasn't defoliated. Iran and Turkey are new tea lands. Turkey's plantings date to 1939, and now cover some one hundred thousand acres. Iran has extensive tea estates near the Caspian Sea and in 1978, the last year for which we have figures, over forty million pounds were produced. Like Russian tea, Iranian tea has always been considered well made but of poor cup quality, and like Turkish tea, it is raised mostly for the home market.

GREEN TEAS

Only this much, therefore, have I to say in praise of your beauty, omitting a great deal.
—*Demosthenes (384–22* B.C.)
DIALOGUE ON THE EROTIC

The world produces over two and a half billion pounds of tea a year, 90 percent of it Black and the remainder divided between Oolong and Green teas. Hard as it is to reconcile these generally accepted figures with the fact that most Chinese drink Green Tea, that need not detain us. Virtually all Green Teas come from China, Japan, and Taiwan and their variety is nigh infinite. Green Tea is to Black as white wine is to red, if you'll forgive an overly broad generalization. Though all are harvested from the same plant, Green Tea—unlike Black or Oolong—is never allowed to wither and ferment. The leaf is killed by heat as soon as possible after plucking, and by the end of the day it was picked it is ready to go into a pot. As a result of bypassing the fermentation process, the dry leaf retains its natural dark olive-green color and all of its natural tannin and is only 1 percent caffeine by weight. For the same reason Green Tea also contains substantial amounts of vitamin C, chlorophyll, and minerals. The Orient has long claimed that Green Tea refreshes and quiets rather than stimulating or "picking you up," and given all these attributes the claim makes sense. It is an undeniably different kind of delight, somewhat more astringent and subtler to the taste usually, and the perfect meditative aid. The same Black Tea may be sifted into every grade from Orange Pekoe to Dust, but Green Tea names denote specific teas and leaf styles.

GUNPOWDER is so-called because that's what some long-gone John Company agent in China thought it looked like, though whether on account of its granular appearance or grayish-green complexion I cannot say. It is for these reasons, at any rate, that the Chinese themselves have always called it Pearl Tea. Gunpowder is a special style of Green Tea in which each leaf has been rolled into a tiny, compact pellet. If only the very tenderest buds and tips are used it's generally known as Pinhead Gunpowder. The only two Gunpowders you're likely to find outside your tea dealer's bins—Twinings and Wagners—should really be labeled Imperial, which is the old-timey name for the loosely balled older (and therefore larger) leaf that's sifted out of Gunpowder proper. Although one man's Gunpowder remains another's Imperial, this distinction was lost during the years of the China embargo and to add to the confusion the name Imperial Gunpowder is often used nowadays to describe either or both. What makes this point worth belaboring is that poor Gunpowder is very raw to the taste and nothing you'd confuse with the sweet aroma, clear amber liquor, and penetrating flavor of a fine one.

North and inland from Shanghai and roughly on a parallel with Japan is China's Anhwei Province, where the tea-growing season is an especially short one. Anhwei produces China's four special grades, or standards, of Gunpowder. Much of it is exported to Morocco, Algeria, Turkey, and other Moslem lands, but some also finds its way to us. United States importers wholesale the top grades as Pinhead Gunpowder for up to $4 per pound, but it's no longer impossible to find them in packages in Chinatown shops. Evergreen Brand Gunpowder is Grade IV, Sprouting Brand is Grade III, and Temple of Heaven Brand Special Gunpowder is the best of all. Temple of Heaven is unbelievably full-bodied and rich for a Green Tea and far outdistances any Formosa Gunpowder I've tried. I don't believe Japan produces any. Being more delicate than Black, Green Tea is prone to going stale, but because of its tightly rolled leaf Gunpowder has the best keeping quality of any tea made.

HYSON, YOUNG HYSON, & COUSINS A rich East India merchant named Hyson was the first to sell a certain style of Chinese Green Tea in England and it has borne his name ever since. Somewhat shiny, it is a long, bold twisted leaf and the best of it is now called Young Hyson, Hyson pure and simple being older and poorer leaf pan-fired and rolled the same way. The Chinese have designed special machinery for Young Hyson manufacturing. There are three other China Green Teas that I find very similar to these: Chunmee, Sowmee, and Pan-Fired. It's hard for me to tell one from another just by looks without a chance for comparison, but Chunmee is the most distinctive. It's a hard leaf, slender, and very fine and curled. Special Chunmee, available in China's Evergreen Brand in beautiful three-and-a-half-ounce tins, brews a golden cup that's one of the most flavorful Green Teas I know. There are also Formosa versions of all these.

DRAGON WELL, PI LO CHUN, & THE WELL-KNOWN TEA OF ZHEJIANG Lung Ching, which I'm drinking at the moment, means "dragon well," and as all but the most foolish of us agree, dragons are real. According to the Taoists they are elementals that rank among the deified forces of nature. Until eclipsed by the red star, the dragon had always been the national symbol of China and the emblem of her imperial family. Since it was well known that dragons dwell partly in water and partly on land, the Taoists usually built them shrines on river banks. They made an exception in the case of this particular well outside the city of Hangchow because it obviously harbors an especially benevolent dragon. Lung Ching or Dragon Well Tea grows all around and for centuries Chinese tourists have paid reverent visits to the gardens that produce one of their most highly prized teas.

Lung Ching looks remarkably flat and smooth and is slick to the touch. When it is infused and opens up, you can see that the leaf consists almost entirely of intact buds. Lung Ching, or Dragon Well if you prefer, gives a light emerald liquor with a most intriguing vegetative aroma and taste. The Chinese have a real penchant for vegetative flavors and I sometimes find them downright raw, but here they've got it just right—ethereally complex with a haunting, distant sweetness. No wonder it's the most famous China Green Tea. You could drink it all day long.

Even though we can't brew it as custom dictates, with water from the well it's named for, we should beware of substitutes. I was buying a "Dragon Well" for years before I discovered it was just a blend my dealer made to go with the name. Very good tea, mind you, but it bore no relation to the real thing. China sells only the fourth and fifth grades in bulk and the top grades in tins only. I notice my six-ounce can of Sprouting Brand Lung Ching cost $6.95—about a dime a cup! Handsome tin, too, with pictures of Hangchow's famous West Lake on it.

Pi Lo Chun means "Green Couch Spring" and is the name of another superb China Green Tea. China produces three grades of which the best is sold in round black tins under the Sunflower Brand label. This rare tea is made only once a year from the tenderest shoots of the first spring flush, and it's another of those for which the Chinese have developed special manufacturing equipment. The leaf is tiny and comes out spiral shaped, and the brew is clear and golden and of exceeding delicacy. They say Chinese connoisseurs eagerly await its appearance each year. It's easy to see why.

Until a few weeks ago as far as I was concerned The Well Known Tea of Zhejiang was Zhejiang's best kept secret. I discovered it rambling through San Francisco's

"Leaning on a rock,
they wait for tea to
be brewed."

"Face to face the two drink and serve
each other among the flowers
on the mountain!"

Chinatown and judged from its high price and careful packaging in a foil-sealed nitrogen atmosphere that I should make its acquaintance. The shop lady assured me that this was a very rare tea reserved in former times for the emperor himself. My neighbor Andrew Fong is the latest among my Chinese-American friends I've tried it on and all of them pronounce it terrible. Perhaps it's my delight at discovering a taste so singularly Chinese that not even Andrew et al can abide it, but I've decided I like the stuff. It tastes like the leaf died on the bush in the vintage Year of the Dog—you've truly got to dig earthiness to get into it. Clearly for very special occasions but undeniably extraordinary. That's all I know about it. Zhejiang Province is the same one that produces Lung Ching.

OTHER CHINA GREEN TEAS All the tea in China belongs to and is sold by a single organization: The National Native Produce & Animal By-Products Import & Export Corporation of the People's Republic of China. Everybody who buys tea direct from China orders from this one corporation's catalog, in other words. The preface to the latest edition of this catalog mentions Mao Feng and Yu Hua Tea among its Green Tea "products of distinction." I've never heard of them before and the fact is these are but two out of some dozens of China Green Teas hardly known in the West. The catalog lists at least thirty-five different Green Teas for export and most of them are available in at least six different quality grades, or standards. For a rough idea of average quality try Tit Koon Yum. "Drinking it straight gives you a true cup of China tea which is a very common tea for everyday drink," claims the advertisement of its purveyor, the Kwong Sang Tea Company, established over forty years ago in Hong Kong. Tit Koon Yum and Kwong Sang's Shui Sin represent the *ordinaire* most overseas Chinese have lived on for years—uncommonly high standards "for everyday drink."

JAPANESE TEAS I've never had a tea from Japan that wasn't Green. The rarest, much less than 1 percent of her production, is the powdered leaf used for the tea ceremony. It is called Tencha (or Matcha) and though not exactly exported, it is obtainable through tea ceremony students and masters. I disclaim all chauvinism in saying this, but I have found it can be used to make a strangely delicious ice cream. I cannot honestly recommend you drink it, however, even ceremonially.

The most prized nonceremonial Japanese tea is called Gyokuro, which means

Pearl Dew. This is grown where the first Japanese tea was planted in the Uji district of Honshu near Kyoto. Tencha is grown in this same district and in much the same way as Gyokuro. Everything connected with tending and making the tea is done by hand. Three weeks before plucking the bushes are covered with straw shades, a practice that apparently lowers the tannin while slightly increasing the caffeine content of the leaf. This is one explanation given for the intensity of Gyokuro. After steaming, about five pounds of the leaf at a time is basket-fired by hand and rolled. The young leaves emerge looking like short pine needles, and this is why basket-fired teas are often sold as Spiderleg Green Tea. Fewer and fewer Japanese are willing to stay on the farm and practice the laborious old ways, however, and tea professionals complain that both the quantity and quality of Japan's Spiderleg Tea declines with each passing year. So do Japan's tea exports, which declined by over one and a quarter million pounds between 1978 and 1980. With hardly enough for home consumption, it's no wonder Gyokuro costs about thirty dollars a pound here. The other Spiderleg Teas are also expensive, but none cost more.

If you imagine that a pale Green Tea has to be weak and flavorless, Gyokuro will surprise you. It's mouthfilling and rich, with a very complex herbaceous quality to it. This herbaceousness, if there be such a word, is the hallmark of Japanese teas. If the Chinese lean toward flavors somehow reminiscent of root vegetables in Green Teas, the Japanese just as surely prefer theirs to suggest brewed yard grass. It's a cleaner taste, you might say, but a thinner one, sometimes evanescent almost. I find this generally characteristic of Sencha Teas. Sencha comprises about three-quarters of the two hundred million-odd pounds of tea Japan produces each year. It is made from the first and second flushes only and the first flush, or I-Chiban Cha, is especially delicate and grassy. Except with basket-fired Sencha, machines usually steam and fire it in pans as it is rolled. The Japan and Formosa teas you see called simply Pan-Fired Green get a special going over in the hot iron pans that gives them a polished look. As far as I can tell, however, the manufacturing method determines the tea's appearance only and not its taste. This varies from year to year, just as different vintages of wine do.

Depending on the weather, Japan's tea flushes three or four times a year, and the coarse older leaf of the last pluckings goes to make Bancha. Bancha, the workingman's tea so to speak, has little to recommend it and is rarely exported. The last picking is really a sort of cleanup of the bushes before dormancy sets in, but the frugal Japanese even find a use for this in Kuko-Cha or Stem Tea, which is really awful. The stems add only weight, no flavor, and the leaf has obviously had a long and difficult life. The Japanese also enjoy a doctored tea called Gen Mai Cha, which is Sencha with barley popped like popcorn in it. Hoji-Cha, or Roasted Tea, is another of their inventions and the one I like best. It brews a dark cup that combines the flavor of nuts and toast. Yamamoto of the Orient sells it in this country.

Any good Japanese tea is always pricey and beautifully packaged. About 80 percent of all that's exported comes to the United States. None had ever been exported until 1611, when the Dutch East India Company established a factory on Hirado Island just off Kyushu. The Dutch fleet would put in there once a year, arriving in April and remaining until September. They brought everything from sugar to spectacles, telescopes, and clocks, and carried away mainly copper, camphor, laquerware, and tea. The English maintained an agent at Hirado for a time—that first Englishman to call for "a pot of the best sort of chaw"—but his Dutch competitors soon put him out of business. Inspired by the arrival of the Dutch, the Japanese built two seagoing ships and sent one to Rome and the other across the Pacific to Mexico. Soon after they returned from these voyages, however, the feudal government of the Tokugawa shoguns faced the threat of civil war over the teaching of Christianity by missionaries. To isolate Japan from further alien influence, all ports except the Christian stronghold of Nagasaki were closed to foreigners in 1638. The only outsiders allowed to carry on limited trade at Nagasaki from then on were the Dutch and the Chinese and no Japanese ship was permitted to visit a foreign shore and return. When Admiral Perry paid his memorable visit to Japan in 1853, he brought back with him samples of tea supplied by a Nagasaki merchant, Madam Kay Oura, and the Japanese-American tea trade began.

CHINA TEAS

How many types of China black tea is it possible for the tea merchant to furnish? We answer, after careful enumeration of the kinds and grades, about 500.
—*W. H. Ukers, writing in 1935*
ALL ABOUT TEA

To talk about Chinese tea in general is just as meaningless as generalizing about French wines, for China is to tea what France is to wine and I doubt if there's anybody in China even who's sampled the whole bewildering array. According to the best authorities, peak production of China tea before the Revolution occurred in 1886. That record was exceeded for the first time in 1972, the year that also saw the lifting of the United States–China embargo. Until 1890 British buyers had dominated China's export tea market, but inexorably the duty-free, empire-grown teas of India and Ceylon usurped China's position in the trade. In 1892 only four British vessels called at Hankow, six hundred miles up the Yangtze from Shanghai, to load cargoes of NorthChina Congous and in 1901, there were none at all. The Russians took up the slack for a time after the opening of the Trans-Siberian Railroad in 1900, but this market too collapsed with the revolution of 1917. By this time China tea had already gone into a catastrophic decline as the country lurched from its own revolution into factionalism and civil war, followed by the Japanese invasion of the 1930s. Tea was still grown on an enormous scale for local consumption, of course, but exports dried up altogether with the outbreak of World War II. Then, little more than a century after the Opium Wars had opened China to international commerce by force, she managed to restore her longstanding isolation under the rule of Mao Tse-tung. After almost three hundred years, the China trade that had seen the East Indiamen and clippers come and go seemed dead at last.

Along with everything else in the country, the Communist government set about reorganizing China's tea industry. In the old days Chinese tea merchants recognized fully eight thousand different teas. "This incredible number," write the tea merchants Schapira, "arose from the fact that each tea was classified by how it was manufactured (5 ways), the quality of the leaf (4 grades), the quality of the manufacturing (2 grades), and the number of places of origin (200 grades)." Moreover, China's tea was not grown on estates, as elsewhere, but haphazardly by peasants on small holdings scattered around sixteen different tea-producing provinces. The new Chinese government set out to bring some order to this national industry if only to keep from going completely mad. Progress was such that by 1956, Mr. Edward Bramah was engaged as China's tea agent in London, then still the center of the world tea trade, and put in touch with China's commercial representative there, Mr. Liao Run-chu. As Mr. Bramah recounts his adventure:

> There was certainly no established tradition of international friendship to build on. I soon found there was no common professional experience either. Liao knew nothing about tea!
>
> All discussions took place through an interpreter at first, but there were inevitably difficulties about the terms used in tea-tasting. I also had to teach Liao to taste in the English fashion, with milk. At the same time I had sent a lot of samples to China to inform the Tea Corporation of the standards expected on the London market. Strange as the post-war China teas were to the London brokers, the British blends must have been even stranger to the Chinese tea experts, who had been isolated from the rest of the world for years and had in any case never regarded other countries' teas with much interest. The high quality of the Indian and Ceylon teas dismayed them as, so far as I could discover, their rolling machines were of wood and hand-operated, vastly different from the modern plant used in Ceylon and India. However, they studied my tasting reports and gave careful consideration to all my suggestions. They asked for detailed information about processing plant used in other parts of the world.... [Finally,] on Wednesday, 22nd October 1958, exactly 300 years after China tea had first been drunk in this country and 20 years after its last appearance in the auctions, China tea came under the hammer in Mincing Lane.... [It] was the first time the Chinese producers had put their tea in the London auctions themselves.

Personnel from Seattle's China Products Northwest were among the first Westerners to visit a China tea estate in 1975; Mr. Ronald Phipps and his associates have made numerous trips to China since, sampling and buying tea, visiting tea estates, and forming first-hand impressions. Their reports and articles constitute almost the only up-to-date source material available and I'm most grateful for the use of it in what follows. China's tea production is becoming steadily more mechanized, they have found, and all tea-producing provinces now have at least one major factory turning out tea-processing machines. China now has forty different kinds of machines for the different stages of production, including specialized equipment for the manufacture of her finest gourmet teas.

The record crop of 1972 has been surpassed by significantly increasing margins every year since 1975, and exports have risen steadily as well. Chinese teas are now remarkably well made—you almost never find a stem in one, for instance—and are also remarkably consistent. China achieves this consistency by selling its tea by "standards," preestablished levels of quality for every variety of tea. This minimizes the season-to-season and year-to-year variations that always exist in the teas of other countries sold by district or garden names. All the tea in China is divided into six basic categories: Green Tea, Black Tea, Oolong Tea, Scented Tea, White Tea, and Pu-Erh or Compressed Tea. Having already discussed Green, let us now examine some of the many other gourmet teas again available from tea's original homeland.

KEEMUN, which First Colony somewhat overenthusiastically calls "the world's finest Black Tea bar none," is the most famous of all China's Blacks. They say it comes from the district or county of Keemun in Anwhei (Anhui) Province, though none of the maps I've consulted show such a place. The Romanized spelling of Chinese names varies depending on whether your mapmaker subscribes to the Yale or Pinyin system of transliteration and apparently Keemun is no longer recognized in either. The word persists only because tea of that name has been famous around the world for well over a century. Mr. W. H. Ukers has asserted that until the nineteenth century Keemun produced only a nondescript Green Tea. Then for some reason the district switched to Black Tea manufacturing and one of the world's great teas was born. It quickly became known in Europe as English Breakfast Tea and only after supplies were no longer available did English Breakfast become a generic term meaning tea of any origin whatever. It was during this same period Formosa Keemun came into existence. Mark T. Wendell and Grace Rare Tea market Formosa Keemuns of great distinction and the Grace Winey Keemun is one of my favorite teas, but these are exceptions. Most Formosa Keemuns have little in common with the real thing.

Real Keemun is a low-grown tea that's sweet, fruity, and unusually full-bodied. The aroma is unsurpassed, and it's the only one I know of that acquires additional character

with a little age—a Keemun that's been kept for perhaps a year before selling is often described as a Winey Keemun and is a noticeably mellower tea. Fine Keemun shows slender, tightly curled leaf that's black as asphalt after dark. China produces five standards of Keemun and reserves the fanciest for sale in tins. It is the best-known North China Congou.

"Congou," according to my usual reliable sources in these matters, is but one possible anglicization of the ideograms *kung fu,* which also stand for the martial art anciently propagated by the Shaolin Temple. Consider too that "Confucius" is a Jesuit Latinization for Kung fu-tzu, the name of perhaps the greatest of China's sages, and you'll agree that Congou—or *kung fu,* Chinese for "time and labor"—means more than meets the eye. Bastardized or pidgin though it may be, Congou is a tea name the Chinese themselves still recognize today and Keemun is the one Congou that almost every firm and dealer carries.

I CHANG is another North China Congou that comes from western Hupeh (Hubei) Province where it is grown around Yi-Chang, as modern maps spell it, just below the Yangtze (Chang Jiang) gorges. This scenic jumble of rushing water and towering cliff faces, the subject of innumerable Chinese landscape paintings, is no longer famous in the West for its formerly celebrated Black Tea: Fortnum & Mason is the only outfit I know that offers one by name. When I was unable to locate any, a company representative offered to send me some but never did. Is it wholly legendary I wonder?

CHING WO, which is sold us by Country Spice, First Colony, and Jacksons, is one of the more distinguished South China Congous. Like Lapsang Souchong and others including Panyong, a South China Congou which I think only Mark T. Wendell sells in the United States, Ching Wo comes from Fukien (Fujian) Province opposite Taiwan. Ukers described the North China Congous of his day as "the Burgundies of China tea" and designated their southern relatives "the clarets." This remains a pretty apt comparison I think. Compare Keemun and Ching Wo and you see the difference soil and climate can make—it's a Chinese version of the contrast between topnotch Assam and Ceylon. Ching Wo gives a bright-red infusion with a wonderful flavor and aroma but for all its great strength, the Keemun body is lacking. Dunno if I miss it but I do know it ain't there: What do you think?

PINGSUEY is a Black Tea from the same neighborhood as Lung Ching, the Hangchow (Hangzhou) district of Zhejiang Province just south of Shanghai. Pingsuey, which means "ice water" in Chinese, is just as unusual among China Black Teas as Darjeeling is among Indian and sure to find a wider and wider market among Western connoisseurs. At present it is sold in the United States by Country Spice, The Coffee Bean & Tea Leaf and the Pannikin shops, Starbucks, and Mark T. Wendell, plus a few farsighted others. Pingsuey is exceptionally mild for a Black Tea and the flavor is correspondingly delicate. Like nothing else and highly recommended!

YUNNAN is China's cloud-misted, mountainous province that borders Vietnam, Laos, and Burma. The tea plant is thought to be indigenous to this area and bushes the size of large trees have been found growing there. Yunnan now leads all other provinces in Black Tea production and the best of it makes you feel like you're drinking God's own original. It can be almost unbelievably tippy and it has a peppery quality I associate with no other. The tea bushes grown in this province produce a broad, thick, and glossy leaf; raised elsewhere the same bush produces the typical "China leaf," which looks narrow, thin, and dull in comparison. Transplant said bush back to its native province, however, and it produces the broad Yunnan leaf again. I don't know what to make of this curious information, but I do know Yunnan is clearly the finest of the world's recently discovered teas. It is not a classic China Black, having been fully developed only since 1949. Twinings new Yunnan is the nineteenth tea in its line.

As we have seen, China's teas are exported according to certain "standard" numbers that represent varying levels of quality. To compensate for seasonal and other variations and to maintain the quality of a given standard, teas of different origins and flushes are blended together. Maintaining the ten basic Yunnan BOP standards, for example, requires several hundred teas, the main component determining quality being the kind and amount of high-grown tea used. The *yun* in Yunnan means "cloud" and most tea there is raised at elevations of three thousand to seven thousand feet. The quality of the best has improved to such a point that China is now exporting unblended Yunnan: You can spoil yourself with a First Colony or Mark T. Wendell or even Twinings 275th Anniversary Tea—all beautiful stuff! The leaf is usually at least half an inch long and full of tip; it gives a rich, reddish-orange infusion with an exquisite fragrance. According to the people at China Products Northwest, the Chinese have also begun growing coffee in Yunnan Province.

OTHER CHINA BLACK TEAS mostly come, in descending order of total production, from the provinces of Hunan, Kwangtung (Guangdong), Kwangsi (Guangxi), and Anwhei. Anwhei, of course, is the home of Keemun; I've never had a Hunan tea. Canton is the capital of Kwangtung Province where the prized Yingteh is produced. Yingteh is a remarkably robust and flavorful high-grown tea that's increasingly popular in Europe. Along with Yunnan and Hainan, a tea grown on the island at the southern extremity of Kwangtung Province, Yingteh is not only sold by standards but sometimes unblended as well. The people from China Products Northwest estimate that some 15 to 20 percent of all China Black Teas imported into the United States are of Kwangsi origin; they will probably be used in increasing quantity to add distinction and character to our better blends.

TI KUAN YIN & OTHER MAINLAND OOLONGS tend toward roughness and are no match for the better Formosa Oolongs. That said, allow me to confess a partiality for Ti Kuan Yin all the same. Kuan Yin is the Taoist-Buddhist equivalent to the Madonna, very roughly speaking, and her name is generally mistranslated "Goddess of Mercy." *Ti (teh)* means "iron," a reference to the thick, weighty leaf. Like most China Oolongs, Ti Kuan Yin comes from Fukien, the province where this sort of tea manufacture was invented. The leaf shows no tip and much of it looks downright green, the rest almost black. It tastes invigorating and full-bodied and the flavor is especially long lingering. It is not a taste or aroma you'd confuse with the typically peachy quality of a Formosa Oolong, the Chinese preferring as always an undertaste of earthiness nobody else on the planet seems able to approximate. It's a taste I relish every so often, especially when it's as subtly understated as it is in Ti Kuan Yin. My objection to the other "name" Oolongs the Chinese prize is that they carry earthiness too far for my Western country boy's palate. Ming Xiang and Min-Pei are among these, but if you really want to see how far out a flavor can get, hunt down some Ta-Hung-Yen. Any one of them will make you grateful that Chinese restaurants do not serve what they'd consider gourmet China Oolong.

WHITE TEA is in a class unto itself and is produced in China exclusively. It is neither fermented nor rolled and comes mainly from Fukien Province. The costliest, and a truly rare tea even in China, is called Silvery Tip Pekoe, produced from full-grown buds of a special tea bush known as "Big White." One hundred-percent tip, the leaf looks lustrous and silvery and brews a pale golden cup that tastes mellow and has a hint of sweetness to it. White Peony or Pai Mu Tan is almost as rare. It is made from the leaf of the Big White mixed with buds from the Shui Hsien White Tea plant. The leaf shows some silver tip but is predominantly greenish brown in color and very flat. The tea tastes mild and pleasant enough but does not compare with Silvery Tip Pekoe. As far as I know, these are imported by the East Horizon Corporation exclusively. There is also a Sow Mee White that I have never tried.

TEA BRICKS, OR COMPRESSED TEA, is a Chinese invention antedating the T'ang Dynasty: Tea had been compressed into cakes long before Lu Yu published the *Ch'a Ching* circa 780. Under the Ming, loose leaf tea became popular throughout the Celestial Empire, but the inland tribes of Mongolia and Tibet clung to the tastes of former days. The Chinese, who had also evolved the earliest central banking system and were circulating various coins and paper bank notes, found that in commercial transactions with the border peoples their currency had no value. Their ingenious solution to this problem was to make their most valued consumer product—tea—into bricks. This made the tea easy to transport inland where it was used as a form of currency for barter, the reverse side of each brick being scored so that it was easily broken for purposes of making change.

"Tea money" of this description is still used in parts of Asia and the Tibetans remain especially fond of the tea itself. They shave it off the brick and boil it up into a kind of soup, with salt, yak butter, and other ingredients. China's compressed tea has one uniform design nowadays and consists of tea dust hydraulically compressed into a one-kilo brick. Non-Tibetans are unlikely to enjoy this tea for its flavor, but the bricks are widely available and make interesting conversation pieces. If you buy one, make sure to apply a light coat of clear lacquer to prevent its crumbling with the changes in humidity over time. Let me repeat, however: It makes a thoroughly unsatisfactory tea.

SCENTED, FLAVORED, & DECAFFEINATED TEAS

Indeed, Madame, your ladyship is very sparing of your tea; I protest the last I took was no more than water bewitched.

—Jonathan Swift (1667-1745)
in conversation

JASMINE TEA The best-known Scented Tea in the West by some margin is Earl Grey, which we have already discussed under Trade Name Teas. In the East, far the best known is Jasmine Tea, the bulk and the best of which comes from China. Jasmine Tea can produce one of the subtlest or one of the foulest of all brews, depending on its quality. In making it, the Chinese are said to throw away the first water sometimes and use the same leaves to brew a second pot, which they then drink. I doubt that even this would improve some of the vile (non-Chinese) examples available in this country. On the other hand, Yin Hao Jasmine, China's finest standard, which wholesales here for about twenty dollars per pound, is indubitably among the world's great teas and you wouldn't dream of throwing away a drop of it. James Bond drank Yin Hao.

Jasmine Tea was apparently invented some eight hundred years ago under the Sung Dynasty. Today it comes chiefly from the counties surrounding Foochow in Fukien Province, a district Lu Yu included in his list of outstanding tea-producing areas. The best tea there is plucked from early April to late May and that which is destined to become Jasmine Tea is manufactured into steamed (not pan-fired) Green Tea; steamed leaf alone will properly absorb scenting. The best leaf is then stored until the blazing heat of Fukien's summer brings the jasmine flowers into bloom in August and September. (Less pungent and lower grades of Jasmine Tea are also made, but these use spring and early summer blossoms gathered before the heat has intensified the flower's natural flavor and aroma.)

Since jasmine opens only at night, it is plucked around noontime, when the blossoms are most tightly closed. Then between six and eight that evening, as the temperature cools, the flowers begin to open. According to Mr. Paul Kresting of China Products Northwest who has witnessed the process, the buds emit a popping sound when they open and this sound is the signal for the scenting to begin. Flowers and tea are mated in machines that control temperature and humidity. It takes four hours or so for the tea to absorb the fragrance and flavor of the blossoms and for the highest grades this process may be repeated as many as five times over the period of a month. Since the tea has also absorbed moisture from the flowers it must then be refired to prevent spoilage. The spent flowers may or may not be removed from the final product—in the lower grades they generally are not. Being completely dessicated and containing no more aroma, i.e., moisture, the flowers add only visual appeal anyway. They're no clue to quality.

China produces seven numbered quality standards of Jasmine Tea, plus limited amounts of three special or extra-fancy grades for connoisseurs. These latter are available only in tins and the finest one is called Chung Feng Premium Jasmine Tea. Of the seven quality standards, the highest are named Yin Hao and Chun Hao. The experts at Seattle's China Products Northwest report that the people of Fukien Province drink

The Orient

little of the Jasmine Tea for which they are famous, preferring Oolong, which they also produce. On the other hand they also say that 90 percent of the people living in Peking (Beijing), China's capital, are confirmed Jasmine Tea drinkers. One taste of Chung Feng and you're grateful there's any left over for the rest of us. The finest Formosa Jasmines use Pouchong, not Green Tea, as a base and these attain an excellence of their own. One of the best examples I know is the Grace Tea Before the Rain Jasmine.

ROSE TEA The rose, the favorite flower of poets from Horace to Rilke and William Carlos Williams, exists today in some ten thousand identifiable varieties. From the flower's point of view it must appear that the whole point of human civilization has been simply to multiply its petals, for Horace's roses in the days of imperial Rome had only four to six petals and one must assume that their contemporaries in ancient China were no better endowed. As man has bred more complexity and odor into the rose over the centuries, it has gradually found more and more employment as a scenting and flavoring agent in everything from sauces and condiments to—yes—tea. China produces only one standard of Rose Congou Tea and knowing nothing else about it, I am positive American Beauty is not the rose variety employed. The roses impart such heady and overpowering floral aroma and flavor, the otherwise quite decent tea is undrinkable as far as I'm concerned. One assumes the scenting is carried out much the same as in making Jasmine Tea, with the difference that the base tea is Black. This is also true of the Himalayan Rose Teas you see occasionally that come from India. A friend assures me a pinch of Rose Tea adds depth and mystery to any tea blend, and this is something I mean to try once my aversion to it lessens somewhat. You have to drink the damnedest things to write a book like this.

LAPSANG SOUCHONG, drunk by itself, is what might once have been called "a man's tea." Its character is assertive and you love or detest it on its own not-uncertain terms. Souchong, of course, means that the leaf is the largest possible size, black with a bold, raggedy look. Nobody's ever defined Lapsang for me, but by rights it should mean "smoky," since any proper Lapsang Souchong is scented and flavored with smoke (though cheap ones may simply have smoke flavor added). It would be interesting to find out what kind of fire gives such a distinctive smoky and tarry taste, but nobody seems to have asked the Chinese and Taiwanese who make it.

Sam Twining says he enjoys Lapsang Souchong most when he's taking a break from gardening or tennis out-of-doors and I agree it's the best possible outdoors tea. I myself was introduced to it aboard my friend Lyle Bongé's boat in the Gulf of Mexico. Mr. Bongé is a famous sailor in those parts, having set the record for the fastest single-handed crossing of the Gulf from Mérida in the Yucatán to Biloxi, Mississippi, and one of the invariable rules aboard his boat is that Lapsang Souchong is served at four every afternoon, often with a tot of Barbados rum. I once had the misfortune to be sailing with Lyle when a hurricane came up, and he decided to anchor in the lee of a ridiculously small island for shelter. Soon the wind commenced to roar like a Manhattan subway, the waves sloshed over us from mountainous heights, and the boat, judging by its protests and gyrations, feared for its life. Sick at heart and stomach I tossed about in the forward bunk and feared for my own, which was rapidly passing in front of my eyes. Each hour was a week long and more hellish than the last, until finally Mr. Bongé made his way to my side with a mug of Lapsang Souchong at four o'clock. It was the best tea I've ever drunk. It not only settled my stomach and assured me I was still alive but also offered proof positive that we were going to survive Neptune's wrath. How could it be otherwise if Lyle was calmly preparing his prescribed tea as usual, I thought, and joined him in another cup. Only after the weather cleared did I reflect that he would have fixed us Lapsang at that hour regardless of whether we were going to go down or not.

According to *Twinings Tea Guide,* Lapsang's unmistakable flavor "comes from the mineral-rich soil in the province where it's grown." You may consider this twaddle until someone's actually seen it made in Fukien sans smoke, but it's worth citing as an example of the misstatements even tea packers make, so pervasive has our ignorance of tea become in the West. Fukien, where it is said to have originated, remains the source of the two standards China sells—Lapsang Souchong and Tarry Souchong, the latter even smokier than the first. That from Taiwan may or may not be called Formosa Souchong, but the leaf is certain to have a grayish tinge and contain some stems. The Chinese is black as sin, utterly devoid of stems, and a rather more twisted, less open leaf. Like the Chinese, the best Formosa produces a rich, syrupy liquor of a clear bright orange and like Scotch whisky, which also has a smoky taste to it, you either like it or you don't. Yet people who swear they can't stand it are often beguiled by Russian-style blends and others in which it's sometimes used. And although every tea dealer seems to carry one, it's actually rather rare: the Food and Drug Administration records no year in which the United States has imported more than ninety thousand pounds. China Lapsang Souchong is available from First Colony and China Products Northwest, among others, but the one I swear by is the Mark T. Wendell Hu-kwa Tea, which is made in Taiwan.

OTHER SCENTED TEAS Lychee Tea is another scented Black Tea from China, made much the same way as Jasmine and Rose, with the difference that the lychee fruit, mistakenly called a nut in the West, is used instead of the blossom. Just because I find it loathesome is no reason for you not to try it. The Chinese have also made Gardenia and Yu-lan teas, the latter being a species of magnolia, but these are no longer exported at least. It is curious that they left it to us American Southerners to invent Mint Tea. Spearmint and peppermint both seem natural complements to fine Black Teas, especially when it's iced-tea time in summer. The Coffee Bean & Tea Leaf stores in Los Angeles have a particularly fine example and if your own dealer doesn't, you can order Mark T. Wendell Mint Tea by mail. Truly refreshing stuff.

SPICED TEAS Unlike Mint Tea, Spiced Tea should always be served hot I think—for the spices' sake. The Chinese have an adage that only ordinary tea needs to be scented, even though they ignore it when it comes to fine Jasmines or Lapsang Souchong. All the same, a judicious spicing is probably the best thing that can happen to most ordinary tea—it can even rescue it from ordinariness. The most popular one must be orange and clove Spice Tea, which everybody seems to sell with orange rind in it. The leader in this field is surely John Wagner & Sons, which in addition offers Cinnamon & Spice, Nutmeg & Cinnamon, Fruit & Spice, Spiced Apple, and Lemon teas. Like Twinings Spice Tea and Lemon Tea, they're all well made and—well—differently spicy: The indifferent tea doesn't matter. Some people drink them all the time and others just for a change of pace, but they're nothing to sneer at. Somewhere hereabouts, however, we have crossed the line into Flavored Teas and here my lip does begin to curl.

FLAVORED & DECAFFEINATED TEAS To the best of their knowledge, John Wagner & Sons was the first company in the United States to offer Flavored, Decaffeinated Teas and the first to sell Decaffeinated Tea in bags. Flavored Tea in this country goes back to 1944, when Ruth Campbell Bigelow introduced the first little black jars of Constant Comment on the national market. Shortly after World War II, Boston Tea came along with more Flavored Teas. Both brands survived but nobody paid their example much mind until the dawn of the 1970s. After a large investment of time and money, Wagners introduced their spice-flavored teas in the United States and something else happened in England.

London received a consignment of tea that had shared a ship's hold with a cargo of oranges. The results were predictable and the tea was sold at write-off prices, but to the amazement of the tea merchants their customers began pestering them for more. This set the director of a long-established London firm thinking, and in 1975, four years of experiments later, James Ashby & Sons introduced fruit-flavored teas to England. Apricot, Black Currant, Lemon, Lime, Orange, Peach, Pineapple, and Vanilla are numbered among the flavors in the Ashby Rose Brand line, which does include a Rose Tea whose flavor is reinforced with the petals of Bulgarian roses, the most aromatic perfumers use. These are now competing in this country with Flavored Teas from Liptons, Crosse & Blackwell, First Colony's Susan's Tea, and many newer entries. Big firms with big money are winning their bets in this market: One educated guesstimate credits Scented and/or Flavored teas with about two-thirds of specialty-tea sales. More than sixty-five varieties are currently available and it appears this number is limited only by the imaginations of the essential oil manufacturers.

The essences used may or may not be derived from the plant they're named for. The scenting-flavoring is often done with a spray gun, though Ashby uses a system whereby the tea is impregnated inside a prescented rotating drum. More sophisticated still are the methods probably employed in West Germany, where a sizable percentage of our Flavored Tea is produced in Hamburg by Halssen & Lyon, almost certainly the world's largest specialty tea brokers. Now a lover of fine tea cannot help reacting to these soda-pop teas the way a wine connoisseur would to a glass of Gallo Thunderbird. But the flavored wines of the 1950s were the precursors of the wine revolution of the '60s, which changed American drinking habits to the point that in 1980 we consumed more wine than spirits for the first time in our history. That Flavored Teas may do half as much on behalf of tea consciousness is the only good thing I can think to say for them. Let us pray.

The Halssen & Lyon aforementioned also produce virtually all the world's Decaffeinated Tea. I'm told methylene chloride is used as a wash to leach out the caffeine and that the redried tea retains only about five parts of the chemical per million—considerably less than naturally occurring contamination from dirt and insect fragments. Needless to add, there's no such thing as a "natural" Decaffeinated Tea, but then neither did God mean man to fly. Wagners avers that the caffeine level of their decaf Black Teas is considerably less than two-tenths of 1 percent, surely a negligible amount. They also claim that side-by-side comparisons reveal that decaffeination affects neither taste nor aroma. As one who craves his caffeine, I have yet to taste these miracles of technology, but clearly they have their place, if only to allow an M.F.K. Fisher the pleasure of drinking tea again.

BARKS, TONICS, DECOCTIONS, INFUSIONS, & TISANES

When I makes tea I makes tea as old mother Grogan said and when I makes water I makes water.

—*James Joyce (1882–1941)*
ULYSSES

Tea is the name for the plant *Camellia sinensis,* for the plucked and dried leaf it yields, and for the infusion made from that leaf—and none other. Since language cannot be legislated, "tea" has also been a slang term for marijuana and used occasionally as a substitute for the word "extract," as in "beef tea" for example. It bears repeating, however, that tea is the beverage made from the leaves of the tea plant and can no more come from any other plant than it can from the flesh of cattle. Tea is tea. An Herbal Infusion is something else entirely and properly speaking should not be called a "tea" at all. Just what to call one is the subject of ongoing negotiations between the Tea Council of the United States and the herbals industry, but in the light of progress to date we are entitled to ask: If herbal beverages are not teas, what are they?

In France herbal drinks, which are far more popular there than *thé*, are called *tisanes,* as good a word as any for them and one we might do well to ressurect in English. Tisane derives from Greek, via the Latin *ptisana,* and anciently referred to a drink made from husked barley that R. Gordon Wasson and other scholars consider the psychotropic secret behind the mysteries of Eleusis. Alternative names seem pedestrian in contrast. A decoction means anything that's boiled in contrast to an infusion, which is made by merely steeping the ingredients. Tinctures and elixirs are defined as extractions using or containing alcohol—that lets them out—and a tonic is any old pick-me-up. You can see why tisane gets my vote as the best word for herbal beverages.

Whatever name they go by, herbals are not to be taken lightly. Some, like Yerba Maté, contain more caffeine than coffee. Also, as Dr. R. K. Siegel of the University of California School of Medicine, Los Angeles, has written: "There are at least 396 herbs and spices available commercially for use in 'herb tea,' and some of them contain psycho-active substances capable of producing intoxicating effect." More specifically he found that "42 of these herbs contain mind-altering agents, although behavioural effects are not seen in short term use." In most instances, I'm sure, this is much ado about nothing. Decoctions have been made from the benign and flavorful bark of the sassafras for centuries and it's still available everywhere despite the federal government's having banned its use in 1960. It's no doubt true that staggering quantities of sassafras would do *something* to you—who knows what—but then what would not? On the other hand, brew up a beverage from mistletoe and it's a clinical certainty that you can kill erstwhile friends and lovers with it. Wolfbane works even quicker, but then with good luck or ill you're bound to find somebody deathly allergic to chamomile, too.

The history of herbs and spices is far more ancient than that of tea, even, and I touch on the matter not for toxicology's sake but to distinguish between tea, which is what it is, and everything else which, whatever it is, ain't tea.

TEA TIMES

What Is The Meaning Of This?

A COMMENTARY ON TEA WAYS & MEANS

. . . In short, her scandalous reputation
Has shocked the whole of the Hellish nation;
And every turbaned Chinoiserie,
With whom we should sip our black Bohea,
Would stretch out her simian fingers thin
To scratch you, my dears, like a mandolin;
For Hell is just as properly proper
As Greenwich, or as Bath, or Joppa!
                    —*Dame Edith Sitwell*
                    from FACADE

S WITNESS THE BATTLE OF WATERLOO, tea is demonstrably good for the spirits and the brain. It is well known that Napoleon was a great lover of Burgundy and never went into battle without a bottle of the greatest, Le Chambertin, in his saddlebags. Barely noted but nonetheless the fact is it that Wellington drank only tea. Tea cleared his head and left him, so he told his generals at Waterloo, "with no misapprehensions." Battlefield tea must be the only kind accompanied by no ceremony whatever. Of tea off the battlefield, one might think Horace's most quoted line had been amended to read

Dulce et decorum est pro forma to fix tea.

Tea is fixed pro forma not just because tea calls for ceremony, which it may, but also because good tea demands and deserves it. Only on the battlefield is there need for haste. Tea doesn't have a flavor so much as it produces an effect and it takes a quiet palate to appreciate it. I think this is why people all over the world take their time in making tea, as if to acknowledge that making it is part of drinking it and drinking it represents a refuge, a moment's respite, from the demands of our lives. Wine and coffee are tea's only rivals when it comes to drinks meant to stimulate and accompany conversation, but ceremonial has never been associated with either one to the same extent as with tea. Indeed, unlike wine or coffee, tea itself is oftentimes much less important than the ceremony surrounding it or, as that English humorist once put it, "The trouble with tea is that originally it was quite a good drink."

I think the Japanese tea ceremony is a good example of what he means. I say "I think" because life is too short to attend enough Japanese tea ceremonies to form an intelligent opinion of them. One's first impression is of tediousness in the extreme and the second and third impressions confirm this—Tedious, Tedious, Tedious. In addition, the frothy pea soup of a tea that's served resembles nothing unmedicinal I've ever tasted: Simply Ghastly. Let others become tea masters if they must as long as when I meet them we drink wine. If my account of the Japanese tea ceremony has not been sympathetic, it has at least been mercifully briefer. It is, to be sure, an interesting topic in the abstract and in the bibliography I have listed the best books I found on it.

I fear my interest in other tea etiquettes is equally academic. The call of the eskimo housewife to announce tea time in Greenland and the bunch of bananas Sri Lankans hang over their tea-house doors are alike matters of indifference to me. Yet nowhere in my study did I discover tea customs more bizarre than those prescribed for previous generations by Emily (Mrs. Price) Post. One of Mrs. Post's favorite subjects is the tea dance, for instance—from her description a likely opportunity to meet young men with no pressing need to earn a living. Suppose your hostess has arranged for two of her friends to "pour" and as a non-tea drinker you go up to the one pouring chocolate.

> It is merest good manners on her part to make a few pleasant remarks. Very likely when asked for chocolate she says, "How nice of you! I have been feeling very neglected at my end. Everyone seems to prefer tea." Whereupon the guest ventures that people are afraid of chocolate because it is so fattening or so hot. After an observation or two about the weather, or the beauty of the china or how good the little cakes look, or sandwiches taste, the guest finishes the chocolate.

Apparently *all* of Ionesco's characters studied under Mrs. Post at one tea or another.

Tea Sick Ladies, a comedy performed and published at Amsterdam in 1701, is the earliest satire on this sort of thing I've discovered. The glossy, green hypocrisy of overly rehearsed "manners" makes me feel like Cushat-Prinkly, the hero of "Tea," one of Saki's more ironic tales:

> Thousands of women, at this solemn afternoon hour, were sitting behind dainty porcelain and silver fittings, with their voices tinkling pleasantly in a cascade of solicitous little questions. Cushat-Prinkly detested the whole system of afternoon tea. According to his theory of life a woman should lie down on a divan or couch, talking with incomparable charm or looking unutterable thoughts, or merely silent as a thing to be looked on, and from behind a silken curtain a small Nubian page should silently bring in a tray with cups and dainties, to be accepted silently, as a matter of course, without drawn-out chatter about cream and sugar and hot water. . . .

The nearest I've come to realizing this ideal tea is reading about those characters of Proust's who haunt the Rumpelmayer's *salon de thé* on the rue de Rivoli in Paris. It is still there, by the way, under the name of Angelina now but still filled with *le beau monde* of Paris. The *grande dame* of Parisian tea shops, however, is Pons, established in 1865. It overlooks the Luxembourg Gardens and serves chocolate candied chestnuts (also called Pons I think) with your tea. Tea has always had a certain following among

Duke of Wellington

prosperous French (and homesick English) in Paris and other French cities. These tearooms probably account for a good deal of the few ounces of tea France consumes per capita each year. Since 1848 about the only tea available to the French populace at large has been that imported by La Compagnie Coloniale. In one of her famous letters, however, Madame de Sévigné (1626–96) was already referring to *thé de cinq heures* about the same time Charles II and Catherine of Braganza—during whose reign forks also came into general use for the first time in England—set about introducing the English aristocracy to their first tea.

Afternoon tea, which Anna the Duchess of Bedford is credited with inventing in England over a century after Mme. de Sévigné mentions it in France, rapidly became *the* characteristic British institution. If "invented" is too strong, Anna at least may be said to have appointed the hour and ordained the snack format for the occasion we now know as "low tea." The "high tea" or "meat tea" of the less exalted classes was less of a social occasion and more like a proper supper, sometimes with dishes specially invented for tea time—Welsh rarebit, for instance, or Bakewell tart, a cross between cake and pudding. I have spent very little time in England, but the high teas I've read about featured things with names like treacle, Scotch woodcock, plum pudding, kidneys, kippers, bangers, rashers, shepherd's pie, and syllabubs. The kind of food more likely to be eaten at low tea includes savories like marrow or mushrooms on toast points or finger sandwiches of cucumber and watercress, things you can never get enough of! One presumably "correct" way to serve tea is that described by Charles Oliver in *Dinner at Buckingham Palace*:

> The ritual of the English tea-time was brought to perfection by the late Queen Mary, for whom it was the favorite time of day. Everything had to be fully ready by 4 P.M. punctually, with sandwiches, cakes and biscuits invitingly set out on gleaming silver dishes upon a smoothly-running trolley. The teapot, cream jug, hot-water jug and sugar bowl were always the same antique silver service which had been a favorite of Queen Victoria. . . . [Later] Queen Mary would take over and meticulously measure out her favorite Indian tea* from a jade tea-caddy she kept locked in a cupboard.

---

*Apparently this was the Queen Mary Tea Twinings sells as "the personal choice of the late Queen Mary." It is a fine Darjeeling with a pronounced muscatel flavor.

Then she would pour on the boiling water and complete the tea-making ritual by snuffing out the spirit stove before sitting back for the footmen to pour tea and hand round sandwiches and cakes. But before Queen Mary gave the signal for this to begin she would always let exactly three minutes elapse from the moment she poured hot water on the tea leaves so that the tea would be perfectly brewed.

As Queen Mary clearly understood, the thing of first importance at any tea time is to make your tea in the right and proper way—enjoyment is sure to follow.

Just when one thinks every possible device for preparing tea has been invented, another comes on the market. Most belong in the same category as the teapot Mrs. Sarah Guppy patented in 1812, with a wire basket in it for boiling eggs. People before and since have applied themselves to the task of complicating the making of tea, but it was left to our own generation to come up with the one accessory that really does simplify procedure and produces a better pot or cup in the bargain. This miracle of rare device is the stainless-steel wire-mesh tea ball. Please note that I said "stainless-steel wire-mesh"—I do not mean the perforated aluminum tea infuser with its too few holes and unhappily metallic taint. Buy the largest tea ball you can get into your pot; in fact, since they seem to have the lifespan of your average light bulb, it's a good idea to buy several at a time. Use two per pot if necessary, but avoid filling the ball more than roughly half-a-hemisphere full. This gives the leaf inside sufficient room to expand in the water. Remove the ball when the tea has brewed long enough and drink the tea at your leisure—you don't have to worry that your last cup has steeped five times as long as your first. Neither are you hassled with rinsing your pot to death to get all the old leaves out—simply empty the ball.

The only variable you have to take into account in fixing good tea is the size of the leaf. The larger the leaf, the longer you must steep it; the smaller the leaf, the more surface it exposes to the water and the more quickly the goodness is drawn out of it. Dust, which is only used in tea bags and is the very smallest grade of leaf, yields an infusion almost instantly. Being so fine, Dust also releases virtually all the tea's tannin if you let the tea bag steep much more than half a minute, and the result, as we all know, can be undrinkably harsh and astringent. For reasons chemical and otherwise, tea bags rarely give a really satisfactory brew in any case. Brewing good tea takes longer—two to three minutes for the flaky small grades and five to seven for the twisted larger grades. You simply cannot brew a pot of proper Oolong in no more time than a BOP Ceylon requires, this is to say, because the heart of the larger leaf is less exposed and needs to soak longer. Experiments along the lines I've indicated will show you the optimum steeping times for the teas you use. If you observe this one rule, the rest amounts to directions: Start with fresh, cold water and bring it to a bubbling boil; warm the teapot well by rinsing it out with the hot water; pour the boiling water over the desired amount of tea, preferably enclosed in a tea ball or two; let steep for the right length of time; remove the tea ball(s); and voilà—that's that!

This procedure is certain to get the most out of the tea you use and it is equally certain that neglecting it yields inferior brew. As to the little matter of the desired amount of tea, "one teaspoonful per cup and one for the pot" is not graven on stone anywhere outside the tea companies' prescriptions. I have just returned from making some measurements. I find that our teapot holds slightly over a quart or approximately as much as seven of our cups. The eight level teaspoonfuls of tea that conventional wisdom calls for is almost twice the amount I actually use per pot! It always has been my firm conviction that good tea goes further. Nobody needs to tell you how much to use either—just beware of a Deadly Underdose. If it's on the strong side you can always add a little hot water a lot more easily than you can coax more life out of a used tea ball. Oversteeping will not turn Green or Oolong bitter the way it does Black Tea. Tea men call it "stewed" or "stewy" tasting once the liquor has overstayed its welcome on the leaves, a thing to be most diligently guarded against. On the other hand, of course, who's to say we always want our tea full strength? What's too weak? The Orientals who drink it day-long prefer it "no more than water bewitched."

When it comes to preparing tea for a crowd, the thing to do is make a concentrate. A recipe good for around two dozen cups is two-thirds of a cup of dry tea and one quart of boiling water. Steep five minutes, stir, strain liquor off leaves into a teapot, and use within a couple hours. Add boiling water to about two tablespoons of concentrate per cup to serve. This is the principle of the samovar. I used to think they were giant teapots until, for a price too scandalously low to record, I actually acquired one from a fellow undergraduate at Chapel Hill. It was a multipiece brass contraption that was a combination teapot and hot-water heater and had a capacity of forty-odd cups. It was a chimney through the middle of a boiler, basically, and the apparatus was so efficient it would boil that vesselful in about twenty minutes if you weren't looking. This was from the time you half-filled the chimney with charcoal and got it glowing by adding an extra length of stove pipe for additional draw. Once the water boiled, you brewed your tea to Goliath strength and—taking care not to burn your fingers—you removed the extra length of chimney and replaced it with the teapot where it was supposed to sit and stay hot. You'd now be in business, diluting your concentrate in the direction of drinkability with hot water from the little tap. You'd need more water and charcoal every couple hours, but it's far and away the most convenient means I've found yet to keep tea hot and ready at hand for yourself and/or a horde of comrades—Mother Russia's own gift! If you've ever owned a samovar you would share in the regret I felt on discovering this sentence in the September 1980 *Tea & Coffee Trade Journal:* "Tea is regarded as a prestigious beverage in the Soviet Union, and people who can afford such an expensive item are considered aristocrats." Alas for the people of the samovar! It is sad to think these handsome urns steam no longer in the land where they were invented.

I have no opinion, really, on the tea topics little old ladies of both sexes debate: Whether 'tis better the milk precede the tea into the cup or vice versa, that sort of thing. Tea professionals discuss the very real differences the water makes to the tea, but in these first decades of worldwide acid rain I think it would be ludicrous to pursue the differences between hard water and soft—just don't boil the hell out of it. Once you've boiled all the air out of the water you use, the tea you make with it tastes flat, and neither underboiled nor overboiled water produces a full extraction. (This is the reason the Japanese always add extra tea leaves when they use very hot, instead of boiling, water to brew their most delicate Green Teas.) Earthenware seems to hold heat best, but any sort of teapot will do. About the only other thing is, don't add sugar unless you want your tea sweet. I usually agree with Henry Fielding's *Tom Jones* that "love and scandal are the best sweeteners of tea" but the proper thing in all such matters is to suit yourself.

A large part of the pleasure tea affords is that it gets you high, as M.F.K. Fisher knows. It is a high so gentle that we seldom notice either lift or letdown, yet it is for the sake of this high that the drink has been developed and constantly refined by generations of tea lovers over the centuries. Tea increases mental alertness and agility,

Georgian
Victorian

brightens the spirits, sharpens sensations, and enhances intellectual discrimination. I believe it is the most benign stimulation of the nervous system possible. Tea's effects were never better described than by William Gladstone, Disraeli's great rival whom Queen Victoria despised so and who only once ever said anything in Parliament that she approved of—his challenge that he consumed more tea between the hours of midnight and four than any two other men in the House (by way of saying none worked longer hours). Anyway, on this or some other occasion Gladstone is recorded to have said of tea: "If you are cold, tea will warm you; if you are heated it will cool you; if you are depressed it will cheer you; if you are excited it will calm you." The tea high can take any of these forms, so subtle and variable is it.

The color of tea tells you nothing about how strong or weak it is. Tea's active ingredients are caffeine in combination with the tannin that gives it its pungency and much of its aroma and flavor (which essential oils also enhance). Tea tannin is not the same as tannic acid and does not have the same properties, by the way, but what matters is the effect these ingredients have on us. In 1955, the New York Academy of Medicine held a symposium on "Pharmacological and Physiological Effects of Tea" and confirmed what tea lovers have claimed since Lu Yu's day. These eminent scientists found that the peculiar combination of caffeine and tannin in a cup of tea is a happy one: For reasons they could not explain, tea, unlike coffee, does not cause nervousness, insomnia, or stomach irritation when drunk in quantity. Their tests showed a cup of tea gives both an immediate and a delayed lift without secondary depressing effects later on. They agreed tea is as good an agent for relieving fatigue as we've found and that it aids clearness of thought and digestion alike.

The doctors were so intent on medically describing the feeling of well-being tea gives mind and body that they never once mention tea also tastes good. Mostly they analyzed the caffeine question. A pound of tea contains more caffeine by weight than a pound of coffee. That pound of coffee is good for about forty cups, however, compared to the two hundred cups and more you can easily make from a pound of tea. A cup of tea may be said to hold rather less than half as much caffeine as the same amount of coffee therefore: roughly three-quarters versus one and half grains, or forty-eight versus ninety-six milligrams. The medical dosage is two hundred milligrams of caffeine for drowsiness, fatigue, etc. It's worth noting that this comparison was made using Black

Tea, which has approximately three times as much caffeine as Green Tea and half again as much as Oolong. This has obviously brought us to the subject of tea selection.

Tea is a mood drink. If it's rainy you like one kind and if it's sunny you prefer a different one. You want different teas with different foods or at different times— perhaps strong Black Tea at breakfast and delicate Green Teas at night, for instance. The tea you want depends on how you feel and for this if for no other reason you need to keep a number at hand. A couple dozen is not excessive. Once you get used to having a range of different teas to turn to, you even begin traveling with your favorites in your luggage so you never have to do without. Also, it's neat having a pantry shelf full of teas to play with: It's endlessly intriguing to invent new tastes by blending your teas together. I have, to illustrate, just recently created a Green Tea of great beauty by wedding my doggy China tea, The Well Known Tea of Zhejiang, to a Japanese Spiderleg—Incredible Stuff! I've known for a long time now that a strong dash of Darjeeling makes my breakfast Keemun fairly sparkle and have many other examples— the number of blends possible is probably infinite. Finally, then, the more teas you buy and try and allow yourself to know the more favorites you gradually acquire. Fine tea is the least costly of all the world's great luxuries, don't forget—only water is cheaper to drink and not even that when bottled. When it comes to your favorite teas therefore, you will naturally want the best examples procurable. A man can keep himself in elegant teas more cheaply than he can smoke cigarettes, but with tea the trick is getting what you pay for.

Tea is an orphan product, a sideline of coffee roasters and specialty food shops that rarely makes up more than 10 percent of their total sales. This is part of the reason most tea dealers are only slightly less ignorant than their customers where tea is concerned. (At least one other reason tea merchants and consumers remain so ignorant of tea and its delights is a nigh-total lack of readable and reliable writing on the subject.) Tea companies continue to make innocent misstatements of fact in their literature, meanwhile, and many a tea dealer can't even tell if his tea goes stale and certainly wouldn't know, for example, whether his Darjeeling is average or superior. With sound advice hard to come by, you have to figure things out for yourself.

You'll find any number of teas packed by British firms that are not worth the asking price, at least by the time they get to these shores. I have heard it estimated that many's the one that's been a year or two in the can by the time you buy it, and the curious fact is that tea dries out and grows stale in small tins more quickly than in large chests and such. Thus it's always the ideal to buy from your dealer's bins and put your tea in tins of your own on your pantry shelves. *Keep your tea airtight and protected from the light.* Bristolware, the tins I like best, satisfy these essentials and look handsome, too. But come by your tea as you will, the thing is to make comparisons and observe and enjoy. The world drinks more tea than anything else except water, and yet gourmet teas are among the few goods our supermarkets do *not* carry in the United States. How then do you shop for tea?

With ease and excellence as my two main criteria, I think I'd recommend ordering teas by mail, two at a time, to compare with what's available locally. Eventually you'll know whether your dealer can equal the Grace Rare Tea Formosa Oolong Supreme or MTW Keemun or the First Colony deluxe Gunpowder or what you will. It's even interesting to find out what teas you don't like—and you'll easily find somebody who would enjoy the gift. Before you know it you'll find yourself as shameless as any other hardened tea lover about the peculiarities of your taste. You will have become a member of that tiny minority in the Western world, the happy few to whom tea is not simply a staple, like salt or oatmeal, but also a delight—a trip—even a revelation now and then! ❧

TEA TRADE

Whose Business Is It Anyway?

A MISCELLANY OF CURIOUS LORE

Banking is business, oil is industry, tea and coffee are trades, but the tea trade in particular has always had a special aristocratic position in the world of buying and selling.
—Edward Bramah
TEA & COFFEE

HE FORSYTES of John Galsworthy's *The Forsyte Saga* founded a large part of their family fortune on tea. Those who have read the book or seen the TV series will remember old Jolyon did so well in Mincing Lane that he maintained a large house in Stanhope Gate, Park Lane, and died leaving one hundred forty-five thousand pounds. It's doubtful if any independent tea broker in the world could amass the modern equivalent to such a fortune in the international tea trade today. Before World War II only about ten countries in the world produced tea as a cash crop; today there are almost forty. It was a far different trade in those old days.

Because of the great quantity and variety they used to handle, the thrice-weekly London auctions virtually set the world price for all teas. Even when a consuming country like Canada, Australia, or the United States bought directly from a producing country, London set the price it would pay. Except for the few sales privately arranged between tea importers and the most prestigious tea estates, tea is still sold at auction, like tobacco, but most* of what we drink today is traded not at London but at a dozen or more nerve centers of the international tea trade around the world: Calcutta and Cochin in India, Colombo and Trincomalee in Sri Lanka, Djakarta and Medan in Indonesia, Nairobi and Mombasa in Kenya, Singapore, Yokohama, and elsewhere. The only European cities that conduct tea auctions are Hamburg, Amsterdam, and London.

The procedure at all auctions is generally the same. A hole is bored in each chest† and a sample removed for tasting by the bidders. These must be astute men—few if any women are involved in the trade—who are familiar with the district and garden each tea comes from, how each is made, and what characteristics to look for or defects to look out for. They must have a place in mind for each tea in a preexisting blend or have a special buyer looking for exceptional lots of a certain quality; in addition they must know what each tea is worth just then on the world market. Everybody knows all he needs to about

---

*Taiwan teas are handled by brokers, while all the tea in mainland China is controlled by the China Native Produce & Animal By-Products Import & Export Corporation.

---

† Chests are made of plywood and lined with tin or aluminum foil to keep moisture out. They weigh from 80 to 130 pounds, depending on the country of origin, and smaller "half chests" hold 50 to 90.

the teas by the time they come to auction, where the buying broker frequently acts for a number of buyers, a practice that keeps the actual purchaser a secret. The auctions proceed quickly and quietly and outsiders find them difficult to follow. Each lot, usually thirty or forty chests, is succinctly and unemotionally described. (The better the tea, the smaller the lot, and vice versa; extraordinary teas may be sold in lots of five or fewer chests.) The bidding itself usually takes only about twenty seconds per lot, and the tea is on its way to the consumer.

Sometimes a lot of tea is bought by agents for a major packing and marketing company like Brooke Bond, Liptons, or Twinings to be a constituent part of one of their blends. Sometimes the buyer is not a tea packer at all but simply a tea importer. The tea importer distributes standards to buying brokers at the various auctions, standards that represent what quality teas he's seeking from each. The buying brokers keep the importer informed as to when tea equivalent to one or another of his standards is available and what it's likely to go for at auction. The importer will telex as to how much, if any, he needs of which and the most he's prepared to pay. Sometimes the importer is simply buying for others (and to the standards of others) who lack his good connections in certain markets. In this case the United States importer charges a 3 percent commission and directs that the tea be shipped direct to his client-buyer. If he finances the transaction and takes delivery himself he charges a flat fee over and above the purchase price. His margins are slim at best.

The importer, of course, competes for orders from tea firms within his own country. There are five or six who have standards for each Wagners tea, for example, and keep that company abreast of supply and price in each category. When Wagners decides to buy one hundred or so chests of a certain standard Darjeeling, therefore, they can count on receiving samples from at least three or four of the importers they've engaged. The Wagners tea consultant, for many years now Mr. Herman Preston, will select the one he thinks best or alternatively enough of each to blend into the desired quality and the company orders accordingly. A little of the finest quality of any tea goes a long way in most blends, but tea being an agricultural commodity and one with far wider quality variations from year to year than most, Wagners will need sometimes more and sometimes less of any given standard of Darjeeling to maintain the overall consistency of its blend. As with vintages of wine, the quality of a given flush is wholly dependent on the weather and other unpredictables. Poor would be a charitable description of the 1981 first flush Darjeeling, for example; you can imagine the juggling of standards Wagners went through to keep their Darjeeling up to par that year. Supermarket quality teas seem to constitute the bread and butter for everybody concerned, to be sure, but the buying brokers and importers keep their eyes open for the small lot, gourmet-quality teas that specialty dealers can be relied upon to buy no matter what the cost and regardless of the major tea packers' interest in them at the time.

As you will have gathered, except for a certain few in fine merchants' bins, virtually all teas are blends, those of gourmet quality included. Were tea sold direct from the estate factory to the household we'd sometimes get a superlative brew—as Robert Fortune did on the summit of a Bohea hill—and other times a most indifferent one. There are well over six thousand tea estates outside of China. Even if their produce were sold strictly according to country or district, you'd still notice sizeable differences from one batch to the next, for no two seasons or pluckings are exactly alike, *even from the same tea bush*. But the fact is, if you've bought a given type under a particular brand name before, you know exactly what you're getting when you go back to buy that same tea again. This bit of wizardry is the work of the tea blender.

Tea packers do not buy a lot of tea to resell it as is, but to be a constituent part of one of their blends. Each blend must be consistent as to appearance, taste, body, color, aroma, and strength. The blender accomplishes this by juggling anywhere from fifteen to thirty teas from perhaps four or five different countries. He must also make sure the larger and smaller grades are evened out to fit his company's standard package and that the average price per unit of this blend remains the same. It's said that it takes seven years to master the arts of tea tasting and tea blending, mainly because it's only possible to note the seasonal variations in each tea as and when it becomes available.

Tasting is largely a matter of comparison, and in tasting a number of teas together it's essential for each one to be brewed exactly the same way—equal weights of tea, equal quantities of freshly boiled water, equal time for brewing, equal size and style of pot and bowl. The professional tea-tasting pot rather ressembles a coffee mug with a lid that's serrated on one side. The teas are allowed to brew for either five or six minutes exactly and the pots with the lids still in place are tipped over the bowls so that the liquid drains off through the serrations and the infused leaf can then be tipped onto the reverse side of the lids, which are then replaced atop the pots. Now the taster has the liquor in the bowl, the infused leaf on the lid, and a sample of the dry leaf to examine at the same time. He smells the infused leaf and compares its color and appearance with the dry. Then he quickly slurps a spoonful of the tea onto the taste buds at the back of his tongue and after a second or two, in which time his palate has completely registered the tea, he spits it out into a spittoon.

Tasters always work with assistants. The taste of a tea cannot be photographed or tape recorded, but a taster will remember it for years with complete accuracy. Having a second trained palate to record it is the only way to make a carbon copy. Once each tea is precisely evaluated in this way, the taster-blender contrives the proportionate combination of teas that exactly duplicates the standard for the blend he's working on.

In the old days tea was sold from open chests and blended either by the tea grocer or the customer himself. One of the present volume's earliest ancestors was published in 1785 under the awesome title *The Tea Purchaser's Guide to the Lady and Gentleman's Tea Table: Useful Companion in the Knowledge and Choice of Teas. To Which is added the Art of mixing one Quality with Another as Practiced by A Tea Dealer.* But old-time tea dealers were no more alike than types of tea. Some of them were scrupulously honest, like one Maria Tewk, a woman living in the north of England who set herself up as a tea merchant in 1725. Denied a license to trade and fined for doing so without one, she paid the fine and went on doing business. The John Company and the officers of the Crown had so much trouble from her that she was finally granted her license and founded a firm of such repute it remained in her family for seven generations. But in the absence of Tewklike integrity, selling from the open chest was wide open to abuses. These had become so endemic by 1826 that another tea merchant, John Horniman, was able to found his fortune on the sale of packages guaranteed to contain a certain net weight of unadulterated tea *of a certain quality*. And the blender has been essential to the trade ever since.

We in the United States are protected against really bad tea by the Food and Drug Administration's tea examiners, who test all our tea shipments before clearing them for entry into the country. This system is the result of the oldest consumer-protection law on the national books and perhaps the only one ever enacted at the request of the industry involved. Though really designed to protect the trade against having to accept shipments of adulterated or worthless tea, the Tea Act of 1897 has spared American consumers countless tons of unsound or substandard teas over the years since. During the Depression the packers and importers volunteered to pay inspection fees rather than see the program discontinued and they continue to pay them today, to the tune of three and a half cents per hundred pounds of tea.

The examination consists of trying each tea against the standards set for each type by the seven members of the United States Board of Tea Experts appointed by the FDA commissioner. Since these are minimum standards, the tea examiners' only concern with quality is the negative one of judging when a tea is too bad to enter the United States market. Richard Nixon decided to eliminate the board in 1970 as part of an economy drive. (Board members receive a lordly fifty dollars per year.) It took Chief Tea Examiner Robert H. Dick only a month to get the mess straightened out and return to his kettles. "What they didn't understand," he explains, "is that the Tea Board was created by the Tea Act of 1897 and Congress would have to amend or repeal the Tea Act to do away with us." No Board, no standards, no tea. Nixon hastily reversed himself.

If the three-hundred-fifty-dollar-a-year Tea Board has been retained, Reaganomic cutbacks have reduced the examiners themselves to two in number, Mr. Dick in New York and his colleague James Barnett in New Orleans. Every tea packer and importer in the land submits samples of his latest tea shipments to them. Mr. Dick is sixty-eight years old as of this writing, but he and Mr. Barnett are expected to slurp their way through the one hundred eighty to two hundred million pounds of tea the United States imports each year: perhaps another pennywise, pound-foolish decision.

"The supermarket shopper, in selecting his box of tea bags, is forced to choose between the mediocre and the vile" wrote the tea merchants Schapira in their 1975 guide, *The Book of Coffee & Tea.* Mr. William MacMelville, a leading American tea professional for over forty-five years, objects. He points out that Tetleys, for instance, has steadily improved the quality of its tea bags over recent years and that Liptons, with over 50 percent of the market long since, has never allowed its quality to decline; he says there are other examples also. Just because a tea does not proclaim itself gourmet quality doesn't mean it has to be bad, he points out. All these are points well taken, but none alter the fact that tea has come down in this world. I have just returned from a respectable restaurant that served me, so they thought, a respectable tea after dinner—

an Orange Pekoe & Pekoe Cut Black Tea tea bag packed by MJB. By the time it had steeped less than one minute it was undrinkably harsh. The most popular tea bag in the Near and Middle East, I'm told, is Sunflower Brand packed in Calcutta by Madhu Jayanti Private, Ltd. It would be too painful to belabor the difference between what the lowliest Iraqi can take for granted and the best that I can expect. Perhaps this is a case where, as the poet Gary Snyder says,

> Men like that
> Ought to stick to making money.

America's six-hundred-odd wholesale tea distributors handle between one hundred eighty and two hundred million pounds of tea a year. We enjoy governmental assurance that none of it is of the very worst quality; the challenge is to identify that fraction of it which is of the best.

A DIRECTORY OF TEA FIRMS

We had a kettle; we let it leak;
Our not repairing it made it worse.
We haven't had any tea for a week . . .
The bottom is out of the Universe!
—*Rudyard Kipling (1865–1936)*
NATURAL THEOLOGY

UNITED STATES TEA BRANDS

According to a list sent me by the Tea Council of the United States, Tetley and Brooke Bond are the only British firms that also rank among leading tea packers in this country. Thomas J. Lipton, Inc., which is generally believed to have over 50 percent of the United States market, has always been a separate company from its sister firm in England. Nestlé, a Swiss-based firm that sells only tea "mixes" and instants, is considered the second largest tea importer and packer in this country, and Tetleys is third. Other leading packers are the Kellogg Company (Salada), McCormick & Company, and Nabisco, which now owns Standard Brands and its Tenderleaf Tea. Also on the list are Boston Tea, with its line of Flavored Teas, and R. C. Bigelow, a family-owned firm that originated in the late 1930s when Ruth Campbell Bigelow began packing her Constant Comment at home. It is interesting that this list no longer includes the formerly big name Great Atlantic and Pacific Tea Company—

the A&P chain. There is nothing else sufficiently interesting, however, about any of these mass-market teas to detain us. Not all of them are contemptible—some are beneath contempt—but few attain mediocrity. Wagners is the only real specialty tea firm on the list.

JOHN WAGNER & SONS, founded in 1847, has been deeply rooted in the social fabric of the elderly and aristocratic city of Philadelphia for over one hundred thirty-five years, catering to epicurean tastes for wine, cigars, spices, condiments, and tea. It's only within recent decades that the firm abandoned its original shop on Dock Street with its twenty-three moose, elk, deer, and mountain goat heads mounted on the walls and its practice of billing customers only in January and July. When John Wagner, Jr.—locally beloved as "Johnny Wag"—succeeded his father in the firm he also inherited his position as quartermaster of the socialite First Troop, Philadelphia City Cavalry, a swanky mounted militia that antedates the Revolution. This military duty involved nothing more strenuous than a keen appreciation of fine vintages and the position was handed down in the firm until Prohibition put Wagners out of the wine and spirits business.

The government took no note of Wagners tea business, however, until the World War II–era Office of Price Administration required merchants to make out estimates of prospective sales of all goods. The OPA inspectors deemed the volume of Wagners' tea sales downright un-American and descended on the shop in the conviction that nobody excepting possibly restaurants and hotels bought five and ten pounds of tea at a time. Johnny Wag's son and heir was obliged to fish out yellowing accounts going back to the 1840s to prove that some of America's first families have always done just that; the bemused bureaucrats went away. The introduction of Lapsang Souchong in America is credited to one of these early customers, by the way—a Mr. Borie. He'd been sent some by a cousin then living in China; soon he found himself so besieged by friends who loved its smoky flavor that, in order to protect his own supply, he begged John Wagner to bring some in on the next clipper.

Wagner did and today Lapsang Souchong—a surprisingly good one—is among the twenty-six teas Wagners markets coast to coast under the guidance of its president, Ralph Starr, who joined the company in 1950. Although the company continues to sell spices, preserves, and other specialty foods, Mr. Starr has seen to it that Wagners is nationally known for its extensive line of teas. Besides packaging his teas attractively and going national with them, Mr. Starr's innovations extend to the introduction of Flavored and Decaffeinated teas and he has made his firm the country's leading supplier of tea gift packs.

Wagners does no consumer advertising and does not sell through supermarkets, but rather through gourmet and gift shops and department stores. All the same, there must be several million Americans like myself whose first taste of gourmet tea came out of a Wagners' tin.

FIRST COLONY is the only American firm besides Wagners to enjoy significant nationwide distribution of its specialty teas. It is a new-old company, tracing its roots to a nineteenth-century Scotsman who apprenticed himself to the tea trade in London in 1877. Having emigrated to Virginia, he established the James G. Gill Company in Norfolk in 1902; Gill's Hotel Special Coffee Blend is still a byword for quality in the Virginia-Carolinas region.

In 1977, Mr. Gill's descendants established First Colony Coffee & Tea Company as an independent offshoot, with headquarters in Norfolk and San Francisco. Their coffees are the most expensive in the land and widely considered the best, but tea represents the fastest-growing segment of the business. Company president Gill Brockenbrough, Jr. claims First Colony maintains the widest stock of fine China teas held in warehouse in the United States. Mr. Brockenbrough is particularly impressed with China's quality control: "They are the only teas I can reorder by lot number and know that they will never vary from the standard originally submitted for tasting," he told me. "All the other teas I buy I must sample again and again, year after year." Bowing to the demands of the market, First Colony has recently introduced a line of nine flavored varieties called Susan's Tea. On the other hand, the company steadfastly continues to market its Queen's Blend Tea, a Southern favorite that Mr. Brockenbrough's great-grandfather originated and named in honor of Queen Victoria.

UNITED STATES TEA IMPORTERS

Most of First Colony's business comes from supplying teas in bulk to retail merchants. Very few such middleman companies are known by name to the consumer, but they are crucially important to him all the same. Thanks to the complexity of the international tea trade, direct importing is simply out of the question for a retail dealer. He has to obtain his tea from first-line importers or through brokers in the world's tea centers who are willing to add some chests of the desired teas to the volume shipments that make up the vast majority of the business. Comparatively few retailers who sell loose tea "cup-sample" their wares and fewer still

are competent to do so. The quality and consistency of any given merchant's teas, therefore, depends as much on the shop's suppliers as it does on the shop itself. For whatever it's worth, here is a list of a few such suppliers that I know to be quality conscious in the extreme.

COUNTRY SPICE TEA COMPANY
Portland, Oregon

CHINA PRODUCTS NORTHWEST
Seattle, Washington

O. H. CLAPP & COMPANY
Westport, Connecticut

DOUWE EGBERTS SUPERIOR COMPANY
Bensenville, Illinois
(United States branch of Holland's leading tea company)

EAST HORIZON IMPORT CORPORATION
New York City and Los Angeles
(Handles only top-quality teas)

FORMOST-FRIEDMAN, INC.
New York City
(Tea importers and blending specialists for numerous private labels)

HALSSEN & LYON
Hamburg, West Germany
(Largest specialty tea firm in the world and supplier for certain United States dealers)

G. S. HALY COMPANY
San Carlos, California
(Chiefly Ceylon, India, and Formosa teas)

STARBUCKS COFFEE & TEA
Seattle, Washington

TIFFINY GOURMET COFFEE
Mt. Vernon, New York

YAMAMOTO OF THE ORIENT
Los Angeles
(Chiefly Japanese and Formosa teas)

GOURMET TEAS BY MAIL

O. H. CLAPP & COMPANY, INC.
47 Riverside Drive
Westport, Connecticut 06880

This is the mail-order department of a major United States tea importer, but despite an occasional advertisement in the *New York Times Magazine*'s Shopping Mart, they supply very little information about themselves. Besides their Vintage Teas they sell assorted tea infusers and a three-piece white porcelain professional tea taster's set. The six teas are much above average quality and are available by the half pound or in a six-tea sampler chest. All are attractively packaged in wooden chests.

TEAS: China Keemun, Darjeeling, China Jasmine, Rose Congou, Formosa Oolong, China Yunnan.

GRACE TEA COMPANY
80 Fifth Avenue
New York, New York 10011

"We sell only loose tea and that only by the half pound," says Grace president Richard Sanders, "probably the worst possible approach to 'marketing' tea in this country. But we succeed in selling this way because our customers would probably order our particular teas even if they were FOB Alaska." Mr. Sanders took over Grace in 1979, from his Harvard classmate Frank Cho, a tea importer and past co-chairman of the United States Board of Tea Experts who continues to oversee quality control for the company. Mr. Cho founded Grace in 1962 with the intention of selling "simply the best tea in America," some of which is made specifically for Grace in Taiwan and elsewhere. The seven Grace teas are all extraordinary and packaged in elegant black tins.

TEAS: Superb Darjeeling 6000, Winey Keemun, Lapsang Souchong Smoky No. 1, Grace Connoisseur Blend, The Original Earl Grey Mixture, Formosa Oolong Supreme, Before the Rain Jasmine.

SARUM TEAS
White Hart Inn, Village Green
Salisbury, Connecticut 06068

After forty-odd years as a professional tea man in London and New York City, Mr. Stanley Mason retired with his wife to Salisbury, Connecticut, only to discover that he couldn't shake the tea trade. He started a minuscule tea company of his own under the name of Sarum, the old Roman name of Salisbury, England, to represent, as he explained, "joint tribute to my native land and the Connecticut village of my choice." Dear Mr. Mason, full of years, died in 1981, filled also no doubt with amazement that the business he had begun in his living room was by then selling some six thousand pounds of tea a year. This makes it one of the smallest operations I've ever heard of, to be sure, but while Sarum Tea would merit mention if only as an elderly tea man's hobby, it is also more than that.

"Mr. Mason taught me how to produce a quality tea," says his successor John Harney, quality having been Mr. Mason's sole concern after all. "It took me years to talk Stanley into selling a spiced tea," Mr. Harney says. "He thought I was prostituting the damned stuff." John Harney has inherited all of Mr. Mason's extensive contacts in the quality end of the trade and while he does sell a spiced tea, any of his teas will tell you he doesn't prostitute "the damned stuff." The teas are packaged in formal black-and-gold cannisters.

TEAS: Ceylon & India Special Blend, Earl Grey, Keemun, Darjeeling, Jasmine, Lapsang Souchong, Formosa Oolong, Countess of Salisbury, Gunpowder Green, Orange Pekoe & Pekoe Teabags, Spiced Tea.

SIMPSON & VAIL
38 Clinton Street
Pleasantville, New York 10570
After decades in midtown Manhattan, where it was established in the 1920s, New York's most prestigious tea merchant has been forced to move to the suburbs. The stress of the move just as this was being written prevented the present proprietors from answering my requests for detailed information. Suffice it that their reputation stands high among New Yorkers and their J. P. Morgan Tea is famous. Catalog on request.

MARK T. WENDELL, IMPORTER
P.O. Box 1312
West Concord, Massachusetts 01742
The Boston area's oldest and most reputable tea firm, Mark T. Wendell dates back to 1904. Mr. Eliot Johnson, the present owner, continues the founder's policy of importing only the best and generally the costliest teas available and offers a wider variety than any of his competitors. The best-selling and most famous of them is the Hu-Kwa Lapsang Souchong. MTW teas are sold by the pound and half-pound caddy.

TEAS: Earl Grey, English Breakfast, Formosa Oolong, Indonesian, Irish Breakfast, Mountain Kenya, Mint Tea, Cinnamon & Spice, China Yunnan, Russian Caravan, Boston Harbour Tea, China Jasmine, Cheericup Ceylon, Darjeeling, China Lapsang Souchong, China Keemun, Assam, China Pingsuey, China Oolong, China Panyong, MTW Keemun.

Outstanding merchants who offer catalogs and invite mail-order business include the following.

THE COFFEE BEAN & TEA LEAF
361 North Larchmont
Los Angeles, California 90004

FREED TELLER & FREED
1326 Polk Street
San Francisco, California 94109

NORTHWESTERN COFFEE MILLS
217 North Broadway
Milwaukee Wisconsin 53202

THE PANNIKIN
645 G Street
San Diego, California 92101

BRITISH TEA BRANDS

DAVISON, NEWMAN & CO., LTD. was already 127 years old when Messrs. Davison and Newman gave it their names in 1777. The two partners had themselves buried together in one vault, inseparable even in death. The firm's peculiar trademark represents three sugar loaves suspended from a crown, the sign at which it had always done business in London. It was this historic old house that exported the famous chests of tea that occasioned the Boston Tea Party. The firm is represented on the American market today by its excellent Boston Harbour Tea, which goes far toward making amends for its namesake.

TWININGS dates to Thomas Twining's purchase in 1706, of Tom's Coffee House in the Strand, London. Twining first promoted fine teas as a novelty, but before long had to expand his business to retail loose tea and coffee next door at the sign of the Golden Lion. Twinings Tea has been sold there ever since. Thomas Twining was followed into the business by his son Daniel, whose premature death left Daniel's widow in charge of the company. She ran it for twenty years, one of the very few females in business in her day, and reared her son Richard to understand the arts of tea blending and the intricacies of the trade. Richard took over from her in 1783; a year later he was chairman of the Dealers of Tea and in that capacity persuaded Prime Minister Pitt to repeal the ruinous English tea taxes. Within a year, legal imports had risen from six to sixteen million pounds and Twining and his friends had put England's smugglers out of the tea business.

At the present moment in its long and illustrious history, the House of Twining is said to sell less tea per capita in Britain than it does in the United States, where the only other widely available line of specialty teas is Wagners. Twinings' preeminence in this regard is comparatively recent and largely due to the brilliance of a national sales manager named Jim McGilloway and a publicist named Ruth Morrison. Among other things, they

Argentinian Mate Cup

Twinings and Wagners have much in common. There are many places in this country where they represent the only specialty tea brands ever heard of and that they're there at all is ample grounds for gratitude when I stay, for example, in Mississippi. Both lines— Twinings eighteen teas and Wagners twenty-six—are also extensive. In trying to satisfy a variety of tastes within a given price range, however, they inevitably sell some teas that are poorer than others. Twinings Vintage Darjeeling is an example of how successful it can be in the quality department. On the other hand, neither Twinings nor anybody else can mass market the *very* rarest Darjeeling, or Fanciest Formosa Oolong, and the fact that it doesn't cannot be used to impugn the overall quality of the line. R. Twining & Co., Ltd. is presently planning the introduction of a positively beautiful Yunnan as its nineteenth tea.

FORTNUM & MASON is the result of William Fortnum's taking lodgings with one Hugh Mason in 1707 while he looked around London for a job. He found one as a footman in the household of Queen Anne and upon retirement put his connections with the royal household to use by going into the grocery business in nearby Piccadilly with his old landlord Mason. There was no aspect of the provisioning, catering, and grocery business they and their successors failed to enter. With the Napoleonic wars the firm found itself in the mail-order business, supplying

rescued an honest-to-God descendant of old Tom's, the amiable Mr. Sam Twining, O.B.E., from the firm's export department and got him out front as the company spokesman and symbol—a living ad. It's a great job, of course, and one Mr. Twining clearly delights and excels in.

the needs of British officers and gentlemen all around the world. By Victoria's day the name was a household word, if you ran a rich household I mean, as witness these lines by one of F&M's regular customers, Charles Dickens.

> Well, to be sure, there never was such a Derby Day as this present Derby Day. Never, to be sure, were there so many carriages, so many fours, so many twos, so many ones, so many horsemen, so many people who have come down by "rail," so many fine ladies in so many broughams, so many of Fortnum & Mason's hampers, so much ice and champagne. If I were on the turf, and had a horse to enter for the Derby, I would call that horse Fortnum & Mason, convinced that with that name he would beat the field. Public opinion would bring him in somehow. Look where I will—in some connection with the carriages—made fast upon the top, or occupying the box, or peeping out of a window—I see Fortnum & Mason. And now, Heavens! All the hampers fly open and the Green Downs burst into blossoms of lobster-salad!

It is always a comfort to reflect that after over two hundred fifty years in a violently changing world, Fortnum & Mason is still there in Piccadilly laying out all the good things the world provides, fine teas not least among them. F&M does not market its finest teas in this country, however, and all except the Assam Superb, I Chang, and proprietary teas can easily be equaled.

MELROSES was established in Edinburgh, Scotland, in 1812, and that's about all the company seems to want known about itself. Melroses teas seem generally comparable to F&M's.

LYONS-TETLEY is an amalgamation of not two but three of England's best-known mass-market tea companies. The honest Quaker John Horniman had been the first to sell tea by the packet, each "of guaranteed consistency and net weight." This was in 1826, at a time when grocers enjoyed a widely deserved reputation for selling poor quality and short-weight tea. Horniman started out selling his packets in the hinterlands by peddler, but rapidly became a major brand name. The brothers Tetley were a couple of Yorkshiremen who'd started as teenage tea peddlers and by 1837, managed to set themselves up as nonperipatetic tea merchants hoping to rival Hornimans. Tetleys entered the United States market in the 1880s, and by the end of World War I was in a position to buy Hornimans out (though it perpetuates the brand name to this day). Soon after the opening of the first Lyons Teashop in 1894, however, Tetleys was facing another competitor; by the 1920s Lyons had the largest tea-packing plant in the world. Lyons acquired Tetleys in 1973. From the Channel island of Jersey they export specialty teas to the Continent under both brand names, but their United Kingdom and United States products are of supermarket quality only.

RIDGWAYS was established in London in 1836, soon after the East India Company lost its monopoly on the tea trade with China. Fifty years later Ridgways was appointed purveyor to Queen Victoria, since which time their most famous tea has been HMB—Her Majesty's Blend. I think they're pretty good on the whole. However, there's no telling who owns the line.

JACKSONS OF PICCADILLY, more formally Robert Jackson & Company, Ltd., was founded by a family that moved to Piccadilly in 1680, when it was still a suburban village. Succeeding generations followed a variety of trades that were finally consolidated under one roof in 1840 at 171–172 Piccadilly, just down the street from Fortnum & Mason. Then as now Jacksons sells not only teas but everything else from groceries, fish, meat, and game to tobacco, soap, and hardware. In 1931, ownership of the company passed from descendants of the first Jacksons to Francis Stonor, whose heirs own it today. For many years a number of the famous Jacksons teas were blended and packed for them by James Ashby & Sons. This is no longer the case, but it continues to be the consensus among American tea professionals that Jacksons is generally the best of the British tea lines sold in this country and their China teas are particularly praised.

BROOKE BOND, founded in 1870, is today the world's largest tea company. At present they market one-third of all the tea sold in Great Britain, while a subsidiary, Bushnells, named after a cousin of Arthur Brooke's, accounts for 50 percent of all the tea Australia drinks. The Brooke Bond Red Rose Brand is Canada's best seller and claims a considerable share of the United States supermarket tea business. Apart from multiple other interests, the Brooke Bond-Liebig conglomerate owns over forty-two thousand acres of tea and coffee plantations in India, Tanzania, Malawi, and especially, Kenya. The company has contributed much to the Kenya Tea Development Authority's effort to help Kenyan small landholders and cooperatives develop their own tea estates.

DRYSDALES of Edinburgh, Scotland, is a small family concern founded in 1878. As of this writing, its tea has just entered the United States market, being imported and distributed by New York's Dean & DeLuca of culinary fame. Tea for tea, one is forced to wonder if Drysdales is not the finest line currently being imported from Great Britain.

TY-PHOO TEA is now owned by the Cadbury chocolate people, another firm that can trace its origins to the tea business. Ty-phoo owes its own beginnings to a digestive disorder suffered by the sister of a Birmingham grocer, Mr. John Sumner. His sister discovered or imagined that a certain small-leaf Ceylon tea helped her condition and at her urging he began selling this tea under the name Ty-phoo in 1905. Her Invalid Tea became so popular that within a short time families in the neighborhood were calling themselves Ty-phooites, and Mr. Sumner's company went on to win a major share of the national market. Ty-phoo Tea is a somewhat above-average supermarket blend today.

JAMES ASHBY & SONS of London has been in existence since 1855, and has long enjoyed a back-room reputation among tea men as blenders and packers of fine China and Darjeeling teas for other firms and brands. The firm, which is wholly owned and run by an old Quaker family, first began marketing its own Rose Brand teas in the 1970s. With the exception of a Pure Russian, a Gunpowder Green, and two others, all their teas are scented and flavored and probably represent about the best that can be done in that department. Too bad.

NOT BRITISH they would be quick to say, is Dublin, Ireland's McGrath Brothers, Ltd., the only Irish tea company competing in the United States market. In existence since the early part of this century, McGraths offers four blends only, all of them exceptional.

A CHRONOLOGY OF TEA FORTUNES

It is of course absurd to decry scholarship. Accuracy of mind and a certain erudition are as necessary to the imaginative writer as is native genius.
                                    —*Ford Madox Ford (1873-1939)*
                                              PROVENCE

CIRCA 2700 B.C. A legendary Chinese emperor roughly contemporary with Moses, Shen Nung, is credited with discovering tea.

CIRCA A.D. 350 A description of the tea plant and tea making by Kuo P'o constitutes the earliest definite reference to tea yet discovered in Chinese writings.

476 Fall of the Roman Empire in the West beneath the Gothic *Völkerwanderung*; the Turks, to whom the Eastern capital of Constantinople will fall almost a thousand years later, are reported in Chinese writings to have arrived on Mongolia's borders, where they barter with the Chinese for tea.

CIRCA 725 *Ch'a*, the distinctive ideograph for tea, first appears in Chinese, in an herbal.

CIRCA 780 Lu Yu publishes the first tea book, the *Ch'a Ching,* and comes to be regarded as the patron saint of China's tea, Taoist division.

805 Dengo Daishi, the Buddhist patron saint of Japanese tea and a contemporary of Charlemagne, introduces tea growing in Japan.

815 The Japanese emperor Saga orders tea cultivated near his capital.

850 *An Account of Tea by Two Arabian Travellers* is written in Arabic by one Suleiman, the first account of tea published outside China.

906 Fall of China's T'ang Dynasty (618–906) and close of the so-called classic, or Taoist, era of (brick) tea use in the Orient.

960 Accession of the Sung Dynasty (960–1127), whose first emperor received brick tea in gold boxes as tribute and whose last emperor, Hui Tsung, wrote a treatise on rare tea and patronized its cultivation. This largely Buddhist Sung period, considered the "romantic" era of tea use in the Orient, is the first to use loose leaf tea. In the south of China Sung rule continues until 1280.

1191 After centuries of neglect, the cultivation of tea in Japan is reintroduced by the Buddhist abbot Yeisai, who subsequently publishes the first Japanese tea book. His friend and brother abbot Myo-e pioneers the famous Uji tea-growing district in 1200.

1206–1280 Mongols under Genghis and then Kublai Khan progressively conquer Chinese territories, ousting the Sung and establishing the Mongol, or Yuan, Dynasty (1206–1368). For the first time China's ruling class neither knows of nor cares for tea, so much so that Marco Polo, who'd first arrived in China in 1275, never encounters it. Tea traditions and connoisseurship are maintained during this period in Japan, where the luxurious tea tournament is a Japanese tradition of long standing by the early 1300s.

1368 The native Chinese Ming Dynasty (1368–1644) takes control of China. It is during the Ming period that Europe first tastes "the Chinean drink." The corresponding Muromachi period under the shogunate of the Ashikaga clan (1338–1568) in Japan sees the retired shogun Yoshimasa become the first patron of the *chado* or tea ceremony, with the Zen master Shuko as its first high priest in the year 1473.

1498 Portugal's Vasco da Gama rounds the Cape of Good Hope and sails to India. By 1517, Portuguese mariners become the first Europeans to reach China by sea; half barterers, half pirates, they carry on trade of a sort with China and Japan for decades before winning any form of legal recognition in those countries. Portuguese Jesuit missionaries first set foot in Japan in 1549.

CIRCA 1500 The first teapots of which positive records exist date from this period, being made in imitation of spouted earthenware wine ewers at Yi-Xing, a spot famous for its clays near Shanghai; the potteries of Yi-Xing later become famous with the patronage of the Mings. These pots become popular all over China and are exported in great numbers to Japan and the West. The purpose of making them very small is that each person should have his own pot.

1557 Portugal is ceded use of Macao as a base down river from Canton in China. In Japan, Christianity has found so many converts by 1567, that a feudal baron establishes Nagasaki as a center and refuge for them.

1559 The first mention of tea in Europe is published in a collection of travelers' tales and reports compiled by Ramusio in Venice. Within succeeding decades it is followed by other accounts, the first notice of tea in English appearing in 1598, translated from a Dutchman's Latin.

1588 Hideyoshi, military dictator of Japan and tea connoisseur, orders a national tea party to be held for ten days under the pines of Kitano. It is organized by Sen-no Rikyu (1521–91), the tea master whose doctrine of *wabi*, "simple and natural," spilled out of his tea cup into every aspect of Japanese life. The Japanese tea cult persists to the present in the form he gave it.

1600 Elizabeth I of England charters the Honorable East India Company, granting it monopoly over all British trade from Cape Horn the long way round to the Cape of Good Hope. The first John Company ship to penetrate the Orient returns from Sumatra in 1603, and turns a profit. A Company agent at a Dutch trading station at Hirado Island off Kyushu, Japan, one R. L. Wickham, becomes the first Englishman to refer to tea, writing to request some from Macao in 1615.

1610 Tea reaches Europe for the first time, carried by the Dutch from a trading station they've established at Bantam, Java, where they buy tea from Chinese merchants who speak the Amoy dialect and thus do not call it by its customary Chinese name, *ch'a.* Thenceforth it is known in Europe by its Amoy name of "tea," except in Portugal. Its use becomes popular enough by 1635, that a German doctor, Simon Paulli, publishes an attack on the beverage from the medical standpoint, while from the commercial standpoint the "Lords Seventeen" of the Dutch East India Company order the regular importation "of Chinese as well as Japanese tea with every ship" by 1637.

1644 Manchurian warriors are admitted through the Great Wall to help quell a rebellion and wind up unseating the Ming Dynasty. The Ch'ing, or Manchu, Dynasty is dated from this year and remains in power until 1 January 1912, when Sun Yat-sen enters the republican capital of Nanking as president of a provisional government, and brings the dynastic history of China to a close.

1649 Charles I of England loses his head and Cromwell becomes Lord Protector of the British Commonwealth. The royal family is in exile in Holland, where tea is fashionable and where the future Charles II grows up. That French high society has taken to tea by now is evident from a Parisian doctor's decrying it as "the impertinent novelty of the century" at this time. The Dutch introduce their New World colony of Nieuw Amsterdam to tea about 1650. Cromwell's mercantile wars with Holland delay its introduction into England, where the first coffee house is established in 1650, at Oxford.

1658 The first solid evidence of tea being sold in England appears in the form of an advertisement in a newspaper for Garway's Coffee House. The new drink catches on quickly. In 1660 Garway publishes a broadside on the "Vertues of the Leaf, Thea," and Samuel Pepys notes ms first taste of tea in his *Diary*.

1664 The recently restored King Charles II receives about two pounds of "thea" from the East India Company, anxious to win his favor with a gift of his favorite exotic beverage. His Portuguese queen, Catherine of Braganza, who had also grown up with tea at home, becomes England's first tea-drinking queen.

The fashion the royal couple begins receives considerable impetus in aristocratic society in 1666, when certain nobles return from a mission to The Hague and give lavish parties featuring tea they bought there. The following year Mr. Pepys comes home to find his wife "a-making of tea," bought from a pharmacist. The John Company begins importing it directly from the Orient in 1669, and by a curious coincidence importing tea from Holland is outlawed that same year.

1670 The earliest known "Silver Tea-Pott" is presented to the board of directors of the East India Company by Lord Berkeley.

1679 The Dutch physician Cornelius Bontekoe publishes a tract urging everybody to consume tea in quantities and is handsomely rewarded by the Dutch East India Company.

1684 The John Company succeeds at last in establishing the first English trading post on China's mainland at Canton. The following year, 1685, sees the Manchu emperor for the first time able to exercise authority throughout his realm. He decrees all ports except Canton closed to international trade and establishes the co-hong system there, whereby thirteen hong, or warehouse, owners under the supervision of one of their number, the hoppo, will be responsible for all trade with the *yang kuei-tzu* or "foreign devils." The co-hong system will continue to operate and be the West's sole source of tea until 1842.

1689 Following the Treaty of Nerchinsk nego-
tiated by Western Jesuits between China
and Russia, even the Russians begin importing tea overland via the obscure border
outpost of Usk Kayakhta in Outer Mongolia.
In 1690, two Bostoners become the first
English colonists in the New World licensed
to import tea, one being Z. Boylston.

1698 Celia Fiennes, riding around Staffordshire,
reports in her diary going to see "the making
of fine teapotts, cups and saucers of the fine
red earth, in imitation and as curious as that
which comes from China." She is speaking of
the pottery of the Dutch brothers Elers, who
pioneered the Staffordshire pottery industry
in 1693. Their wares imitated the Yi-Xing
pots from near Shanghai.

1702 After a decade or so of tea imports
averaging twenty thousand pounds per year,
the John Company orders its first full ship's
cargo of tea, including the first sizable shipment of Green Tea to the West. English
grocers begin taking over the tea business
from apothecaries.

1703 J.-F. Böttger presents his patron the
elector of Saxony with a fine red teapot, the
first product of the first firing of his newly
established kiln at Meissen and the first
piece of "china" made in Europe. By 1709 he
perfects the production of white porcelain
and by 1713, Meissen china is being sold in
quantities.

1707 William Fortnum lodges with Hugh Mason
in London and a great partnership is formed.

1714 Upon the death of Queen Anne, George
I accedes to the British Crown and founds
the Hanoverian-Windsor dynasty.

1717 Thomas Twining expands Tom's Coffee
House to include England's first retail tea
shop at the sign of the Golden Lion in the
Strand, London. English tea imports exceed
a million pounds for the first time in 1721. In
1735, Czarina Elizabeth of Russia inaugurates
privately backed tea caravans from China
and by 1740, the value of the tea Holland
imports exceeds that of all other goods
brought from the East. New York establishes
special municipal "tea water" pumps.

1742 The king, Horace Walpole, Dr. Johnson,
and all London society turn out for the
opening of Ranelagh Tea Gardens, one of
dozens such establishments that do much to
popularize tea. Tea smuggling, which flour-
ishes throughout most of the century, popu-
larizes it even more.

1751 The Worchester Royal Porcelain Works
is established in England. A porcelain works
is founded at Sèvres, near Versailles, in
1756, and is soon taken over by the state at
the behest of Mme. de Pompadour.

1756 A John Company clerk, Robert Clive,
leads Company forces to victory over the

army of the French East India Company at Plassey in India, clearing the way for India to be ruled as a Company fief for a century. The uncirculated wealth Clive dispatches to Britain finances the Industrial Revolution in the West.

1757 The celebrated Dr. Samuel Johnson becomes the most vociferous in a long line of tea-loving English men of letters, answering an attack on tea with a description of himself as "a hardened and shameless tea drinker" and recommending its use to all thinking men and women. In 1762, the Swedish botanist Linnaeus declares in his *Species Plantorum* that Black and Green teas come from two different plants.

1760 Josiah Wedgwood founds his Etruria Pottery Works; the neoclassical designs he champions exercise an immediate and continuing influence on tea wares of every sort.

1767 Parliament passes the infamous act imposing duties on tea and other commodities imported by the colonists in America. The act is resisted and proves unenforceable; the colonists turn to bootlegging their tea from Holland. All duties except the one on tea are repealed in 1770; the colonists continue buying from Holland. By 1773, the John Company is sitting on a surplus of some seventeen million pounds of tea that's rapidly going stale. Parliament grants the Company a monopoly on shipping tea to the colonies and selling it there. Colonial agents are appointed and ships dispatched.

1773 On 16 December, certain citizens disguised as Indians dump the entire Boston consignment of the John Company's tea into the harbor, turning the colonial tax resistance into open rebellion. American patriots discover a large consignment of tea stored at Greenwich, New Jersey, and, after disguising themselves as Indians also, burn it in the town square.

1773 On 26 December, a tea ship bound for Philadelphia is halted within sight of the city and sent back to London under threat of burning. The first of the Charleston tea ships lands its cargo some days later, but without payment of duty. Obliged by law to seize the tea, the tax collectors store it in the dampest available basement to rot.

1774 In April, two tea ships arrive at New York. Eighteen chests of tea in a general cargo aboard the smaller ship are dumped into the harbor; the larger ship, fully laden with tea, escapes similar treatment by returning to London. In August, a ship bound for Annapolis with general cargo including some tea is sent back to England; in October the *Peggy Stewart* reaches Annapolis with two thousand pounds of tea and is burned at her anchorage by the owner under some duress. On 1 November, the *Britannia* arrives at Charleston with eight chests of tea aboard, which the ship's owners are compelled to break open and dump overboard in full view of the populace.

1775 The Declaration of the Ladies of Edenton, North Carolina, "not to Conform to the Pernicious Custom of Drinking Tea, until such time as all Acts which tend to enslave our native country shall be repealed," is published in a London paper to the considerable consternation of the ladies' families and social connections. By the time the American Revolution begins, the populace as a whole has renounced tea drinking.

1784 After a long climb, England's tea duty has reached 120 percent ad valorem. Richard Twining, as chairman of the Dealers of Tea, persuades Prime Minister Pitt to reduce this ruinous duty to 12 percent, effectively putting England's tea smugglers out of business. Legal imports over the following year rise from twelve to thirty-two million pounds and there are thirty thousand registered tea dealers.

1793 Lord MaCartney's mission to the emperor of China fails to win trade concessions of any sort for the John Company.

1796 The death of Catherine the Great sees Russia importing some three and a half million pounds—over six thousand camel loads—of tea annually.

1800 The emperor of China issues first edict forbidding importation of the "foreign mud,"

Indian opium, a John Company product. John Jacob Astor earns fifty thousand dollars as his half of his first China venture, tea constituting a large part of the cargo. America's first three millionaires all make their fortunes in the China trade.

1810 Chinese from Amoy introduce tea growing in Formosa.

1815 British depose the 186th and last native Sinhalese king of Ceylon, which becomes a fully occupied Crown Colony.

1819 Sir Stamford Raffles of the English East India Company founds Singapore on the straits joining the Indian and Pacific oceans to protect the Company's sea lanes from India to China.

1823 Major Robert Bruce discovers tea growing wild in Assam.

1826 John Horniman markets the first prepackaged, guaranteed unadulterated tea.

1830 The John Company is exporting about ten thousand cases of opium a year from India to China. England's annual tea consumption reaches thirty million pounds. Imports by all other countries are estimated to total twenty-two million pounds.

1833 Parliament decrees an end to the East India Company's monopoly of British trade with China. The following year the first tea auction is held in Mincing Lane and the Company appoints its Tea Committee to assess the possibilities of growing tea in (its) India. They soon announce the discovery of tea in Assam and begin importing seeds from China to plant there under the supervision of Charles Bruce, who wisely starts a nursery of native tea plants also.

1837 Victoria's coronation ushers in the Victorian era.

1839 The first lot of Assam-grown tea—eight chests altogether—is auctioned at London and the Assam Company is promptly formed.

1840 Robert Jackson & Co., Ltd. takes up quarters down the street from Fortnum & Mason and grows into Jacksons of Piccadilly.

1842 The First Opium War is concluded by the Treaty of Nanking, which puts an end to the hong system, opens four additional Chinese ports to international trade, and cedes Hong Kong to Great Britain.

1845 The *Rainbow,* the first "extreme" clipper ship, is launched in New York and makes her maiden voyage to China and back in record time. Clippers rapidly become the queens of the seas.

1847 John Wagner & Sons is founded in Philadelphia.

1848 An experimental planting of tea is made in Russian Transcaucasia and another in Greenville, South Carolina. The John Company's government of India sends Robert Fortune to China for tea plants, expert workmen, and tools.

1853 George Williamson, who will become known as the "Father of India's Tea Industry," takes over Charles Bruce's job for the Assam Company and soon begins propagating the Assam tea *jat.*

1853 Commodore Perry establishes direct commercial relations between Japan and the United States, carrying home tea.

1856 The first tea is planted in India's Darjeeling district.

1857 The Second Opium War ends with British burning the emperor's summer palace in Peking by way of forcing imperial legalization of opium. The number of addicts grows tenfold over the following decade in China and imports of opium approach one hundred thousand cases. Opium is to remain a legitimate article of commerce until 1908.

1858 The United States government sends Robert Fortune to China for tea seeds to be cultivated in the southern states.

1858 On 2 August, possession of India is formally transferred from the East India

Company to the British Crown, effectively marking the end of the greatest multinational corporation the world has yet known. India's independence from Britain comes a century later.

1866 The greatest of all the tea clipper races, ninety-nine days and sixteen thousand miles by the log, ends with three clippers that had left Foochow on the same tide entering the Thames on the same tide and docking.

1867 James Taylor makes the first experimental planting of tea in Ceylon. The first tea is also planted in Japan's principal tea district, **Shizuoka** Prefecture, and Formosa Oolong is **first exported** the following year.

1869 The opening of the Suez Canal transforms world shipping; 1871 will be the year of the last tea clipper race.

1870 Coffee blight descends on Ceylon, preparing the way for the "rush into tea" by desperate planters there. In England, Brooke Bond is founded, destined to become the world's largest tea company.

1872 William Jackson, the pioneer inventor of tea machinery, produces and installs his first machine and finds it works.

1878 Assam tea seeds are introduced into Java and prove the solution to successful tea growing there. Experimental plantings are made in East Africa, and Robert Drysdale sets up shop in Edinburgh.

1884 London's first tea shop opens and an English social phenomenon is born. Exactly ten years later, the Lyons chain of tea shops is established and catapults Lyons into the ranks of major tea firms.

1886 Peak year of China's tea production and trade.

1890 Dr. Charles Shepard plants a tea garden and builds a tea factory in South Carolina; some of his tea still grows on the campus of Clemson University. Halfway around the world, Sir Thomas Lipton is investing in Ceylon tea estates preparatory to launching Liptons Tea.

1891 Ceylon tea establishes a record price of £25 10s. per pound when the first fine lot is auctioned in Mincing Lane. Ceylon's reputation for high-quality teas dates from this sale.

1897 According to Mr. W. H. Ukers, United States tea consumption reaches its highest point ever in this year—1.56 pounds per capita.

1900 The last camel caravan carrying tea for Russia leaves Peking in the same year the last link of the Trans-Siberian Railroad is completed. Usk Kayakhta passes into history. Tea cultivation spreads to Iran and French

Indochina exports its first.

1902 The parent of First Colony, the James G. Gill Company, is formed in Norfolk, Virginia.

1904 Iced tea is invented at the St. Louis World's Fair. Dr. Shepard's South Carolina-grown tea wins a "Best in Show" medal.

1908 Mr. William Sullivan, tea merchant of New York, inadvertently invents the tea bag.

1925 Africa passes the million-pound mark in tea shipments. Brooke Bond begins buying land and planting tea in Kenya. Russia resumes tea buying on a large scale in all markets. The glut begins.

1958 Three hundred years after China tea was first sold in England, it is sold there for the first time by its Chinese producers.

1972 For the first time since her revolution, Chinese tea production exceeds all previous records and the United States resumes trade with China.

1982 With almost forty producing countries, worldwide tea production averages well over two and a half billion pounds per annum.

A GLOSSARY OF TEA TASTER'S JARGON

DRY LEAF
Bloom: sheen or luster on black leaf
Bold: large leaf or sometimes pieces of leaf too big for a grade, outsized
Chesty: resinous odor/taste imparted by uncured wood in tea chest
Common: poor quality
Dull: leaf without sheen, i.e., "bloom"
Flaky: poorly made leaf that's flat and easily broken; nonpejoratively, small grades
Shotty: well-made Gunpowder; sometimes also applied to Souchong
Tippy: generous amount of white or golden tip, i.e., budding leaf

Well-twisted: fully withered, tightly rolled leaf
Wiry: stylish, thin whole leaves; quite often OP grade

INFUSION
Agony of the leaves: unfolding of the leaves in boiling water

TEA LIQUOR
Bakey: unpleasant taste caused by firing leaf at too high a temperature; not as strong as "burnt"
Biscuity: pleasant characteristic often associated with Assam teas

Bite: not a taste but the astringent puckeriness that gives Black Tea its refreshing quality

Body: viscosity, the strength of the liquor combined with its weight on the tongue; body may be "full," "light," etc.

Brassy: unpleasant tang caused by under-withering

Bright: sparkling liquor characteristic of all fine teas; also describes taste opposite of "dull"

Brisk: lively, not flat

Complex: the harmonious mélange of various flavors characteristic of the very finest teas

Dull: muddy looking liquor, the opposite of "bright"; "flat" tasting

Flat: soft, rather flabby-bodied tea lacking "bite" and "briskness"

Fruity: piquant quality characteristic of good Oolongs, some Keemuns, etc.

Gone off: tea that's been spoiled by improper storage or packing or is simply past its prime and stale

Malty: a subtle underlying flavor often characteristic of Assam

Peak: the high point of the tasting experience when, some instants after the liquor enters the mouth, its body, flavor, and astringency make themselves fully felt. Greens and Oolongs do not peak but stand immediately and fully revealed.

Pointy: a liquor is said to "have point" if it shows some desirable property—for example, briskness or fine fragrance

Pungent: astringent; what gives a tea its bite

Self-drinking: any tea with sufficient aroma, flavor, body, and color to stand alone and in no need of blending for improvement

Stewed or stewy: poorly fired tea giving soft liquor without "point"; also used of tea that's brewed too long and has become bitter

Tarry: smoky flavor associated with Lapsang Souchong

Thin: lacking body and/or color

Weedy: may be applied to thin, cabbagy Black Teas; nonpejoratively, a Green Tea may be called weedy if it has a not-unpleasant vegetative aroma and flavor, varying from simple "herbaceousness" to scents of new-mown hay

Winey: usually descriptive of a mellow quality fine Darjeelings or Keemuns acquire with six months to a year or more of age; more rarely used to describe overfermented tea

TEA PRODUCING

Why Does It Taste Like That ?

A SOMEWHAT TECHNICAL EXCURSUS

If we had paid no more attention to our plants than we have to our children, we would now be living in a jungle of weeds.

—*Luther Burbank*
HOW PLANTS ARE TRAINED TO WORK FOR MAN

HE FLAVOR OF TEA begins on the tree, or—to wax botanical about it—the bush or shrub. Tea is an evergreen shrub, and from the look of its leaves and conical shape you might think it a myrtle. In the springtime its faintly fragrant white blossoms with their yellow stamens resemble wild roses. Then the blossom fades to make fruit, and concealed inside each fruit grow one to three seeds a little smaller than those of an apple. It is a plant that grows in climates ranging from Mediterranean to tropical and at altitudes from sea level up to eight thousand feet. Generally speaking, the nearer the equator, the higher the altitude has to be if the tea produced is to be good. It requires lower elevations in zones where frost occurs. The largest specimen ever discovered was found in 1939, growing wild in China's Yunnan province, which borders Vietnam, Thailand, and Burma. Standing over a hundred feet high and with a trunk better than a yard in diameter, this "King Tea Tree," rightly so-called, was over seventeen hundred years old. It is clearly an exception. Left to its natural inclinations, the tea plant will grow to a height of fifteen to thirty feet, surround itself with little tea plants, and live upwards of a hundred years. It is a hard plant to kill.

The Swedish botanist Linnaeus, who invented our double-barreled Latin names for plants, believed there were two kinds of tea: the *viridis,* which produced Green Teas, and the *bohea,* which produced Black. Robert Fortune proved that both Green and Black teas are made from the same kind of leaves provided they are treated differently. Later, it was established that both the China and the Assam *jat* belong to the same species. Thus every tea bush in every tea garden is a certified *Camellia sinensis,* but this is not to say any two are exactly alike. Unlike some, tea is not a self-fertilizing plant; each one must be pollinated by another. And as with every other plant or animal, its tiniest cells contain a number of threadlike things called chromosomes, of which tea has thirty-two, fourteen fewer than humans. When one plant pollinates another, their two sets of genes and chromosomes are shuffled together like two decks of cards and then dealt out to the offspring as they fall. The descendant inherits certain qualities from each parent, along with others that were latent in them, handed down from more or less distant ancestors. Only about 1930 was it proved that a tea plant that looks no different from its brothers or cousins might still produce twice the yield or a leaf worth somewhat more—or less—per pound. One wonders why this general principle *needed* proof. Isn't this the reason our parents always harped on "good breeding," and why the Indian tea planters deplore the China *jat* to this day as "the curse of the India tea industry"? Sexual reproduction remains about as chancy with tea plants as it is with human beings.

The only way to reproduce a bush exactly is "layering," which is burying a branch that's still on the bush until it roots. The advantages of reproducing superior plants in this way have induced more and more tea planters around the world to employ it. Since reproduction by seeds from selective cross-fertilization is much cheaper, however, most tea planters still grow shrubs from seeds in nursery beds. The seedlings are transplanted to the tea garden after about six months when they stand six to eight inches tall. The young plants are set out in rows at three- to six-foot intervals and allowed to grow unimpeded for some two years. A fairly level tea garden will be inhabited by three to four thousand bushes per acre.

For luxuriant growth, tea requires a climate that's hot and very wet—at least a hundred inches of rainfall per annum. In China it is often still grown on bits of wasteland unsuitable for other crops, just as in the days when the *Ch'a Ching* was written. Lu Yu was wrong to recommend this practice, however, for while tea can and does grow in soil of every description, it takes best to the richest earth. Regardless of where you grow it, any tea plant must be carefully tended to give good tea. Tea bushes grow best in the shade in most places; specially selected shade trees help discourage weeds and keep the sun from scorching the tea. The best Oolong always comes from bushes that are covered for protection from the sun for some little while before plucking, and some of Japan's finest Green Tea is grown entirely in the shade. Gardens must be fertilized from time to time, but insecticides and the like are rarely used since the assorted pests and diseases to which the bush is subject are relatively harmless, at least in comparison with other crops. Interestingly enough, tea will not grow for some time where lightning has struck or on the site of former human habitation, or so I am assured, and it ill becomes any mere writer to doubt a farmer's lore. In Louisiana, for instance, it's well known that to grow really hot peppers you should plant them in the full of the moon after you've had a fight with your wife and you're still mad as a dull razor.

The end of the long process of tea growing and tea making comes when boiling water is poured over the leaves in a pot; the leaves unfold and release their flavor, tannins, and caffeine. Tea men call this "the agony of the leaves," but if the tea is any good this must have been preceded by what can only be called "the torture of the plant." After two years of pampering, the tea plant is six feet tall, more or less, depending on climate and altitude. At this point it is cut back drastically. After another year or more, again depending, it is ready for its first plucking. From now on it will be kept plucked and pruned to a height of three to five feet. This renders plucking easier, but also and more importantly it stimulates the growth of "flush," the tender young leaves from which tea is made. Unpruned, the plant would stop yielding "flush" as it aged, the sap passages would gradually block up, the twigs would harden into wood, and the existing leaves would simply grow larger and tougher until only a primitive Assamese could make tea from them. Constant pruning and plucking keeps the bush desperately striving for full treehood and perpetually producing new leaves and buds. Every Southern farmer employs basically the same principle when he beats his nut trees with a two-by-four each year to increase their yield. What happens is, you panic the plant into thinking its last days are at hand and it puts all its energy into reproducing itself. The poor tea bush is kept in this state of unrelieved anxiety from age two to something over fifty, when its yield begins to decrease and, to avoid labor and sorrow, it's uprooted and replaced. It dies without once having been allowed to flower and seed. The most it could possibly produce is under ten ounces of finished dry leaf a year.

"TWO LEAVES AND A BUD"

The one goal of all crop cultivation is the harvest. In the case of tea this means plucking the new leaves, or flush. The Russians, who have long raised tea in Soviet Georgia just north of the Caucasus, have invented a self-propelled, mechanical tea plucker. I can confidently predict that this is an idea whose time will never come. In the first place, virtually all the tea-producing countries are desperately poor and cannot afford to throw their tea pluckers out of work. Secondly, with few exceptions the best teas are all high grown and the terrain of the estates precludes mechanization. Even industrialized countries like Japan and Taiwan never machine-pluck their fine teas, though for some time now the Japanese have used shears instead of fingernails for plucking, employing a machine to remove the woody stems hydrostatically once the tea is manufactured.

Tea must be plucked evenly so that the leaves will wither and dry uniformly, as fine shoots mixed together with coarser will not, with poorer tea the result. The quality of the tea also depends on the planter's decision either to try for a small amount of good to fine or a larger quantity of ordinary leaf. "Two leaves and a bud" is the golden rule for plucking average to good tea. This is "normal" or "medium" as opposed to "fine" plucking, in which only the growth bud and the next youngest leaf are taken to produce a superior-quality tea. "Coarse" plucking is to take the bud and the first two leaves and the "old leaf" below them, along with that much more of the twig.

In Indonesia and other lands where there is no cold season, tea flushes all year round and may be picked every seven to ten days. Elsewhere, the bush must rest part of the year and tea men refer to their harvests as first, second, or whatever flush. In Japan, where the season is shortest, there are usually no more than three or four pluckings between May and early October. In northern India, China, and Taiwan, the harvests begin earlier and last longer. The first and second flushes in these countries are usually fine plucked and produce exceptional teas, but the quality decreases with each flush thereafter and the coarse, old leaves of the final pickings are rarely exported. Along with elevation, this matter of the best-sized leaf and the best time of year for plucking it is a crucial one when it comes to quality.

Regardless of which flush it is or what kind of plucking is ordained, it is humbling to note that God has yet to invent a better instrument for the task than human fingernails, generally female. Most tea pluckers in Sri Lanka are Tamil-speaking Hindus, the Sinhalese Sri Lankans being too proud for such menial work. The workers even bury their dead between the tea rows. The indefatigable Mr. W. H. Ukers has reckoned that the average Sri Lankan plucker, using both hands, can pick about thirty thousand shoots a day. Since it takes approximately thirty-two hundred shoots to make a single pound of finished tea, that's only a fraction over nine pounds of tea per day, somewhat more than the average tea drinker consumes in a year. I figure it requires at least five hundred tea drinkers to support that one worker year round. For garden and factory combined, a thousand-acre estate of average yield needs about fifteen hundred workers.

Nowadays the British "sahib" is most conspicuous by his absence from the Indian and Sri Lankan tea estates he pioneered, but the work of plucking has not changed appreciably since Mr. A. R. Ramsden described it in his excellent and unfortunately long out-of-print *Assam Planter*:

> We went to see the women start the work of plucking. They were trooping up from the coolie lines—the tin shanties where they lived—in single file, each carrying a large basket on her head. In the shade at one end of a twelve-acre block of tea ready to be plucked they halted and put down their baskets. Each woman had to pluck three rows of tea two hundred forty yards long. This meant one hundred and sixty women to every twelve acres. The best pluckers jealously defended their right to the same three rows in every block as by good plucking the yield could be considerably increased....
>
> As we forged our way through the more than waist-high dripping wet tea, Jack [the superintendant] corrected a woman here and there, cracked jokes with them mostly of the rather robust kind, and asked about their families and such things as the rice prospects on their holdings. Although he had only been in the country eighteen months, I was lucky to have him to show me the ropes. He had the natives feeding out of his hand and could raise a laugh or smile from them at any time, which is the way to handle native labour.
>
> Back at the bungalow we changed and had breakfast, a substantial meal as it was too hot at lunchtime to eat much. By then the men had finished their daily hoeing task and were turning out to the work of plucking green leaf. Each man carried two baskets hung from the end of a whippy bamboo slung across his shoulders, and being empty they bounced up and down as he almost ran in his eagerness to start work, for it was considered overtime and paid for daily in cash at so much per seer [two and half pounds] of green leaf. This meant more supervision for us, and we went through the long lines of men, women and children plucking the lower and younger tea bushes....

The work is, if anything, heavier now. An acre in Assam that produced three hundred pounds of tea in 1865 will yield up to fifteen hundred pounds today. Tea production has increased enormously since India's independence, though existing acreage has expanded only slightly.

But if human labor is required to work tea estates, it is dwarfed by the elephant labor that went into developing most of those estates outside China and Japan. I cannot in conscience leave Mr. Ramsden's tribute to this beast of burden unquoted: "As tempermental as a racehorse, as placid as a pumpkin, as blind as a bat and as clumsy as a camel, the elephant is lovable in spite of being as savage as a hell cat. Not the sort of

animal to have about the house, you might well say; but the elephant nevertheless inspires much real affection and is far more reliable than many of your women friends." Anyone who's seen *Elephant Walk,* that memorable film starring Elizabeth Taylor and Peter Finch set on a tea estate in what was then Ceylon, will appreciate the writer's understatement. Hell cats or no, elephants must also be numbered among the workers who provide us our tea.

THE MAKING OF BLACK TEA

On a warm, damp day the aroma of tea suffuses the gardens. Since no vineyard smells of wine, one may correctly deduce that the chemical changes involved in making tea are less drastic than those of wine making. A tea made from fresh leaf would be harsh, raw, and thin—as different in flavor from manufactured tea as maple sap is from maple syrup. It was Lu Yu, as usual, who laid down the law for proper tea making, and the Chinese followed it religiously for a thousand years. When the British began tea growing and tea making in India, they too consulted the *Ch'a Ching* for instructions. What they found was a twelve-step operation that required three days. Once the raw material—the fresh leaf—was on hand and in the proper condition—the leaves fresh from the bushes and unbruised and those too the right leaves evenly plucked with extraneous matter like twigs removed—only then could manufacture produce the best results.

The ancient prescription for manipulating the leaves began with spreading them in the sun as soon as they were plucked, to be turned by hand from noon to six o'clock. The next day they were spread in the shade and gently rolled, still and always by hand. By this time the leaves were withered and rolling cracked their surface, exposing their juices and cells to the air and starting their fermentation and oxidation. A little more sun and they were spread out in the shade again and again rolled any number of times, as all the while the fermentation continued. When, *judging by the smell,* the tea maker decided the right point of fermentation was reached, he put the leaves into hot pans to "kill" them and somewhat arrest further fermentation. More cooling, roasting, and rolling completed the process. With each rolling, fermentation proceeded a little further; with each roasting, fermentation was checked. The withering process required a worker to hand toss each trayful of tea three to four hundred times. To complete the rolling process, he had to work his way around the tray, hand rolling the leaf another three to four hundred times. The leaves were then exposed to the *poey long,* or "fire fierce," until they were 80 percent dried. Any old yellow leaves and stalks were then picked out, and the leaves were yet again "poeyed" over a slow fire, turned once, and finally packed in chests. All the Black Tea in the world was made by this laborious process up until about a century ago. Consider that even the most expensive bottle of champagne requires fewer than two hundred handlings by the time it's sold to you.

Black Tea is now made in six steps instead of Lu Yu's twelve, and machines have greatly reduced the time and labor involved. The first step is withering, which the Chinese accomplished by simply spreading and tossing the "green" or "fresh" leaf out in the sun. Withering machines have never produced very satisfactory results, apparently, and the process still takes eighteen to twenty-four hours. By the end of this time, the leaf will have lost a third to a half of its weight through evaporation. It is now limp and soft enough for the second step, rolling.

Perhaps some China Congous (the name means "time and labor") are still rolled by hand as Lu Yu prescribed. A good man might roll thirty to forty pounds in a good day's work. Outside of China, the Jacksons' tea-rolling machines and those of their successors have almost universally replaced hand rolling; each machine does the work of seventy-odd men a day. The object of rolling is to bruise and crush the leaf and give it the proper twist. Twisted leaf produces a less pungent but more flavorful brew than flat, open leaf. The bruising and crushing break down the leaf's cell walls so that its enzymes and juices are exposed to the air and fermentation can begin. Rolling can take anywhere from one to three hours, but fermentation, being a natural process, takes its own sweet time. It continues after the leaf leaves the rolling machine in the form of twisted-up balls ready for the third step in the process, variously known as roll breaking or green-leaf sifting. This is done by machines called ball-breakers, vibrating wire sieves that break the clumps down into separate leaves again and sift them through screens to ensure that none are larger than a certain size. If this were not done, the leaf would not ferment evenly. Fermentation gets underway during rolling, as I said, and completing the fermentation process is the fourth procedure in tea making.

Withered, rolled, and sifted by now, the leaf leaves the ball-breaker quite flaccid—not surprisingly—but still more or less green. It goes next to the fermenting room to be spread out on scrupulously clean cement, glass, or tile surfaces. Some teas require faster and some slower rates of fermentation, but in most tea districts it's generally considered ideal for the entire process to last no longer than three and a half hours, rolling time included. Tea tannin undergoes marked chemical changes during this period. In its natural state, it is colorless and pungent; the longer it ferments, the more color it develops and the less pungent it becomes. Tea men must try for either a very aromatic and astringent tea or for one that is more flavorful and deeply colored, since teas very seldom combine these qualities. Much of the flavor, body, and color is determined by oxidation, which is also part of the process. It's like watching the flesh of an apple turn brown after you've taken a bite. The fermentation is considered complete when the leaf has turned the proper "new penny" bright coppery red.

The tea is now ready for "firing." Firing, now that hot air machines have replaced Lu Yu's *poey long,* might more accurately be called "drying." It has to be done just right. If dried too quickly, the leaf remains moist at the center and might go moldy. If the temperature is too high or too low, the tea that results tastes flat or sometimes turns gray, a bad thing in a Black Tea. Firing kills the bacteria responsible for fermentation and stops the process. It leaves only about 3 percent of the red, fermented leaf's moisture content and turns it black.

Important as it is to judge color transformations in the tea making, the identification of smells is also part of the expert tea man's stock in trade. What a cornucopia of odors Mr. C. R. Harler describes in *The Culture and Marketing of Tea*! Imagine:

> Freshly plucked tea-leaf has the same spicy smell as growing leaf, resembling that of ginger root or the concentrated smell of hay with the acrid part predominating. As withering proceeds, the leaf develops a marked fruity smell, as of apples. During the first ten minutes or so of rolling the fruity smell is accentuated and includes the smell of pears, the last being strong when underwithered leaf is rolled. As the leaf ferments, the fruity smell fades, and a nutty aroma, as of almonds, together with the basic spicy smell, becomes apparent. With flowery teas the flower-like smell is also evident at this stage. Freshly fired tea has a smell of burnt toast and also a caramel smell of burnt sugar. . . .

Once the leaf has been carefully fired, it is piled in heaps on the floor to cool and then put in bins for sorting or grading. This is the indispensable sixth and last step in making Black Tea. The fired leaf comes out of the dryer with large and small, broken and unbroken leaves all mixed together. They must be separated according to their size, or "grade," or the tea would be impossible to market. One reason for this is that small leaf is always heavier than larger leaf *by volume,* wherefore packages of different-sized leaves mixed together would differ in weight even though they all held the same volume. It is important that the leaf be sorted by grades for blending purposes also, if the blender is to avoid unpredictable inconsistencies and constant variations from one batch to the next. You would even find noticeable variations from pot to pot if you tried to use an ungraded tea. It is thus easier on us all for the fired leaf to be sifted by machines until each grade is segregated from the others. Since his tea was never sold loose but compressed into cakes, Lu Yu is understandably silent on this point.

By "grade," let me emphasize, we're talking here about the size of the leaf and size alone, not quality. The main division tea men make is between "leaf" grades and "broken" grades, so-called. Leaf grades are the larger of the two and, except for China and Formosa Souchongs, the largest-sized leaf grade is called Orange Pekoe. Now "pekoe" (pronounced pek-oh, not peek-oh) is another bit of pidgin, derived, like the word "tea" itself, from the Chinese dialect spoken in Amoy, the port opposite Taiwan, and signifying "white down" (*pek-ho*), in reference to the downy tips of young tea buds. What "orange" has to do with this I have despaired of ever finding out, but Orange Pekoe or OP is indubitably the term employed for the largest leaf grade of Ceylon tea. The equivalent leaf grade in India is called Flowery Orange Pekoe or FOP. A somewhat smaller leaf grade called simply Pekoe is recognized in Ceylon but not in India; both produce BOP (Broken Orange Pekoe) and BOPF (Broken Orange Pekoe Fannings), which "broken" grades are smaller than any leaf grade. There are other standard names as well, but these are the basic ones. Such minute leaf fragments as may remain are sold either as "Fannings" or as "Dust." (In days before machinery the Fannings were whatever could be fanned aside while the tea was being sifted into grades, and the Dust was what remained to be swept up.) Fannings and Dust are used only in making instants and in tea bags, since their main virtue is that they infuse almost immediately.

The thing to remember is that these grade names are chiefly of interest to the tea blender and packer. Advertising teas to the consumer this way, one merchant has remarked, "is like selling cheeses as sliced, unsliced, and thin-sliced, without any reference to whether they are cheddars or bries, sharps or milds, domestics or imports." I must emphasize again that these terms and the manufacturing procedures I've outlined apply only to Black Tea, which most of the world now drinks.

THE MAKING OF GREEN TEA

Up until very recently, it has always been thought that Black Tea was the earliest kind manufactured. Green Tea was supposed to have been invented during the Ming Dynasty (1368–1628) in China. Nowadays the Chinese assure us the earliest teas were Green and that Black is a comparative latecomer. It is passing strange that the Brits, using Lu Yu's procedures, came up with Black Tea in India, but then who knows whether Lu Yu's cake tea was really Black or Green, anyhow? I don't know who to believe or if it matters.

Black Tea, as we have seen, is completely fermented. Green Tea is not fermented at all. The secret to making it is that the leaf is killed by heat at the start of the process. This is done either by firing it in large pans over high flame or, more often, steaming it in a perforated cylinder or boiler *immediately after plucking.* Green Tea is never withered. The firing or steaming does away with the enzymes and bacteria responsible for fermentation; it also prevents the oxidation of the juices in the leaf and renders it pliable enough for rolling. All this accomplished, the leaf is rolled a little, then steamed again, rolled some more, and again steamed over and over until all its moisture gradually evaporates and it's finally too crisp to withstand further manipulation. Most of its tannin is intact in its original, colorless state and none of the essential oil which gives rise to the aroma and flavor of Black Tea has been allowed to develop, wherefore Green Tea will seem more puckery and more delicate to the taste. It is graded and named, of course, and—if destined for consumption overseas—is pan-fired one last time before packing and shipment.

With Green Tea, in contrast to Black, there is a very definite relationship between grade and quality. Most Green comes from China, with Japan and Taiwan following in

that order. It is graded according to the age of the leaf and the style in which it has been rolled and treated. The first-quality Green Tea from China and Taiwan is called Pinhead Gunpowder, because that's what some long-gone agent of the John Company decided it looked like to him. Gunpowder consists of tiny, gray-green balls rolled from the tenderest young and medium-aged leaves. The loosely balled older leaf that's sifted out of Gunpowder is called Imperial. Young Hyson is also made from top-quality leaf, only rolled long and thin. Old leaf so rolled as to look like a mixture of Young Hyson and Imperial is known as Hyson. It is named after a Mr. Hyson, a rich East India merchant who first imported it; one presumes Young Hyson was his son. The next grade down is Twankay, unrolled old leaf of poor quality. Hyson Skin is considered even poorer, and whatever is left is Dust.

THE GREEN TEAS OF JAPAN

"The history of France is written in wine, the history of Japan in tea," as my friend Lyle Bongé observes. Virtually all the tea Japan produces is Green, and only some 4 percent of it, or less than eight million pounds, ever leaves the country. In fact, to support their tea habit, the Japanese are compelled to import several times this amount each year, chiefly from Taiwan. Far and away the largest part of Japan's export crop is sold to the United States. It accounts for only 4 percent of our total tea consumption, but that's four out of every five pounds of Green Tea we drink. All of this, like most of what the Japanese themselves drink, falls under the Sencha or "regular tea" category.

Japan's finest grades, Gyokuro and Tencha, are simply not for sale in any quantity to foreigners. Gyokuro, which translates "Pearl Dew," is grown around Uji, where tea was first raised in the year 1200. Only the top buds of the first flush of bushes specially tended and grown in deep shade are used, and the rolling is entirely by hand. This same leaf, when dried in its natural, unrolled state, produces Tencha, which is painstakingly ground to powder in a mortar for use in the Japanese tea ceremony. Gyokuro and Tencha together probably account for less than 1 percent of Japan's tea output. In stark contrast to these exotics is Bancha, a coarse and remarkably undelicious tea made from old leaf pruned from the plant at the season's end. The Japanese sometimes brew it with barley or other additives to make it more palatable.

Gyokuro, Tencha, and Bancha are grades unto themselves. The remaining 75 percent of Japan's Green Tea is called Sencha, as we have noted, but this is not to say all Sencha is the same. Of two Senchas I recently bought, for example, one cost $1.50 for six ounces while the other was three and a half ounces and priced at $3.45. This latter was labeled "I-Chiban Cha" to indicate first flush and well worth the difference. Nowadays, the best Sencha is vacuum-packed in a nitrogen atmosphere in foil wrappings to prevent its going stale. The Japanese have discovered over the centuries that certain manufacturing methods are best suited to certain districts, growths, pluckings, and leaf styles. Steaming, rolling, and firing are the three steps in making all Sencha, with firing sometimes substituted for the initial steaming as well. But export Sencha must be refired immediately before shipment to guarantee the leaf will be too dry to turn moldy before it is used.

The different refiring methods produce three distinct types of tea: pan-fired, basket-fired, and natural leaf. Pan-fired tea is refired in metal pans, about twenty pounds at a time, and stirred over the heat for half an hour or more. This is the usual procedure with leaf that is small, well twisted, and curly. Long-leaf tea is usually refired in hourglass-shaped bamboo baskets, some five pounds at a time. Periodically, the basket is removed from the heat and the leaf is turned by hand. This particular curing process turns the leaf a dark olive green. Natural leaf is usually pan-fired also, but it is coarse, older leaf that has had little rolling and so appears almost flat. Little of it is exported. The cup quality of any of these grades, however, depends less on the refiring method than on the quality of leaf used.

THE MAKING OF OOLONG AND SCENTED TEAS

Oolong, which has been called "the champagne of teas," represents a cross between Green and Black. The name is derived from the Chinese *wu-lung*, which means "black dragon." Oolong originated in China but except for that produced in Fukien Province it all comes from Taiwan today. Once upon a time the planters of India and Ceylon hoped to compete with the Taiwanese, but a preliminary study convinced them that Taiwan's soil and climate are chiefly responsible for her Oolong's character. Oolong's subtlety is partly due to its being made from Souchong. Souchong receives the very minimum of manipulation with the result that it is the largest and least rolled leaf possible. Its innate delicacy is thus left intact.

The leaf is withered in the shade for four or five hours until it begins changing color and the applelike odor of fermentation begins to develop. It is then fired in a very hot pan for ten minutes or so and immediately rolled. At this point it is coaxed into another brief fermentation before the leaf is finally killed by basket-firing for some three hours. It undergoes a final refiring of up to twelve hours before it is packed and shipped. The result is a semifermented leaf that looks greenish brown and that produces an intensely pungent and piquant liquor. Fukien Oolongs have a larger, more loosely rolled leaf style and give off an infusion that is more greenish yellow as compared to the brownish yellow of Formosa Oolong. Taiwan produces five crops a year and there is considerable variation among them. The Fancy and Fanciest are made in June and July.

Scenting a tea—making Jasmine and company—involves an additional step that may be taken with any finished tea, be it Green, Oolong, or Black. In the case of Jasmine, at least, it is quite often a Pouchong that serves as the base. Pouchong, to refresh your memory, is Green Tea's closest relative. Green Tea is "killed" by heat immediately after plucking and before it has a chance to wither. If you wait until it's on the point of withering before you kill the leaf, you've got Pouchong. (Wait a little longer and you come up with Oolong.)

The best China tea is made from April through June and the only good Jasmines are made soon after in August when the jasmine flowers bloom. Formerly a given weight of flowers and tea would be mixed together and kept at a particular temperature, with fresh flowers added as needed until the desired intensity of scent was obtained. Today hot air is blown over the jasmine petals directly onto the tea, which absorbs the odor. Only once the petals are exhausted and completely dessicated are they added to the tea, where their only function is to look pretty. Were there any scent and savor, i.e., moisture, left in them the tea would quickly turn moldy. Jasmine, which is a cousin of the orchid by the way, makes the most popular of all Scented Teas. The worst of it is undrinkable and the best unbelievably expensive, as tea goes.

Far the most floral and fragrant of Scented Teas is China Rose, made from a Black Tea in the same way as Jasmine and produced only in China, whence it is orderable as People's Republic Standard Tea #350. I know of no other from China or elsewhere.

While China Rose makes a very mysterious base for further blending, I can't stand it by itself any more than I can the similarly made China Lychee Tea. Lychee, which my dictionary also gives as "Lichee" and "Litchi," derives its wholly indescribable flavor from the Chinese evergreen that is also responsible for those abominable "nuts" of the same name. This plant belongs to something appropriately called the soapberry family. None of this is to say you won't find these products delightful, only that I do not.

Some Scented Teas, Earl Grey chief among them, owe their aroma and taste to an essence that is sprayed directly onto the leaf. In 1830, between the time he had visited China as a diplomat and the time he became prime minister, the second Earl Grey entrusted the original formula for Earl Grey Tea to the tea firm of Jacksons of Piccadilly. Some of Jacksons present-day competitors have departed so far from the formula as to use lavender for scenting, but the true essence is oil of bergamot, bergamot being a pear-shaped citrus fruit grown in southern Europe. Lapsang Souchong, the only one of this lot I like, is probably the least-popular Scented Tea. Properly speaking, Lapsang Souchong is not a Scented but a Smoked Tea, originally from Fukien Province but now produced in Taiwan as well. My best guess would be that pine is the wood used for smoking, but this is a guess only. (Cheap examples merely have an overwhelming dose of smoke flavor added.) Fine Lapsang Souchong is said to taste "tarry"; it bears a certain resemblance to Scotch whisky, which is also smoky tasting and which, like this tea, you either like or you do not. When Formosa Souchong is the base tea used, it's called Formosa Lapsang.

Flavored Teas, many of them treated in England or Germany, have lately grown popular. The flavors—black currant or you name it—are simply essences sprayed onto the tea. Spiced Teas, needless to add, are produced in their infinite variety by the simple addition of so much orange peel, clove, or whatnot.

USEFUL REFERENCES ON TEA

Bramah, Edward. *Tea & Coffee: A Modern View of 300 Years of Tradition.* London: Hutchinson Books, Ltd., 1972. A very readable account of the tea and coffee business from top to bottom by a gentleman and scholar who has been intimately associated with both. Clear, concise, and informative, though necessarily limited to certain areas.

Franklin, Aubrey. *Teatime.* New York: Frederick Fell, 1981. Invaluable as a source of tea snack recipes and ideas.

Harler, C. R. *The Culture & Marketing of Tea.* 3rd ed. London: Oxford University Press, 1964. Indispensable for an understanding of the subject and as readable as it is detailed.

Huxley, Gervas. *Talking of Tea.* Ivyland, Pennsylvania: John Wagner & Sons, 1956. Brief but delightful collection of lore and anecdote by a tea professional, grandson of the famed biologist Thomas Henry Huxley.

Quimme, Peter. *The Signet Book of Coffee & Tea.* New York: New American Library, 1976.

Ramsden, A. R. *Assam Planter.* London: John Gifford, 1945. Well-written adventures of a tea planter in the old days of the British raj in India, with considerable technical information effortlessly conveyed.

Repplier, Agnes. *To Think of Tea!* Boston: Houghton Mifflin Co., 1932. A social, historical, and literary study of tea of rare insight and unsurpassed charm. Now hard to find, but worth the search.

Schapira, Joel; Schapira, David; and Shapira, Karl. *The Book of Coffee & Tea.* New York: St. Martin's Press, 1975.

Scott, J. M. *The Great Tea Venture.* New York: E. P. Dutton, 1965. An historical overview of the story of tea written with great wit and erudition by the only author besides Repplier to convey a sense of the subject's romance. Authoritative and fun.

Ukers, W. H. *All About Tea.* Whitestone, New York: Tea & Coffee Trade Journal Co., 1935. A vast and meticulous compilation in two quarto volumes totaling over one thousand pages and exhausting as they are exhaustive: The author's wealth of information on tea has never been assembled before or since. Although Ukers' descriptions are completely outdated as regards the types of teas available and their characteristics today, this has not prevented them from being repeated as gospel, usually without attribution or acknowledgment. Long out of print and almost impossible to find.

———. *Ukers' International Tea & Coffee Buyers' Guide.* Whitestone, New York: Tea and Coffee Trade Journal Co., annual editions. An up-to-the-moment source of statistics and index to sources of supply for buyers in the tea, coffee, and allied trades.

MAJOR WORKS
RELATING TO THE HISTORY OF TEA

Clark, Arthur H. *The Clipper Ship Era.* New York: G. P. Putnam's Sons, 1910.

Collis, Maurice. *Foreign Mud.* New York: Alfred A. Knopf, 1947. The opium trade and the opium wars.

Fortune, Robert. *A Visit to the Tea Districts of China.* London: John Murray, 1852.

———*Wanderings in China.* London: John Murray, 1843.

Lubbock, Basil. *The China Clippers.* Boston: Lauriat, 1914.

Shore, H. *Smuggling Days & Smuggling Ways.* London: Casell, 1892.

Yu, Lu. *The Classic of Tea.* Translated by F. R. Carpenter. Boston: Little, Brown and Company, 1974.

BOOKS CONCERNING
THE JAPANESE TEA CEREMONY

Iguchi, Kaisen. *Tea Ceremony.* Translated by J. Clark. Osaka: Hoikusha Publishing Co., Ltd., 1975.

Kakuzo, Okakura. *The Book of Tea.* New York: Duffield & Co., 1906.

Kawabata, Yusunari. *Thousand Cranes.* New York: Alfred A. Knopf, 1958. A short novel by the 1968 Nobel Prize for Literature recipient.

Sen XV, Soshitsu. *Tea Life, Tea Mind.* Tokyo: Weatherhill, 1979.

Tanaka, Senlo. *The Tea Ceremony.* New York: Harmony Books, 1978.

Index

Adam, James, Scottish architect, 115, 118
Adam, Robert, Scottish architect, 115, 118
Adam style, influence on silver ware design, 115
Addison, Joseph, English writer, 45, 53
Africa, tea production in, 92, 143, 198. See also specific countries
Africa tea
    in McGraths Original Irish Blend, 121
afternoon tea, 17, 48–49, 175
Afternoon Tea, 122, 123
Agarwala & Son, R. N. See R. N. Agarwala & Son
All About Tea, 58, 83. See also Ukers, William H.
America. See also United States
    Black Tea drunk in, 141
    British taxation of tea in, 54–56
    China tea in, 93
    drinking of tea in Colonial, 53–54
    Green Tea drunk in, 93, 141
    silver ware of, 111–12
    tea parties in, 57–61
    trade with China, 63, 95
Amoy, 32, 139
Anna, the Duchess of Bedford, 48, 175
Annapolis Tea Party, 60–61
Anwhei (Anhui) Province, tea production in, 149, 157, 160
Argentina, tea production in, 92, 147
Assam, tea production in, 83–84, 86–89, 90, 92, 132
Assam Company, 86–88, 90
Assam jat, 88, 92, 142, 212
Assam Planter, 216–18
Assam Superb Tea (Fortnum & Mason), 133
Assam tea, 132–33, 145. See also Assam, Assam jat
    in Breakfast blends, 121, 133
Ashby Rose Brand, 168
Ashby & Sons, James. See James Ashby & Sons
Astor, John Jacob, and China trade, 70, 95, 126
auctions, tea. See tea auctions
Augustus II, 106–07
Azerbaidzhan, tea production in, 146

Balasun tea estate, Darjeeling, 137
Bancha Tea, 153–54, 224, 225
Bangladesh, tea production in, 147
barley, used in Japan tea, 154, 224
Barnett, James, U.S. tea examiner, 188
basket-fired tea, 153, 225
Before the Rain Jasmine Tea (Grace Tea), 165
Bigelow, Ruth Campbell, founder of R. C. Bigelow, 168, 190
Black Tea. See also specific countries, types
    about, 132–39, 140, 146–47
    caffeine in, 180–81
    in English Breakfast Teas, 121, 157
    in London 77 Tea, 129
    making of, 218–222
    popularity in America, 141
    popularity in Britain, 96
    in Russian Caravan Tea, 122
    in Servit Chin Chu Oriental Blend Tea, 127
blenders, tea. See tea blenders
blending your own teas, 181
bohea, 212
Bohea Tea, 42
Bolivia, tea production in, 147
Bombay, leased to East India Company, 80
Bongé, Lyle, 166
Bontekoe, Dr. Cornelius, 17th-century Dutch physician, 33, 105
The Book of Coffee & Tea, 188
The Book of Tea, 21, 27–28
The Book of Tea Sanitation, 24
Boston Harbour Tea (Davison, Newman), 128, 195
Boston Tea Company, 168, 190
Boston Tea Party, 57–58
Boswell, James, Scottish author, 45, 47
Böttger, Johann-Friederich, inventor of European hard-paste porcelain, 106–07
Boulsover, Thomas, rediscoverer of Sheffield plate, 117
Boylston, Zabdiel, Boston apothecary, 53
Bramah, Edward, on China tea, 156
Brazil, tea production in, 92, 147
Breakfast Teas, 120–22, 133

brewing tea, 176–77
Brick Tea, 162
Bristolware tea containers, 182
Britannia, 58
Brockenbrough, Jr., Gill, president of First Colony, 191–92
broken grades, 135, 221
Broken Orange Pekoe, 135, 160, 221
Broken Orange Pekoe Fannings, 221
Brooke, Arthur, 198
Brooke Bond, 96, 185
    about, 190, 198
    Kenya Ragati High Grown BOP Tea, 143
    -Liebig conglomerate, 198
    Red Rose Brand, 198
Bruce, Charles, 78–80, 83–84, 86
Bruce, Robert, 78, 132
Buddhism, influence on tea cultivation and drinking, 17–19, 23, 24, 27
Bushnells (Brooke Bond), 198
Button's coffee house, 45
buying brokers, 185

Cachar tea district, Bangladesh, 147
Cadbury Company, 199
caffeine
    content of coffee, 180
    content of herbals, 170
    content of tea, 180–81
Calcutta, 67, 80, 135, 184
Camellia sinensis, 78, 212
Canton, 32, 42, 62, 67, 90, 96, 126, 160
Catherine of Braganza, 39–41, 80, 175
Ceylon. See also Sri Lanka
    coffee cultivation in, 91–92, 98, 133
    and Sir Thomas Lipton, 98–99
    tea production in, 98, 133–34
Ceylon Breakfast Tea, 121, 134
Ceylon Orange Pekoe (leaf grade), 135
Ceylon Orange Pekoe Tea, 135
Ceylon tea, 92, 133–35
    in Boston Harbour Tea, 129
    broken grades, 135
    in English Breakfast Tea, 121, 134
    in Five O'Clock Tea, 122
    in Lady Londonderry Tea, 127
    leaf grades, 135
ch'a, 16, 31

Ch'a Ching, first book of tea, 17–19, 21, 83, 213
Ch'a Ching Chinese Restaurant Tea (Wagners), 141
chado, 26
chai, word for tea, 31
Chai brand tea, 139
Chakve tea estate, Soviet Georgia, 145
Charles I, 39, 111
Charles II, 39–41, 44, 175
Charleston Tea Party, 58
Cheericup Ceylon Tea (Mark T. Wendell), 135
Chelsea porcelain, 109
Chin Chu Oriental Blend Tea (Servit), 127
china, 20, 106–10
China, 77, 78
  discovery of tea in, 16
  early American trade with, 63, 70, 95, 96, 126
  early dynastic rule of, 17–19, 20–21
  early English trade with, 62–65
  early European trade with, 28–30, 34–37
  early Russian trade with, 36–37
  early teapots of, 104, 105
  Robert Fortune in, 84–86
The China Clippers, 74–77
China *jat,* 88, 212, 213
China Products Northwest, 160–61, 163–65, 167, 192
  report on current China tea crop, 154–56
China tea, 155–62, 192
  Black, 157–61
  Compressed, 162
  discovery of, 16
  in Fortmason Tea, 129
  Green, 148–52, 222–23
  harvesting, 215
  Keemun, 121, 142, 160, 157–58, 159
  machinery for processing, 156–57
  Oolong, 122, 161
  Scented, 163–65
  White, 161
China Tea (First Colony), 192
Ching Wo Tea, 159
Cho, Frank, founder of Grace Tea, 193
chronology of tea history, 199–209
Chun Hao Jasmine Tea, 163
Chung Feng Premium Jasmine Tea, 163, 165
Chunmee Tea, 149
Churchill, Sir Winston, 81
  on British expansion in India, 69, 81

on taxation of American tea imports, 54, 56
Clapp & Company, Inc., O. H. See O. H. Clapp & Company, Inc.
clipper ships, 70–72, 73–77
The Coffee Bean & Tea Leaf Shops, 133, 137, 159, 167, 195
coffee cultivation, 77, 91–92, 98, 133
coffee houses, 41, 42–45, 49, 97
Colonial Dames Tea, 127
color, importance of in making Black Tea, 220
La Compagnie Coloniale, 175
Confessions, 92–93
Compressed Tea, 20, 162
Congou Tea, 74, 158, 219
  North China, 158, 159
  Rose, 165
  South China, 159
Connoisseur blends, 128
Constant Comment Tea, 168, 190
Countess of Salisbury Tea (Sarum), 129
Country Spice Tea Company, 143, 159, 192
Cowper, William, on tea time, 49
Crawley, Eustace, managing director of Jacksons of Piccadilly
  on Lady Londonderry Tea, 127–28
  on Russian Tea, 146
  on use of royal family names, 131–32
Cross & Blackwell Flavored Teas, 168
Crowley, Aleister, on China and Ceylon teas, 92–93
The Culture and Marketing of Tea, 220

Daishi, Dengo, Japanese Buddhist, 23
Darjeeling, tea production in, 90, 135–36
Darjeeling tea, 135–39, 140, 145, 185–86
  in Crown Tea, 131
  in Queen's Tea, 131
Davison, Newman & Company, Ltd., 94, 128
  about, 195
  Boston Harbour Tea, 128, 195
Dean & DeLuca, 198
Decaffeinated Teas, 169
Dehra Dun tea district, India, 145
Delft ware, 105
Dennis, Reg, of Ceylon Tea Centre, 133
Diary, 16
Dick, Robert H., U.S. tea examiner, 188
Dickens, Charles, on Fortnum & Mason, 196
Dictionary, 47, 48

Dimbula tea district, Sri Lanka, 134–35
Dinner at Buckingham Palace, 175–76
Doctor Milton's Tea (Jacksons), 127
Dooars tea district, India, 145
Douwe Egberts Import Corporation, 192
Dowager Tea (Fortnum & Mason), 127
Dragon Well Tea, 149–50
Drysdales
  about, 120, 198
  Breakfast Tea, 120
  Connoisseur Blend Tea, 128, 129
  Fancy Golden Tip Assam Tea, 133
  FOP Vintage Darjeeling Tea, 139
Duncans brand tea, 133, 139
Dust, 176, 221, 224
Dutch. See Holland
Dutch Breakfast Tea, 121–22
Dutch East India Company, 33, 154

Earl Grey, Charles, 123, 227
Earl Grey Tea, 123–25, 162, 227
earthenware tea things, 104–05, 178
East Horizon Corporation, 161
East India Company, 38, 39, 41–43, 50, 52, 54, 65, 78, 86–87, 95, 96, 113, 148, 187, 198, 224
  chartered, 37
  first shipment of tea, 41
  first factory established in China, 42, 62–63
  loss of China trade monopoly, 70–72, 78, 81–82, 89
  and opium trade, 67–70
  Robert Fortune as envoy, 85–86
Easterlings, 111
Edenton, North Carolina Tea Party, 61
"Eight Regulations," 63
elephant, role in tea harvesting, 216–18
Elers, Dutch potters, 105, 106
Elizabeth I, 36, 39
  chartered East India Company, 37
England. See also East India Company, specific subjects
  arrival of tea in, 16, 39–41
  exports of tea to America, 54–56
  and opium trade, 67–70
  porcelain manufacture in, 107–08
  silver ware of, 111–13
  tea smuggling in, 50–52
  trade with China, 62–65
English Breakfast Tea, 120–21, 125, 157
Equador, tea production in, 92, 147
Etruria Pottery Works, 115–17
Evening Tea, 122, 123

Evergreen Brand
  Gunpowder Tea, 149
  Special Chumnee Tea, 149

Faience pottery, 105, 106
Fancy Formosa Oolong Tea, 140
Fancy Golden Tip Assam, 133
Fancy Tippy Gold Flowery Orange
    Pekoe, 137
Fannings, 221
fermentation
  of Black Tea, 218, 219–20
  partial, of Oolong Tea, 226
firing
  of Black Tea, 220
  of Green Tea, 222, 225
First Colony Coffee & Tea Company
  about, 191–92
  Ceylon Orange Pekoe Tea, 135
  Ching Wo Tea, 159
  Gunpowder Tea, 182
  Lapsang Souchong Tea, 167
  London 77 Tea, 129
  Queen's Blend Tea, 132, 192
  Russian Tea, 146
  Susan's Teas, 168, 192
  Yunnan Tea, 160
Five O'Clock Tea (Ridgways), 122
Flavored Decaffeinated Teas, 168
Flavored Teas, 168–69, 190. See also
    specific types
  making of, 227
Flowery Orange Pekoe (grade), 221
Flowery Orange Pekoe Tea (Fortnum
    & Mason), 137
flush, defined, 214
Fong, Andrew, 152
Foochow, 73
Food and Drug Administration (U.S.),
    167, 187–88
FOP Vintage Darjeeling Tea, 139,
    196
Ford, Ford Madox, on British empire,
    131
Formosa, 32, 149. See also Taiwan
Formosa Keemun Tea (Grace Tea),
    157
Formosa Oolong Supreme Tea (Grace
    Tea), 141, 182
Formosa tea, 141–42. See also Taiwan
    tea
  Black, 121
  Gunpowder, 149
  Jasmine, 165
  Keemun, 142, 157, 182
  in Lady Londonderry Tea, 127
  Lapsang, 227

Lapsang Souchong, 166
Oolong, 122, 129, 139–41, 182, 226
Pan-Fired Green, 153
Pouchong, 142
Souchong, 166–67
Formost-Friedman, Inc., 192
Fortnum & Mason
  about, 95, 196–97, 198
  Assam Superb Tea, 133
  Crown Tea, 131
  Dowager Tea, 127
  Flowery Orange Pekoe Tea, 137
  Fortmason Tea, 129
  I Chang Tea, 159
  Queen Anne Tea, 131
Fortnum, William, 95, 196
Fortune, Charles, 78–80
Fortune, Robert, 84–86, 88, 186, 212
France, 80
  China goods in, 30
  coffee cultivation in Martinique, 77
  early tea drinking in, 34
  in French and Indian War, 81
  porcelain made in, 108–09
  tea customs in, 174–75
  tearooms in, 174–75
Freed Teller & Freed, 139, 141, 195
French and Indian War, 81
Fukien (Fujian) Province, tea produc-
    tion in, 139–40, 159, 161, 163–
    65, 166

G. S. Haly Company, 193
Gardenia Tea, 167
Garway, Thomas, 16, 39, 44
Garway's coffee house, 16, 44
Gen Mai Cha, 154
Georges, kings of England, 113–14, 128
Georgia (USSR), tea production in, 145
Georgian style, influence on silver
    design, 113
Germany
  early tea drinking in, 33–34
  porcelain discovery in, 106–07
Girard, Stephen, and China trade, 70,
    96, 126
Gissing, George, on tea time, 48
Gladstone, William, on tea's effects,
    180
glossary of tea tasting terms, 199–200
Grace Tea Company
  about, 193
  Before the Rain Jasmine Tea, 165
  Connoisseur Blend Tea, 128
  Darjeeling Tea, 139
  Formosa Keemun Tea, 157

Formosa Oolong Supreme Tea,
    141, 182
Original Earl Grey Mixture, 125
Superb Darjeeling 6000 Tea, 137
Winey Keemun Tea, 157
grading
  of Black Tea, 221
  of Green Tea, 222–24, 225
The Great Tea Venture, 50, 65, 72. See
    also Scott, J. M.
Green Tea. See also specific countries,
    types
  about, 148–54
  caffeine in, 181
  growing conditions for, 213
  in London 77 Tea, 129
  making of, 221–23
  making of Japanese, 223–225
  popularity in America, 141
  popularity in Britain, 96
Greenwich Tea Party, 58
Grey, Charles Earl. See Earl Grey,
    Charles
Gunpowder Tea, 148–49, 182, 199, 224
Guppy, Sarah, 176
Gyokuro Tea, 153, 224, 225

The Hague, tea at, 33, 41
Hainan Tea, 160
Halssen & Lyon, 192
  Decaffeinated Teas, 169
  Flavored Teas, 168
Hangchow (Hangzhou) tea district,
    China, 150, 159
Harler, C. R., on importantance of
    smell in tea making, 220
Harney, John, president of Sarum
    Teas, 194
harvesting. See tea harvesting
Hauser, Bert, founder of Servit Foods,
    127
Hemphill, Simpson, 111, 118
Her Majesty's Blend Tea (Ridgways),
    131, 198
Herbal Infusions, 169–70
Herbal "teas," 169–70
Hideyoshi, ruler of Japan, 26
high tea, 49, 175
Hoji Cha, 154
Holland. See also Dutch East Indies
    Company
  early tea drinking in, 33
  coffee cultivation in Dutch East
    Indies, 77
  importation of tea to America by,
    54, 56

introduction of tea to Europe by, 30, 32
introduction of teapots to Europe by, 104–05
medical concerns about tea in, 33
missionaries in Japan, 26
tea cultivation in Dutch East Indies, 142
trade with Asia, 37
trade with China, 30, 62, 63
war with England, 39
hong system, 63–65, 69
Honorable Company. See East India Company
Honorable East India Company. See East India Company
hoppo, 63–65
Horniman, John, 96, 187, 197
Hornimans Tea, 96, 129
Houqua, 126
Houqua, Chinese merchant prince, 96, 126
Howqua Mixture Tea, 126
Hui-Sung, Chinese emperor, 21
Hu-kwa Tea, 126–27, 167, 194
Hunan Province, tea production in, 160
Hunter, W. C., on opium smuggling, 68
Hupeh (Hubei) Province, tea production in, 159
Hyson Tea, 149, 224
Hyson Skin Tea, 224

I Chang Tea, 159
iced tea, 93–94
I-Chiban Cha, 153, 225
Imperial Gunpowder Tea, 148–49, 224
Imperial Tea, 42
importers, tea. See tea importers
Indar Boudoir Tea, 122
India. See also specific states
    Brooke-Bond Liebig conglomerate in, 198
    control of by England, 81–82
    early tea cultivation in, 78–80
    East India Company factories in, 38
    French and Indian War in, 81
    opium cultivation in, 67
India tea. See also specific tea districts
    in Boston Harbour Tea, 129
    in English Breakfast Tea, 121
    in Fortmason Tea, 129
    in Lady Londonderry Tea, 127
    in Original Irish Blend Tea, 121
    Rose Tea, 165
    at St. Lopuis World's Fair, 93
Indonesia, 32, 33, 92

Indonesia tea, 121, 122, 142–43
    plucking of, 215
Indonesian Tea (Mark T. Wendell), 143
instant tea, 190, 221
The International Tea & Coffee Buyer's Guide, 146
Invalid Tea (Ty-phoo), 127, 199
Iran, tea production in, 147
Irish Breakfast Tea (McGraths), 121
Isle of Man, role in tea smuggling, 51

J. P. Morgan Tea (Simpson & Vail), 128
Jacksons, tea-rolling machine inventors, 90–91, 92
Jacksons of Piccadilly, 131–32
    about, 96, 198
    Afternoon Tea, 122
    Ching Wo Tea, 159
    Coronation Tea, 131
    Doctor Milton's Tea, 127
    Earl Grey Tea, 123–25
    English Breakfast Tea, 121
    Evening Tea, 122
    Lady Londonderry Tea, 127–28
    Russian Tea, 146
James Ashby & Sons
    about, 198, 199
    fruit-flavored teas, 168
    Gunpowder Green Tea, 199
    Pure Russian, 146, 199
James G. Gill Company, 191
Japan
    Dutch East Indies Company base in, 33
    early government influence on tea, 25–27
    early tea cultivation in, 23–24
    early Western influence on, 26
    first English tea drinker in, 38
    tea ceremony in, 19, 24, 28, 152, 172, 224
    tea tournament in feudal, 24–25
    trade with America, 153, 154
Jasmine Tea, 162–65
    making of, 163, 226
    in Countess of Salisbury Tea, 129
jat, 88. See also Assam *jat,* China *jat*
Java, tea production in, 122, 142
Jesuits, role in tea history, 26, 36
John Company. See East India Company
John Travers & Sons, 94–95
John Wagner & Sons
    about, 142, 185, 190–191, 195, 196
    English Breakfast Tea, 121
    Ceylon Breakfast Tea, 121

Ch'a Ching Chinese Restaurant Tea, 141
Darjeeling Tea, 137
Decaffeinated Black Tea, 169
Gunpowder Tea, 148
Irish Tea, 121
Lapsang Souchong Tea, 191
Orange Pekoe Tea, 135
Russian Caravan Tea, 122
Spiced Teas, 167
Johnson, Dr. Samuel, English lexicographer, 16, 45–47, 48, 49
Johnson, Eliot, owner of Mark T. Wendell, 194

Kakuzo, Okakura
    on Japanese tea ceremony, 26–27
    on tea drinking, 21
Kangra tea district, India, 145
Keemun. See also China tea, Formosa tea
    in English Breakfast Tea, 121, 181
    in Fortnum & Mason Crown Tea, 131
    in Russian-style Tea, 122
    in Servit Chin Chu Oriental Blend Tea, 127
    in Twinings Prince of Wales Tea, 131
Kellogg Company (Salada), 190
Kenya Ragati High Grown BOP Tea, 143
Kenya, tea production in, 92, 143, 147, 198
Kenya Tea, 143
Kresting, Paul, of China Products Northwest, 163
Kuko-Cha, 154
Kwangsi (Guangxi) Province, tea production in, 160, 161
Kwangtung (Guangdong) Province, tea production in, 160
Kwong Sang Tea Company
    Shui Sin Tea, 152
    Tit Koon Yum Tea, 152
Kyoto, 25, 26, 153

Lady Hamilton, 49, 109
Lady Londonderry Tea (Jacksons), 127–28
Lapsang Souchong Tea, 122, 159, 165–67, 191
    in Hu-kwa Tea, 127
    making of, 227
    in Russian Caravan Tea, 122
Late Georgian style, influence on silver ware design, 115

leaf grades, 135, 140, 221
Life of Johnson, 45, 47
Limoges porcelain, 109
Lintin Island, 68
Lipton, Sir Thomas, 97–102, 134, 135
Liptons Tea, 93, 99, 185, 188. See also
    Lipton, Sir Thomas
    Flavored Teas, 168
Lisbon, 30
Lloyd's coffee house, 44
London
    coffee houses, 41, 42–45, 49, 97
    tea gardens, 49, 96–97
London 77 Tea (First Colony), 129
Loolecondera tea estate, Sri Lanka,
    133
Lord Amherst, British envoy to China,
    68
Lord MaCartney, British envoy to
    China, 67–68
low tea, 49, 175
Lubbock, Basil, on clipper ship races,
    74–77
Lung Ching Tea, 149–50
Lychee Tea, 167
    making of, 227
Lyons tea shops, 97, 197
Lyons-Tetley, 188, 190, 197–98. See
    also Tetleys

Macao, 30, 32, 42, 62, 63, 69
Macauley, Thomas, on the East India
    Company, 81–82, 88
McCormick & Company, 1890
McGilloway, James, national sales
    manager of Twinings, 195
McGrath Brothers, Ltd.
    about, 199
    Original Irish Blend Tea, 121
machinery for tea rolling, 91
McKay, Donald, designer of clipper
    ship, 72
MacMelville, William, U.S. tea
    authority, 188
Madhu Jayanti Private, Ltd., Indian
    tea packer, 189
Madras, 80
Makhams Sinbad brand tea, 133
mail order of teas, 182, 193–195
majolica pottery, 105, 106
Malawi, tea production in, 143, 147,
    198
Malaysia, tea production in, 147
Mandi tea district, India, 145
Manchu Dynasty, 62–63
Manchurian Dynasty, 62–63

Mao Feng Tea, 152
Margaret's Hope tea estate, Darjeeling,
    137
Mark T. Wendell
    about, 194
    Boston Harbour Tea, 128
    Cherricup Ceylon Tea, 135
    Darjeeling Tea, 139
    English Breakfast Tea, 121
    Fancy Formosa Oolong Tea, 141
    Formosa Keemun Tea, 157, 182
    Hu-kwa Tea, 126–127, 167, 194
    Indonesian Tea, 143
    Mint Tea, 167
    Mountain Kenya Tea, 143
    Panyong Tea, 159
    Pingsuey Tea, 159
    Russian Caravan Tea, 122
    Yunnan Tea, 160
Marylebone tea garden, 49
Mason, Hugh, 95, 196
Mason, Stanley, founder of Sarum
    Teas, 193–194
Massachusetts Gazette, 58
meat tea, 49, 175
Matcha Tea, 152. See also Tencha Tea
Maturata tea district, Sri Lanka, 134
Maya brand tea, 133, 139
Mazawatee Ceylon Tea, 129
Meissen china factory, 107
Melroses
    about, 197
    Boston Harbour Tea, 128
    Ceylon Orange Pekoe Tea, 135
    English Breakfast Tea, 121
    Queen's Tea, 131
Mid-Georgian style, influence on silver
    ware design, 114
milk, used in tea, 178
Mill, John Stuart, 82
Mim tea estate, Darjeeling, 137
Mincing Lane, site of tea auctions, 92,
    99
Ming Dynasty, 21, 30, 62
    early teapots of, 104
Ming Xiang Tea, 161
Min-Pei Tea, 161
Mint Tea (Mark T. Wendell), 167
Mitre Tavern, 94
MJB Orange Pekoe & Pekoe Cut Black
    Tea tea bag, 189
Mongol Dynasty, 21
Mongols, tea drunk by, 19
Morgan, J. Pierpont, U.S. financier,
    128
Morrison, Ruth, publicist of Twinings,
    195

Mountain Kenya Tea (Mark T.
    Wendell), 143
Murmachi period, 25
Musashi, samurai, 27
Myo-e, abbot, 24

Nabisco Company, 190
Nagasaki, 26, 154
The National Native Produce &
    Animal By-Products Import &
    Export Corporation of China,
    152, 184
natural leaf teas, 225
neoclassicism, influence on silver ware
    design, 115
neoclassic revival, influence on silver
    ware design, 115
Nestlé Company, 190
New Guinea, tea production in, 92
New York, early tea drinking in, 53
New York Tea Party, 60
Nilgiri tea, 144–45
Nixon, Richard, 188
North China Congou, 158, 159
Northwestern Coffee Mills, 139, 195
Nursery Tea, 127
Nuwara Eliya tea district, Sri Lanka,
    134

O.H. Clapp & Company, Inc., 139, 193
"O'Clock Teas," 122
Oliver, Charles, on tea time, 175–76
On Liberty, 82
Oolong Tea. See also China tea,
    Formosa tea
    in Chin Chu Oriental Blend, 127
    in Countess of Salisbury Tea, 129
    growing conditions for, 213
    making of, 139, 225–26
opium trade, 67–70
Opium Wars, 67, 69, 78, 84, 155
Orange Pekoe, 99, 135, 221
orange-flavored Spiced Teas, 167
oxidation of Black Tea, 220

packers, tea. See tea packers
Pai Mun Tan Tea, 161
Pan-Fired Green Tea, 149, 153, 225
The Pannikin shops, 133, 135, 159, 195
Panyong Tea, 159
The Papers of Henry Ryecroft, 48
Papua New Guinea, tea production in,
    147
Paulli, Dr. Simon, on medical dangers
    of tea, 33
Pearl Tea, 148

Pekoe, defined, 221. See also specific teas, grades
Pepys, Samuel, English diarist, 16, 37, 41, 44, 94
Perkins, Thomas Handasyd, and China trade, 70, 96, 126
Perry, Commodore, 27, 154
Peru, tea production in, 147
Philadelphia Tea Party, 58–60
Pi Lo Chun Tea, 149, 150
pidgin English, 65–66
Pingsuey Tea, 159
Pinhead Gunpowder Tea, 148, 149, 224
plucking. See tea plucking
poey long, 219
pollination of tea bush, 212
Polo, Marco, 21, 28
Pons tearoom, 173
Pope, Alexander, on Queen Anne, 43
porcelain. See also china
  English manufacture of, 107–08
  French manufacture of, 108–09
  growth of industry in Europe, 107–08
  hard-paste, 107
  soft-paste, 106
  willowware, 109–10
Portugal, 33, 37, 38, 62, 80
  establishment of base in Macao, 30
  exploration of China, 28–30
  exploration of India, 28
  missionaries in Japan, 26
posset cup, 110
Post, Emily, on tea dance, 173
Pouchong
  in Chin Chu Oriental Blend Tea, 127
  in Formosa Jasmine, 139, 165, 226
Preston, Herman, tea consultant at Wagners, 185
Prince of Wales, and Sir Thomas Lipton, 99–101
Prince of Wales Tea (Twinings), 131
proprietary teas, 128–29
pruning of tea bush, 214
Pu-Erh Tea, 157. See also Compressed Tea
Pure Russian Tea (Ashbys), 199

Queen Anne, 43, 44, 95, 113, 196
Queen Anne style, influence on silver ware design, 114
Queen Anne Tea (Fortnum & Mason), 131
Queen Mary, 175–76
Queen Mary Tea (Twinings), 131
Queen Victoria, 111, 114, 129, 192, 198

Queen's Blend Tea (First Colony), 132, 192
Queen's Tea (Melroses), 131

R. Twining & Company, Ltd. See Twinings
R. C. Bigelow Company, 190
R. N. Agarwala & Sons, Indian tea merchants, 139
Ramsden, A. R., on tea harvesting, 216–17
Ramusio, Giambattista, Venetian author, 31
Ranelagh tea garden, 49
The Rape of the Lock, 43
Rawlinson, Sir Thomas, 94
Red Rose Brand (Brooke Bond), 198
Regency style, influence on silver ware design, 118
Revere, Paul, as silversmith, 117
Reynolds, Sir Joshua, English portrait painter, 45, 47
Ridgways
  about, 96, 198
  Ceylon Orange Pekoe Tea, 135
  English Breakfast Tea, 121
  Five O'Clock Tea, 122
  Her Majesty's Blend Tea, 131, 198
  Imperial Breakfast Blend Tea, 121
Rikyu, Sen-no, tea master, 26–27
rococo style, influence on silver ware design, 115
rolling of Black Tea. 218–19
Rose Brand (Ashbys), 199
Rose Congou Tea, 165
Rose Tea, 165, 168
Rumpelmayer's salon de thé, 173
Run-chu, Liao, commercial tea representative of China, 156
Russia, 32, 34–37
Russia tea, 145–46, 147
Russian Caravan Tea, 122
Russian-style Teas, 122

Saga, emperor of Japan, 23–24
St. Louis World's Fair, 93
Saki, on afternoon tea, 173
samovar, 36–37, 177–80
Sanders, Richard, president of Grace Tea, 141, 193
Sarum Teas
  about, 129, 193–94
  Countess of Salisbury Tea, 129
Scented Teas, 162–67
  making of, 225

Schapira brothers, tea merchants
  on China tea industry, 155
  on tea bags, 188
  on tea drinking in America, 141
Schapira Flavor Cup Tea, 129
Scott, J. M.
  on Assam and China teas, 88–89
  on Chinese business system, 65
  on clipper ships, 72
  on opium trade, 69
  on tea smuggling, 50, 51–52
selecting teas, 181–82
Sencha Tea, 153, 224, 225
Serica, 74–77
Servit Foods, 127
  Chin Chu Oriental Blend Tea, 127
Sévigné, Madame de, on tea drinking, 34, 175
Sèvres porcelain factory, 109
Seychelles, tea production in, 147
Shamrock(s), 101
Sheffield plate, 117–18
Shen Nung, legendary Chinese emperor, 16
Shui Hsien White Tea, 161
Shui Sin Tea (Kwong Sang), 152
Shuko, abbot, 25
side effects of tea consumption, 180
Siegel, Dr. R. K., on herb "teas," 170
silver ware
  American, 111–12
  development during various cultural styles, 114–16
  English, 111–13
  hallmarks on, 112
  tea services, 118
Silvery Tip Pekoe Tea, 161
Simpson & Vail
  about, 128, 194
  J. P. Morgan Tea, 128, 194
Singlo Tea, 42
smell, importance in making of Black Tea, 220
Smoked Tea. See Lapsang Souchong Tea
Smooch, 96
Snyder, Gary, on making money, 189
smuggling tea in England, 50–52
Souchong, 85, 140, 165
South Carolina, tea production in, 92
South China Congou Tea, 159
Soviet Union, 146, 178. See also Georgia, Russia, Russia Tea
Sow Mee White Tea, 161
Sowmee Tea, 149

Special Chumnee Tea (Evergreen Brand), 149
Spiced Teas, 167
 making of, 227
Spiderleg Tea, 153, 181
Spillane, Michael, of G. S. Haly Company, 137
Spode porcelain, 109
Sprouting Brand
 Gunpowder Tea, 149
 Lung Ching Tea, 150
Sri Lanka, 92. See also Ceylon, Ceylon tea
 harvesting in, 215
Staffordshire, pottery industry in, 105–06
Starbucks Coffee & Tea, 133, 159, 193
Starr, Ralph, president of Wagners, 191
Steele, Richard, English writer, 44–45
Stem Tea, 154
stoneware, 104, 105, 106, 107
Stonor, Francis, former owner of Jacksons of Piccadilly, 198
Stonor, The Honorable Georgina, on Earl Grey Tea, 123–25
storing tea at home, 181–82
Sullivan, Thomas, inventor of American tea bag, 94
Sumatra, tea production in, 38, 142
Sumner, John, of Ty-phoo Tea, 199
Sung Dynasty, 20–21
 tea brewing in, 104
 tea bricks in, 162
 whipped tea in, 28
Sunflower Brand
 Pi Lo Chun Tea, 150
 tea bags, 189
Superb Darjeeling 6000 (Grace Tea), 137
Susan's Teas (First Colony), 168, 192
Sylhet tea district, Bangladesh, 147

Ta-Hung-Yen Tea, 161
Taiwan, 32, 139. See also Formosa, Formosa tea
Taiwan tea. See also Formosa tea
 harvesting, 215
 making of Green, 224
 Oolong, 139
T'ang Dynasty, 20, 106
tannin, 180, 220
Tanzania, tea production in, 92, 144, 198
Tarry Souchong Tea, 166
tasting, tea. See tea tasting
taxing of tea, 52, 54

"Tea," 173
Tea Act of 1897, 188
Tea Act of 1773, 56
tea auctions, 184–85
 sites of, 184
 procedure at, 184
tea bags, 168, 176, 187, 188, 221
 invention of in America, 94
 invention of in England, 96, 197
tea ball, 176–77
tea blender, 186, 222
tea brick, 20, 162
tea bush, 212. See also tea cultivation
 botanical description of, 78, 212
 plucking of, 214–15
tea ceremony, Japanese, 19, 24, 28, 172, 224
tea chests, 184
Tea & Coffee Trade Journal, 178
Tea Committee, 78, 79, 80, 82–83
tea concentrate, 177
Tea Council of the U.S., 169
tea cultivation
 altitudes for, 212
 description of early, 17
 fertilization, 213
 pruning, 214
 shade requirements, 213
 soil requirements, 213
 for specific types, 213
tea dance, 173
tea gardens, 49, 96–97
tea harvesting, 214–18
tea importers, 221
 U.S. firms, 192–93
tea packers, 221. See also specific firm names
tea parties in Colonial America, 58–61
The Tea Planters & Importers Company "O'Clock Teas," 123
tea plucking, 214–16
tea shops, 97, 173–74, 197
tea tasting, professional, 186–87
 glossary of terms, 209–10
tea time, 48–49, 109
tea tournaments, in Japan, 24–25
teacup
 early examples of in Europe, 105
 Chinese design for, 20, 110
 English design for, 110
 made in Europe, 107
 origins of, 104
teapot
 early examples in America, 113
 early examples in Europe, 105
 made in Europe, 107

origins of, 104–05
selecting, 178
silver, in Europe and America, 113–18
tearooms, Parisian, 173–74
Temple of Heaven Brand Special Gunpowder Tea, 149
Tencha Tea, 152, 153, 224, 225
Tenderleaf Tea, 190
Terai tea district, India, 145
Tetleys, 96. See also Lyons-Tetley
Tewk, Maria, 95, 187
Thomas J. Lipton, Inc., 190. See also Liptons
Thurbo tea estate, Darjeeling, 137
Tibet, tea drinking in, 19, 162
Tiffiny Gourmet Coffee, 142, 193
 Java OP Select Tea, 142
 Kenya Tea, 143
 Sumatra Bah Butong Tea, 142
Ti Kuan Yin Tea, 161
Tippy Golden Flowery Orange Pekoe Tea, 137
tisanes, 170
Tit Koon Yum Tea (Kwong Sang), 152
Tom's Coffee House, 95, 195
Transcaucasia, tea production in, 146
Travancores, South India teas, 145
Travers & Sons, John. See John Travers & Sons
Treaty of Nanking, 69
Trevelyan, George Macauley, on tea's popularity in America, 53–54
Turkey, tea production in, 147
Turk's Head coffee house, 43, 45
Twankay Tea, 224
Twining, Daniel, 195
Twining, Mary Little, 95, 195
Twining, Richard, 95, 195
Twining, O.B.E., Sam, 123–25, 166, 196
Twining, Thomas, 95, 195
Twinings
 about, 95, 185, 195–96
 English Breakfast Tea, 121
 Ceylon Breakfast Tea, 134
 Choice Formosa Oolong Tea, 196
 FOP Vintage Darjeeling Tea, 139, 196
 Gunpowder Tea, 148
 Irish Breakfast Tea, 121
 Orange Pekoe Tea, 135
 Original Earl Grey Mixture Tea, 123, 125
 Prince of Wales Tea, 131
 Russian Caravan Tea, 122
 Queen Mary Tea, 131, 175

275th Anniversary Tea, 160
Yunnan Tea, 160, 196
Twinings Tea Guide, 166
Ty-phoo Tea, 127, 199
Ty-phoo Tea company, 199

Uganda, tea production in, 92, 147
Uji tea district, Japan, 24, 153, 224
Ukers, William H.
    on clipper ship races, 73–74
    on Greenwich Tea Party, 58
    on India tea, 83
    on Indonesia tea, 142
    on J. P. Morgan Tea, 128
    on Keemun Tea, 157
    on North China Congou Tea, 159
    on tea pluckers in Sri Lanka, 215
U.S. Board of Tea Experts, 188, 193
Usk Kayakhta, 36, 37
Uva tea district, Sri Lanka, 134–35
Vauxhall tea garden, 49
Vietnam, tea production in, 147
Venice, 30, 31, 77
Vintage Teas (O.H. Clapp), 193
Visit to the Tea Districts of China, 86
Voyages and Travels, 31

Wagner, Jr., John, 190–91
Wagners. See John Wagner & Sons
Walpole, Horace, 114, 117
Wanderings Through China, 84–85
water, for brewing tea, 178
Wedgwood, Josiah, 106, 115–17

The Well Known Tea of Zhejiang, 149,
    150–52, 181
White Peony Tea, 161
White Tea, 161
Williamson, George, developer of
    Assam tea industry, 88, 89
willowware, 109–10
Will's coffee house, 44
Winey Keemun Tea, 157, 158
withering of Black Tea, 218–19
Worcester Royal Porcelain Works,
    108

Yamamoto of the Orient, 154, 193
    Roasted Tea, 154
Yerba Maté Tea, 147, 170
Yin Hao Jasmine Tea, 163
Yingteh Tea, 160–61
Yi-Xing, teapots of, 104
Young Hyson Tea, 149, 224
Yu Hua Tea, 152
Yu Lu, 16, 17, 20, 23–24, 104, 137,
    162, 180, 213, 219
Yuan Dynasty, 21
Yu-lan Tea, 167
Yunnan Tea, 159–60, 196
Zaire, tea production in, 147
Zhejiang Province tea, 150, 152, 159
    Lung Ching Tea, 149–50, 159
    Pingsuey Tea, 159
    The Well Known Tea of Zhejiang,
        150–52

OMISSIONS

Bencheley Teas (U.S.)
Boston Tea (U.S.)
Chai Brand (India)
Crabtree & Evelyn (U.S.)
Crosse & Blackwell (U.S.)
Daigo Shoten & Co. (Yokohama)
Duncans Brand (India)
Indar Boudoir Tea (France)
Kardomah Tea (U.K.)
Kwong Sang China Teas (Hong Kong)
Maravilla Brand (Ceylon)
Maya Brand (India)
Redcoat Tea (U.S.)
Runglee Rungliot Brand (Darjeeling)
Sindbad Brand (India)
Ten Ren Tea Company (Taiwan)

These brands are mentioned in passing or not at all in my text. Obviously there are many other brands I've never heard of, but these are the American brands I either never could find or never could enjoy. I have listed these imported brands to recommend them, on the basis of having enjoyed at least one exemplary tea from each. The Ten Ren Tea Company of Taiwan has just opened beautiful salesrooms in Los Angeles and San Francisco as this book goes to press. Ten Ren Teas are clearly among the world's most luxurious and exciting. May their tribe increase!